(Continued)

Close to Home

Oral and

Literate Practices

in a Transnational

Mexicano

Community

Juan C. Guerra

Teachers College
Columbia University
New York and London

Published by Teachers College Press, 1234 Amsterdam Avenue, New York, NY 10027

Library of Congress Cataloging-in-Publication Data

Guerra, Juan C., 1949–
    Close to home : oral and literate practices in a transnational
  Mexicano community / Juan C. Guerra.
      p.   cm.
    Includes bibliographical references (p.   ) and index.
    ISBN 0-8077-3773-9 (cloth : alk. paper). — ISBN 0-8077-3772-0
  (pbk. : alk. paper)
    1. Bilingualism—Illinois—Chicago.   2. Mexican Americans—
  Illinois—Chicago—Languages.   3. Bilingualism—Mexico.   4. Spanish
  Language—Illinois—Chicago.   I. Title.
  P115.5.U5G84   1998
  420′.4261′0977311—DC21   98-14198

ISBN 0-8077-3772-0 (paper)
ISBN 0-8077-3773-9 (cloth)

Printed on acid-free paper
Manufactured in the United States of America

05 04 03 02 01 00 99 98   8 7 6 5 4 3 2 1

For my mother,
Teresa Guerra Tovar,
my wife,
Diane Jackson Guerra,
and the members of all the families
represented in this book.

Para mi madre,
Teresa Guerra Tovar,
mi esposa,
Diane Jackson Guerra,
y los miembros de todas las familias
representadas en este libro.

Contents

Acknowledgments

While writing demands that scholars isolate themselves for long periods of time, it unquestionably remains a social process that involves the financial contributions, intellectual support, generosity, faith, and love of so many others.

For their part in funding this project, I wish to thank the Office of the Dean of the Graduate College at the University of Illinois at Chicago (UIC) and the National Science Foundation (NSF Grant BNS 8812578). Because of their support, I had an opportunity to participate with several colleagues in what for me became the initial phase of this project (1988–1990). I would also like to thank Tom Lockwood, Chair of the English Department, and the deans of the Graduate College and the College of Arts and Sciences at the University of Washington (UW) for providing the funding and the time I needed (1992–1997) to complete this project. Without everyone's generous backing, the project would never have come to fruition.

For their intellectual, emotional, and spiritual support during the many years I worked on this project, I would like to thank the following friends and colleagues: Johnnella E. Butler, Joe Butwin, Susana Carmona and Gustavo Espinosa, Ralph Cintron, Joe and Ann Coglianese, George Dillon and Gail Stygall, Anne Doyle, Lauro Flores, René Galindo, George Guerra and Janie Fong, Carol Eastman and John Jacobsen, Larry and Pam Harb, Gary Handwerk and Nancy Strom, Larry Joyce, Jabari Mahiri, David McCracken, Miguel Palacio, Leonard Ramírez, Therese Saliba and Tom Wright, Carol Severino, Sandra Silberstein and Doug Brown, Caroline Simpson, Keith and Sheri Toussaint, Olga Vásquez, and Priscilla Wald and Joe Donahue. Thank you all for bearing with me whenever I felt the need to share my thoughts and ideas. A special thanks to Keith Toussaint for coming to the rescue when computer problems stopped my project cold, and to Larry Joyce for providing room, board, and conversation during the final three years of this project.

At UIC, Marcia Farr and Lucía Elías-Olivares, co-principal investigators at the Mexican American Language and Literacy Project (MALLP), as well as my fellow research assistants, Susana Bañuelos, Edith Ortega, and María Tristán, played a critical role in establishing a strong foundation on which to build. Thanks also to Scott Moore for developing the Chicago maps and to my research assistants at UW—Olga Hernández, Laura Maldonado, Adolfo Ojeda-Casimiro, and Rebecca Robertson—for spending long and tedious hours transcribing and translating the interviews, letters, and autobiographical narratives. Your patience and hard work made my own job that much easier.

While I take full responsibility for any shortcomings this book may have,

I know that it's much improved because a number of friends and colleagues at UW: Gary Handwerk, Sandra Silberstein, and Priscilla Wald in particular, took time from their busy schedules to read drafts and to provide the kind of input and advice that made all the difference in the world. Just as helpful were the written comments from Teachers College Press's two outside reviewers; their recommendations for revision encouraged me to rethink my project in ways that transformed it for the better. And many thanks to Carol Chambers Collins and her colleagues at Teachers College Press: Carol for her good humor and excellent advice, her colleagues, especially Sarah Biondello and Karl Nyberg, for turning what might have been a chore into a meaningful adventure.

Finally, I want to thank members of my blood, marriage, and research families for making the biggest difference of all. They not only shared their lives with me in ways that provoked my continuing interest in the roles that language and literacy play in our lives; they also demonstrated unwavering interest in and support for my personal welfare and my professional work. First, I want to thank Jaime and Rocío Durán (pseudonyms, because unfortunately, they and everyone else in their social network must remain anonymous), as well as members of their transnational community in Chicago and Mexico, for inviting me into their homes and giving real meaning to the expression *"Mi casa es su casa."* Without their generous hospitality and willingness to share their lived experience with me at all hours of the day and night, this book would have been impossible.

Thanks also to my mother, my siblings, and their families in Texas for reinforcing my lifelong love and appreciation of language. A special thanks to my sister, Berta Cavazos, for introducing me to worlds I would not have come to know otherwise, and to my mother for teaching me by example that it is never too late to live life to its fullest. Many thanks also to my wife's family for helping me become more aware of and sensitive to the beauty of diversity, of the mingling of different tongues, of different ways with words. Special thanks to Bill and Alberta Jackson, Shirley Washington, Larry and Alvera Strong, and their families for providing me with room and board, warmth and comfort, and unwavering support. Lastly, my wife, Diane, and my son, Sean, made the past several years bearable by creating a place in our home where I could go and be myself, where I could go and share my doubts and fears, knowing that somehow, in some way, they would always help me overcome them. No one is more responsible for the completion of this work than Diane, my life companion, who worked at my side in the field and at home throughout the 10 years of the project's gestation and who now joins me in bringing forth, at long last, its timely birth.

Transcription Conventions

The necessary use of transcription conventions in the kind of work represented in this book always requires scholars to make difficult choices about the best way to represent the oral and written language they have collected in the course of their research. Because my primary goal is to focus on rhetorical and discursive practices, rather than on fine-grained issues important to linguists, I have made the following decisions.

Like Farr (1994b), I represent quotations from recordings of the oral language use in everyday life among, as well as the sociolinguistic interviews with, members of Jaime and Rocío Durán's social network in relatively simple, but clear and direct terms. Thus, "the original Spanish is followed by an English translation" in parentheses. I also use standard orthography, "except for features of casual speech (e.g., *m'ija* for *mi hija,* 'my daughter') or those that mark a particular dialect (e.g., *pos* for *pues,* 'well')." Moreover, because they are not relevant to the present analysis, "false starts are edited out" and "omitted material is indicated by ellipsis (. . .)" (Farr, 1994b, p. 34). I also place words or phrases that I had difficulty deciphering in the tape recordings between diagonal lines (/ assistance /) to indicate that they are educated guesses at best. If undecipherable words or phrases appear in a passage I quote, I indicate their presence with a question mark between diagonal lines (/ ? /). Finally, I sometimes add a word or phrase using brackets to help clarify the intended meaning.

As it was for Besnier (1995), my decision to "edit the form of written texts was a difficult one to make" (p. xvi). I was caught between wanting to represent their language as they had actually written it, something I did in an earlier publication (Guerra, 1996) and as it would appear in edited form, an approach that would lessen the demands on readers and encourage them to focus on the rhetorical and discursive features that I am interested in highlighting. Besnier's discussion convinced me to do the latter, especially in light of the fact that almost all of the writing produced by group members went through one draft only. Unfortunately, one of the elements that ends up getting lost is the range of technical skills of which different group members are capable. Indeed, the range suggests that among members of the group, writing conventions, especially those associated with surface issues (spelling, mechanics, and punctuation), are in constant flux.

All of the editorial changes I make in the sample texts that I culled from personal letters (written in Spanish) and autobiographical narratives (written in Spanish and English) occur at the micro level. I mainly add a variety of punctuation marks (commas, periods, dashes, etc.) and capitalize the first letters of sentences or proper names to make it easier for the reader to follow the often complex syntactical structures of some of the writers. I also standardize their orthography, especially in relation to spelling (*llo* for *yo*, or "I") and fused words (*conla* for *con la*, "with the"). And except for occasionally adding a missing word in brackets to clarify the meaning, changing a word ("my father" for "he"), or adding an inflection (*saludo[s]*, or "wish[es]"), I avoid standardizing their grammar and syntax. At the macro level, I avoid paragraphing where none is indicated by the writers and any changes in the overall presentation or organization of their narratives or ideas. In short, I standardize issues of etiquette rather than matters of form, substance, or function.

Close to Home

Oral and

Literate Practices

in a Transnational

Mexicano

Community

CHAPTER 1

Introduction

For some time now, scholars in language and literacy studies have struggled with conceptions of community. Long the centerpiece of countless ethnographies that described, analyzed, and interpreted cultures as autonomous and isolated entities, the notion of community served to join its members on the basis of shared beliefs and ideas, social and linguistic interaction, and a common physical space.[1] Heath's *Ways with Words* (1983), a classic example of how the practice of spatial distancing works, demonstrates how ethnographers can construct broad frontiers between communities to study them individually over a period of time. Not surprisingly, this makes it difficult, if not impossible, for readers to imagine members of the white working-class, the black working-class, and the integrated middle-class communities of Roadville, Trackton, and Maintown that Heath investigated mixing or interacting socially outside of school or work. In composition studies, Bizzell's (1982) contention that we are members of different discourse communities has produced a similar effect. Although Bizzell argued from the outset that we are all members of several discourse communities at the same time and that discourse communities intersect in a variety of ways, scholars like Bruffee (1984) and Bartholomae (1985) who found Bizzell's concept useful for their own purposes refashioned it into an insular, institutional apparatus governed by a set of conventions and constraints consented to by members of a group. In both instances, an inability or unwillingness to resist the processes of reification and essentialism resulted in communities with minimal deviance or disorder.

As more and more scholars have voiced their concerns about the problems with conceptualizing community in these terms, research interests have shifted dramatically from examining discrete and homogeneous communities to investigating the volatile frontiers between them. Spurred on by Pratt's (1991) introduction of the notion of "contact zones," many scholars now argue that people rarely share an isolated, idealized, or segregated communal experience. We are all, they proclaim, caught in a vortex of hybridity and heterogeneity that makes it impossible for anyone to escape to the safe harbors of the familiar. In place of the rigid boundaries that separate the speech communities that Heath investigates, for example, Cintron (1993) declares a porosity impossible to seal. In their critiques of discourse communities, Harris (1989), Lu (1992), and Spellmeyer (1993) challenge arguments that posit consensual and well-defined patterns in the ways members of communities communicate. No matter how isolated these communities may seem, these critics argue, they are profoundly penetrated and disrupted by the voices that enter via the mass media's hegemonic proliferation and by the constant back-and-forth movement of members (and outsiders) who bring with them not only news from and about other communities, but other ways of speaking, thinking, seeing, and being. Of course, whenever we propose either/or arguments of this type, we are left with a dichotomous view of how people act in the world and how the forms of language and literacy they use function. And because we almost always find ourselves attracted to one of a set of diametrically opposed interpretations of the world— that is, that it is either a static reality where everything and everyone follows order and convention or a fluid one where everything and everyone is changing constantly—we end up missing the vast middle ground where the tension between the two plays itself out.

Members of the "closeknit social network"[2] (Milroy, 1987) of *Mexicanos* who are the focus of this book reside neither in a fixed community where habits and routines determine how they will behave, nor in a free-for-all environment hypothesized by some postmodernists where they are overwhelmed, even para-lyzed, by the options available to them. Instead, as I will explain in Chapter 2, they are caught in a quasi-communal configuration of their own creation that crosses national borders: While half of them reside in a spatially isolated *rancho* (a small rural village of small landowners) in the central plateau of Mexico, the other half live in the tumult of Chicago inner-city neighborhoods strongly influenced by the forces of a postindustrial capitalist society. Their transnational community,[3] created by their social, cultural, and linguistic com-mitment to one another, is both steeped in tradition *and* open to the kinds of change and conflict of which its members are not only aware but readily accept as a given in their lives. If language and literacy are, as almost everyone now agrees, deeply embedded in a "lived experience" (Prus, 1996) that influences the forms they take as groups of people engage one another in everyday life, it behooves us to understand the characteristics of the playing field where they unfold and betray their most salient features. Before I review the chapters that comprise the present study on the "communicative practices" (Grillo, 1989; Street, 1993, 1995) of the Mexicanos with whom I have worked over the course of nine years,[4] I want to discuss the concepts of home front and contact zone that frame my theoretical perspective and then describe the various social spaces that members of the Mexicano social network imagine themselves occupying (or not occupying)—the social spaces, that is, that their everyday actions and uses of oral and written language reflect, reinforce, or destabilize.

HOME FRONTS AND CONTACT ZONES

Driven in part by a desire to situate the communicative practices associated with members of particular groups, theorists and researchers have proposed different models of the social spaces in which language and literacy are used. Most of these models are based on a binary system that posits a center and a margin. While the more traditional models place the dominant language-of-power or community-in-power at the center and the dominated "powerless" language or "powerless" community at the margin, some alternative models switch the relationship between the two, because of their interest in examining how so-called subordinate languages operate. Because many of these models have been developed in the midst of what a number of social commentators call the "culture wars" of our time (Gates, 1992; Graff, 1993; Shor, 1986), it may help to refer to the communities from which representatives of the different social, cultural, political, economic, and linguistic groups originate as "home fronts" and the arenas where their differences clash, blend, or intermingle as "contact zones" (Pratt, 1991).

In two highly regarded essays, titled "Linguistic Utopias" (1987) and "Arts of the Contact Zone" (1991), Pratt provides one of the most provocative analyses of the binary model and expressly argues in favor of abandoning our work on the home front and focusing on the contact zone instead. After describing what she perceives as the inherent limitations of modern linguistics' theoretical stance and methodological approach, especially as they are reflected in its "imagined object of study, the [homogeneous and discrete] speech community" (p. 50), Pratt proposes a shift in focus from the centers to the margins of communities, "where cultures meet, clash, and grapple with each other, often in contexts of highly asymmetrical relations of power" (1991, p. 34). Using key aspects from Anderson's (1991) well-known formulation of nationality, nation-ness, and nationalism as "cultural artifacts of a particular kind" (p. 4)—what Anderson refers to in metaphorical terms as "imagined communities"[5]—Pratt demonstrates how utopian and dystopian tendencies among scholars in modern linguistics have led them to reify and essentialize the speech communities they study and thereby ignore the dynamism and heterogeneity that lie at their borders. "The distance between langue and parole, competence and perfor-mance," Pratt affirms, "is the distance between the homogeneity of the imagined community and the fractured reality of linguistic experience in modern stratified societies" (1987, p. 51).

Like Anderson's prototype of the modern nation-state, Pratt believes that "the image in which the speech community often gets conceived by modern linguistics" is characterized by a particular "style of imagining" reflected in its limitedness, its sovereignty, and its "deep, horizontal comradeship." Pratt notes, for example, that "our modern linguistics of language, code, and competence posits a unified and homogeneous social world in which language exists as shared patrimony." Moreover, the

> prototype or unmarked sense of language is generally taken in linguistics to be the speech of adult native speakers face to face (as in Saussure's diagram) in

monolingual, even monodialectical situations—in short, the maximally homogeneous case linguistically and socially. This is the situation where the data are felt
to be "surest", where you can most clearly see the fundamentals of how language
works, with minimal distortion, infelicity or "noise". (p. 50)

While pragmatics and discourse theory are more closely tied to social interaction
than grammar-based linguistics, Pratt argues that even there, we see styles of
imagining reflected in a "tendency overwhelmingly to present exchanges in
terms of single sets of shared rules and understandings, and the orderliness
they produce. Disorders," she laments, "are almost automatically seen as failures
or breakdowns not to be accounted for within the system" (p. 51).

Even sociolinguists, who "have often criticised the homogenising and nor-
malising tendencies of formal grammar and discourse analysis and have placed
the social variability of language at the centre of their agenda," fall into the
same trap. This results, Pratt claims, in utopian and dystopian accounts that
misrepresent how language and literacy actually operate in the communities
they study. In sociolinguistics, Pratt persuasively argues, "styles, registers and
varieties are typically treated not as lines which divide the community, but as
shared property, a communal repertoire which belongs to all members and
which all seek to use in appropriate and orderly ways" (p. 51). In Pratt's view,
for example, Labov's (1972) work on Black English Vernacular not only fits
within the limitations of the three utopian characteristics associated with Anderson's "style of imagining" (i.e., limitedness, sovereignty, and fraternity), but
adds an element of authenticity that creates the expectation that all members
of a group must, by definition, speak in the same register, style, or dialect.
And in Bernstein's (1971) work, Pratt (1987) notes, we have a construction of
"working-class life as a linguistic dystopia whose internal character accounts
for the social disenfranchisement of the working class." Thus, while Labov
"suggests Black English represents no problem," for Bernstein, "working class
verbal culture represents nothing but a problem" (p. 58).

In light of the difficulties that she sees with a traditional approach to the
study of language and literacy, Pratt offers an alternative that acknowledges
what she calls "the relationality of social differentiation" (p. 59). Consider
instead, Pratt tells us,

> a linguistics that decentered community, that placed at its centre the operation
> of language *across* lines of social differentiation, a linguistics that focused on modes
> and zones of contact between dominant and dominated groups, between persons
> of different and multiple identities, speakers of different languages, that focused
> on how such speakers constitute each other relationally and in difference, how
> they enact differences in language. (p. 60)

Here, in my judgment, Pratt is proposing what she purports is the real, rather
than the imagined, circumstances of people's lives. In so doing, Pratt's model

privileges what happens at the margins and devalues what happens at the centers of speech communities. Indeed, a number of theorists and researchers who have taken up Pratt's clarion call (Bizzell, 1994; Cintron, 1997; Miller, 1994; Sullivan, 1995; van Slyck, 1997; Vásquez, Pease-Alvarez, & Shannon, 1994) have added to our growing understanding of how different forms of discourse wrestle with one another in contact zones and often result in hybrid forms that illustrate the increasingly heterogeneous future that awaits us all. I would argue, however, that we still need to learn as much as we can about the actual lived experience of members of marginalized groups in the United States, especially those whose limited economic and educational options give them little choice but to make their homes in highly segregated racial and ethnic communities out of which some members rarely venture.

Most adult members of the close-knit social network of *Mexicanos* who are the focus of this book historically have had limited contact with individuals outside their group. Only on occasion have they entered the contact zone, as Pratt conceptualizes it. Due to those two factors, I find another model more helpful in explaining how their communicative practices function in a range of social spaces. The basic outline for this model, one in which the center and the margins are not dichotomized but interact dialectically, is proposed by Bizzell (1982) in "Cognition, Convention, and Certainty: What We Need to Know about Writing." Like Pratt, Bizzell developed her model as an alternative, in her case, to one Flower and Hayes (1981) used to illustrate their interpretation of how the writing process works. In her essay, Bizzell describes how the innate mental capacities, which normal human individuals possess, allow them to learn a native tongue and form "thought patterns that organize and interpret experience." And because normal human individuals are members of social groups, these "thought and language capacities" evolve as they interact with one another and thereby modify "reasoning, speaking, and writing within" the group. As a consequence, Bizzell concludes,

> Groups of society members can become accustomed to modifying each other's reasoning and language use in certain ways. Eventually, these familiar ways achieve the status of conventions that bind the group in a discourse community, at work together on some project of interaction with the material world. An individual can belong to more than one discourse community, but her access to the various communities will be unequally conditioned by her social situation. (p. 214)

On the surface, the picture that Bizzell paints of how language functions in a community seems very similar to the one Pratt criticizes in her work. One of the more important differences, however, is that in Bizzell's model disorders are not "automatically seen as failures or breakdowns not to be accounted for within the system" (Pratt, 1987, p. 51). As a matter of fact, later in her essay,

residents of Chicago, many of them know that almost 40% of the Spanish-surnamed or Spanish-speaking population of the city of Chicago consists of other Latino national groups. Still, of all the communities of which they imagine themselves members, their connection to this community is probably the most tenuous. I know of only one case, for example, in which someone in the group was personally connected on a long-term basis to a Latino or Latina whose family origins were not Mexican. On occasion, Marisela Padilla, a young Puerto Rican woman whom Jaime's wife, Rocío, had befriended at work, would visit her home. My long-term observations suggest that identification with the Latino community is primarily the result of their familiarity with it through the media. Whenever the radio or television was on in any group member's home and adults were present, they almost always were tuned to one of several Spanish-language radio stations or television networks that offered news, music, sports, soap operas, or variety shows produced throughout Latin America. In short, group members gain most of their knowledge about other Latinos through the mass media rather than through personal contact.[10]

Because many of the adults and children in the social network currently reside in a home front located in two contiguous and highly segregated Chicano/Mexicano[11] neighborhoods in Chicago known as Pilsen and Little Village,[12] they have had an easier time imagining themselves part of Pilsen/Little Village or, in slightly more general terms, part of a group in the city that is described as "people of Mexican origin." While they often imagine themselves members of the same ethnic group, it is important to acknowledge the significant differences between the Chicanos and Mexicanos who often share the same social spaces in Chicago's inner-city neighborhoods. Unlike the members of the social network on which this study focuses, Chicanos in Chicago tend to have limited command of the Spanish language. Moreover, because many of them have lived in Chicago for several generations, they have acculturated to varying degrees. As a matter of fact, the most assimilated among them sometimes contend that Mexicanos are to blame for many of the social problems for which Chicanos in the city are sometimes held responsible. Mexican immigrants, on the other hand, are disturbed by the inability or unwillingness of many Chicanos to speak Spanish, something that immigrants know marks them as recently arrived Mexicans. Chicanos and Mexican immigrants, however, appear to have more in common with each other than either of them does with other Latino groups. Because they reside in the same neighborhoods, demonstrate a similar economic status, and have familial and cultural ties to Mexico, in many respects they are mutually drawn to and imagine themselves members of the same ethnic community.

As a consequence of their recent arrival (the oldest members of the social network settled in Chicago as undocumented workers in the late 1960s and early 1970s) and a shared nationalist perspective deeply rooted in Mexico, adult members tend to feel a stronger sense of communal identification with other Mexican immigrants living in the neighborhood than they do with Chicanos. Their closer ties to this group are highlighted by the fact that during casual conversations and formal interviews with most of the adult members of the social network, all but Mary Ann and Marta identified themselves as Mexicanos or Mexicanas. Although they are bilingual and have access to mainstream culture through the media, the schools, and their peers, the overwhelming majority of U.S.-born children in the group also made a point of identifying themselves as Mexicanos or Mexicanas. To some extent, their tendency to self-identify as Mexicanos is related to the fact that English is rarely spoken in the home and that group members travel back and forth between their homes in Chicago and their ranchos in Mexico on a continuous basis. The biggest influence, however, is probably the fact that they live in highly segregated Chicano/Mexicano neighborhoods where, because of linguistic differences between the two groups, members of the social network tend to interact primarily with other Mexicanos in school, at work, and on social occasions. In short, most of their daily experiences unfold in social spaces where Spanish is the dominant language and where their fellow Mexicanos are the overwhelming majority of participants. There are some exceptions, of course—two children in one family attend a high school that is half Chicano/Mexicano and half African American; three attend a highly mixed state university; and the bosses or managers at many of their jobs are African American or European American—but these contacts tend to be few and far between.

I would argue, then, that members of the social network interact with one another more often in, and therefore imagine themselves most closely allied through, a multidimensional, social space that I am here referring to as a transnational community. Their transnational community is complicated by the fact that it consists of three separate home fronts: the two separate ranchos in Mexico where Jamie and Rocío were born and raised and the contiguous neighborhoods of Pilsen and Little Village in Chicago, where a large number of the ranchos' former residents have established a third home front through marriage and the system of *compadrazgo*.[13] Although the two ranchos are only about four hours apart by car and residents rarely travel back and forth to visit one another, they still are bound by the social relationships that members of the two ranchos residing in Chicago have forged as a consequence of Jaime and Rocío's marriage. From my research perspective, Jaime and Rocío represent the link that unites them all into a single, albeit complex, social network and transnational community. Although the group's patterns have changed over the years as members have had differences of opinion and have gone their separate ways, as men from Rancho Verde have brought their families to the United States, as some members have left the Pilsen/Little Village area and moved into ethnically mixed neighborhoods, and as others have returned to Mexico on a permanent basis, most social network members maintain a linguistic relationship that binds them socially and culturally and is best reflected in the conversations they share and the letters they write to one another. It is these changing facets of their lives—especially their uses of oral and written language, both self-initiated and elicited—that this book proposes to examine.

CHRONICLE OF A TALE FORETOLD

In the introduction to her edited collection, *Making Face, Making Soul (Haciendo Caras): Creative and Critical Perspectives by Women of Color*, Anzaldúa (1990) notes that "the white writing about Native peoples or cultures displaces the Native writer and often appropriates the culture instead of proliferating it" (p. xxi). What Anzaldúa does not say is that Native writers, especially within the academy, often are forced by institutional pressures to appropriate their own cultures. To avoid giving in to this tendency, our goal as researchers and scholars, Native or White, must always be to proliferate information about a culture rather than to appropriate it. For this reason, similar to several book-length studies by other scholars (Delgado-Gaitan & Trueba, 1991; Heath, 1983; Scollon & Scollon, 1981; Taylor & Dorsey-Gaines, 1988; Vásquez, Pease-Alvarez, & Shannon, 1994), *Close to Home: Oral and Literate Practices in a Transnational Mexicano Community* attempts to broaden our understanding of what language and literacy mean as social and cultural phenomena, rather than narrowly linguistic ones, and of how they are acquired and practiced by members of a particular ethnic minority group in the United States. More specifically, it describes the rhetorical strategies that Mexicanos use to represent themselves and their culture in discursive terms and examines the use of such strategies in various oral and written genres, looking especially at how the introduction of discourse styles from outside of the community influences traditional practices. Although its primary focus is on the discursive practices of social network members who reside in Chicago—a city with the second-largest Mexicano and the fourth-largest combined Chicano/Mexicano populations in the United States (Garza, 1994b)—the book moves beyond the confines of their inner-city neighborhoods to explore the social, cultural, and linguistic relationships that connect them to their ranchos in Mexico. As a consequence, readers gain insight not only into specific uses of oral and written language, but also into the ways in which the experiences of some group members as immigrants have transformed their communicative practices.

While it is widely agreed that context is an important element in understanding any communicative practice, Street (1993) is careful to differentiate between immediate and broader contexts within which language and literacy occur. "There is little point," Street stresses, "in attempting to make sense of a given utterance or discourse in terms only of its immediate 'context of utterance', unless one knows the broader social and conceptual framework that gives it meaning" (p. 14). In keeping with Street's perspective, Chapter 2, "Mexicano Communities and Families in Transition," establishes a historical and sociocultural context for my analysis and interpretation of the oral and written sample texts that I present in later chapters. The chapter opens with a historical overview of the immigration of Mexicanos to the United States and, more specifically, to Chicago. After describing how I came to work with members of the social network, the chapter shifts to a discussion of two of the three home fronts where most members of the group reside: Rancho Verde in Mexico and Pilsen/Little Village in Chicago. This section examines the circumstances that led almost half of Rancho Verde's population to abandon their homes and move, primarily to Chicago. On the basis of a demographic survey that I conducted in Rancho Verde and the U.S. Census Bureau data that I gathered about their community in Chicago, I next analyze the group's current, but always fluctuating, patterns of residency. The final section provides a brief overview of the ways in which language and literacy are implicated in the larger context and serves as a transition into the rest of the book.

Chapter 3, "Metaphorical Representations of Orality and Literacy," examines how attempts to define highly contested notions like orality and literacy rely heavily upon metaphorical conceptions and introduces a metaphor that emerges from my work with members of the social network. It argues, first, that we need to acknowledge the role metaphor plays in these varied definitions—especially if we hope to understand how and why the terms shift repeatedly—and, second, that we need to carefully examine the metaphors used for those terms to understand the ideological perspectives invoked. Once an interpretive framework for analyzing the role of metaphor (see Johnson, 1987; Lakoff, 1987; Lakoff & Johnson, 1980) and ideology (Berlin, 1988; Therborn, 1980) is established, the first part of the chapter reviews how scholars have realigned the relationship between orality and literacy by shifting from a spatial trope that distances and separates them (dichotomous) to one that has them intermingle and occupy the same space (continuous). The next section then identifies and analyzes 62 "basic-level" metaphors (e.g., literacy as adaptation, state of grace, power, etc.) that have been used to interpret literacy. The chapter's final section establishes the importance of moving from models that represent the relationship between orality and literacy as dichotomous (Goody & Watt, 1968; Olson, 1977), continuous (Tannen, 1982), or dialectical (Heath, 1982) to one that represents orality and literacy as communicative practices (Grillo, 1989; Street, 1993, 1995). This leads to my description of the components of a metaphor that emerges from my work with Mexicanos: orality and literacy as rhetorical practices.

Close rhetorical and textual analyses of the discursive materials I collected in the field begin in Chapter 4, "Oral Language Use in Everyday Life." In the first section, I develop a conceptual framework that describes how rhetoric and ideology manifest themselves in a variety of oral and written genres (Bourdieu, 1991; Hanks, 1987) practiced by Mexicanos. This framework provides a theoretical model for analyzing and interpreting the sample texts presented in this and the following two chapters. The next section then examines the group members' provisional conception of rhetoric as they described it in a series of interviews. The section also demonstrates the group members' sensitivity to the abstract qualities of oral language and their awareness of how it can be used to entertain, enlighten, and effect change. In the final section, I present a series of sample texts culled from tape recordings of oral language use in everyday life to illustrate three genres of a "secular ritual" (Moore & Myerhoff, 1977) that members of the group refer to as *"echar plática"* (to chat): "self-oriented" personal narratives, "other-oriented" personal narratives (Stahl, 1983), and propositional statements.

Chapters 5 and 6 shift the focus from oral to written language, continuing to demonstrate the facility with which Mexicanos manipulate discursive language in varied contexts and genres. In Chapter 5, "Personal Letter-Writing in a Mexicano Context," I examine and analyze a corpus of 44 self-initiated personal letters written by members of the social network. Because obtaining personal letters from social network members proved a difficult task for me as a researcher, the first section discusses the problems I experienced. To establish a cross-cultural context for understanding these letters, I then review earlier research on personal letter-writing, focusing specifically on Scribner and Cole's (1981) work among the Vai of Liberia and Besnier's (1988, 1991, 1993, 1995) work among the residents of Nukulaelae, an atoll of the central Pacific. The chapter's final section examines the general characteristics and social functions, as well as the specific form and content, of letters written by members of the group. The first level of analysis focuses on the age, gender, and social relationships of the letter writers and receivers, demonstrating how letters serve to maintain and reinforce the personal relations of group members in two distant home fronts and the possible feminization of literacy in the context of this specific genre. The second level then illustrates how the letters I collected are "overtly framed with the help of a number of specific framing markers, which are always present at the *beginning* and the *end* of the text" (Besnier, 1991, p. 70). The last level of analysis demonstrates that while the form of their letters is highly conventionalized, the content is somewhat varied, even individualized, especially in terms of how letter writers represent self and culture.

Chapter 6, "The Autobiographical Writing of *Las Tres Marías*," shifts the focus to examples of elicited writing produced by three young women in the social network. Because this chapter deals with writing that may not be typical of members of the community, the first section presents the rationale for and a brief description of the process I went through in gathering samples of autobiographical writing. In the next section, I discuss the rhetorics of individuality and relationality (Battaglia, 1995) purportedly used by autobiographers, respectively male and female, majority and minority, to position and construct themselves in their writing. I conclude the section with Watson's (1993) argument that theory in autobiography must resist the reification and essentialism of the self, whether they originate in traditional or feminist perspectives. In the last section, I provide background information about each young woman's current life circumstances, to contextualize the ways in which each establishes rhetorical personas that work with and against the rhetorical conventions the young women learned in their social network and in various school settings. While all three young women are cousins and were in their late teens when they wrote the narratives, their life experiences in Chicago and Mexico, language facility in English and Spanish, marital status, extent of schooling, and representations of the world are dramatically different. Consequently, an examination of their writing and its contents provides readers with insights into the degrees of difference that exist in any community of supposedly like-minded individuals.

Finally, in Chapter 7, "Conclusion," I review what we learn from examining the communicative practices of Mexicanos in everyday life and discuss the implications of this knowledge, especially the ways that it can be used by theorists, researchers, policymakers, and educators to provide adult Mexicanos and their children with a relevant education that effectively merges their schooling and lived experience. Because I believe that any successful and meaningful process of education is by definition an act of intervention and transformation, I agree that individuals who go through it, both teachers and students, are inevitably changed by it in a variety of ways. To make the most of an educational experience, students must learn how to manipulate language in a school context in ways somewhat different from those used in their respective homes and communities. At the same time, however, I believe that we must keep in mind that the personal changes participants experience, as well as the differences in language between their home and school communities, are more often matters of degree rather than quality. As Bizzell (1982) and others (Severino, 1992) have argued and as this book suggests, the communicative practices individuals bring from their home communities to educational settings—whether those settings are elementary or high schools, adult literacy programs or universities—share a number of similarities with those institutions' practices. As such, we must remember that moving from one discourse community to another does not simply entail bridging a discontinuity, but more likely suggests a need for adaptation, for reorientation, for what Lu (1992) calls repositioning.

In an attempt to come to terms with the circumstances that marginalize people, *Close to Home* explores the ways in which different members of the social network use oral and written language to negotiate their way through the discursive challenges they face in the United States and Mexico. It attempts to capture the complexities of language and literacy use that modulate between personal/individual aspirations and the social/cultural constraints that inform and govern interaction in their community. In short, it addresses questions about who is expected or has a right to speak or write in a range of rhetorically and ideologically charged genres. In this way, of course, Mexicanos are no different from members of any other group perpetually caught in the dialectic between the voice of Institution and the voice of Inclination (Foucault, 1982). On the other hand, they are different in many other ways, especially in terms of the status of some members of their transnational community as immigrants caught in the twin desires to improve their lives economically and to continue to enrich them culturally. In the end, the book's primary goals are to demonstrate the richness of the linguistic and cultural resources available to adult Mexicanos and to provide a basis for intervening effectively in their own and their children's educational development. For it is only by understanding the extent to which Mexicanos are already capable of manipulating oral and written language that teachers can develop curricula and pedagogical techniques that take into consideration the group's "communicative economy" (Hymes, 1974) and the "funds of knowledge" (Moll & Díaz, 1987) that adults and children bring with them into any classroom.

CHAPTER 2

Mexicano Communities and Families in Transition

According to current U.S. Census reports, the city of Chicago has the second-largest Mexicano population in the United States and the fourth-largest combined Chicano/Mexicano population behind the southwestern cities of Los Angeles, San Antonio, and Houston (Garza, 1994b). Whenever I report this staggering statistic to students or colleagues who are not aware of the size of Chicago's Mexican-origin population, most of them are utterly confounded by my remark. How and why, they often ask, did so many Mexicanos leave their homes and migrate to a distant city outside the southwestern United States? How and why indeed? While most people in this country are familiar with the well-publicized efforts of the U.S. government to curtail the ever-growing Mexican immigrant population in this country, especially by deporting those who enter the country illegally or making it difficult for employers to hire them, very few are aware of this country's complicity over the past 100 years in creating the political circumstances that it now deplores (Betancur, 1996). For many, it is easier to blame the Mexican government or the immigrants themselves for usurping what they consider the "inviolable right" of the United States to monitor and maintain its borders. Rarely, however, does anyone acknowledge the fact that "Mexico is the paramount example of the rise of a working-class immigrant community through external intervention followed by induced labor outflows" (Portes & Rumbaut, 1990, p. 225).

Historically, immigrants who have come to the United States from Europe, Asia, and other continents have described—or have been represented as de-scribing—their journey as one that entails leaving their home country and "coming to America." For many of them, it has been and continues to be, in both spatial and psychological terms, a journey to a "faraway" land. But because they share the same border, believe that the United States government "stole" half of their national territory, and consider Mexico a part of the Americas (and more specifically of North America), most Mexicanos rarely speak of the immigration process in the same terms. When asked about their immigration from Mexico to this country, Mexicanos often describe the experience as one of "coming to the United States" or, more likely, of coming to a specific locale such as Texas, California, Los Angeles, or Chicago. This particular perception is strongly reinforced by the fact that Mexicanos usually refer to a citizen of this country not as an "American" but rather as *un estadounidense* (a United Statesian). While the famous saying usually attributed to Mexican dictator Porfirio Díaz—"*Pobre México, tan lejos de Dios y tan cerca de los Estados Unidos*" ("Poor Mexico, so far from God and so close to the United States")—is an extreme version of this perception, it reflects a relationship that is unlike the assumed or expressed relationship that many other national groups in the world have with the United States.

THE IMMIGRATION OF MEXICANOS TO THE UNITED STATES

The relationship and perception that many Mexican immigrants have developed began quite dramatically with Mexico ceding half its national territory to the United States in 1848. As a consequence, nearly 100,000 Mexican citizens were suddenly presented with the difficult decision of whether or not to become U.S. citizens. Most reports from the time suggest that very few decided to leave the frontier and return to Mexico. Before long, the Mexicanos who chose to remain were outnumbered by European Americans whom the U.S. government encouraged to migrate and settle in the sparsely populated region with promises of land and prosperity. Although the landholdings of the Mexicans who chose to stay behind were supposedly protected by the Treaty of Guadalupe Hidalgo, well before the turn of the century, most of them were "divested of both political and economic influence in all areas except northern New Mexico and south Texas" (Gutiérrez, 1995, p. 14). While the hardships they faced made daily life difficult for them, they also laid the foundation "for the eventual emergence of a new sense of solidarity" among Mexican-origin residents of the Southwest, an event that transformed the sense of isolation they had felt "from the centers of Mexican civilization and society and from one another by the region's vast expanses of mountains and deserts" (p. 14). The social, economic, and political upheavals that occurred in Mexico and the United States over the next several decades also set the stage for what became the first of three massive waves of immigration that brought millions of Mexicanos across the border into the United States and created the complex, and at times seemingly intractable, scenario that we have today (Durand & Massey, 1992).

For generations before the ascension of Porfirio Díaz to power in 1876, *campesinos* lived on communally owned lands called *ejidos* and *peones* lived "on privately owned *haciendas*, both of which had as their economic function the provisioning of nearby urban centers" (Cardoso, 1980, p. 1). Life in the densely populated central plateau region of Mexico was already quite difficult. Because only about 10% of the land in the area could be cultivated, it could not sustain such a large population. Moreover, the introduction and expansion of the railroad in the 1870s and 1880s encouraged the export of luxury food items and discouraged the cultivation of items that could be bought and used locally. To make matters worse, Díaz's sponsorship of "a series of colonization schemes and land reforms that deprived almost all *ejidatarios* of their ancestral rights to whatever remained of their common lands" (p. 5) resulted in the complete collapse of land ownership by campesinos in Mexico. In its attempt to achieve "capitalist modernization of the countryside," the Díaz government encouraged the immigration of European colonists from northern and western Europe, hoping they "would plant the seeds of economic progress in the countryside and have a favorable influence on the 'regressive' Indian and mestizo peasantry" (p. 6). While the colonization plan failed, it opened the door for local landowners, who formed "colonizing companies" and swallowed up all available communal property. By 1910, 97% of the rural families residing in the central plateau did not own any land (Cardoso, 1980).

While the displacement of campesinos from the land by Díaz's "draconian land policies" and the continuing development of a new railway system set the stage, several other factors contributed to the actual unfolding of the first great wave of Mexican immigration into the United States. In addition to the Mexican Revolution of 1910, which led up to 10% of Mexico's population (more than 1,000,000 people) to flee to the United States, and the conscription of 1,000,000 U.S. nationals into military service during World War I (Cardoso, 1980), a mining boom in northern Mexico and the expansion of agriculture through the development of irrigation projects encouraged U.S. employers to exploit Mexican workers willing to fill the low-skilled, low-paying jobs that rapid economic growth in northern Mexico and the southwestern United States was producing. Employers in the United States—who had begun contracting and transporting Mexican laborers to the Southwest via the ever-expanding railway system now connecting the interior of Mexico to northern Mexico and the southwestern United States—grew even more desperate for their labor after nativist hysteria among American workers, growers, and some small businesses led to the passage of the Chinese Exclusion Act of 1882 and the Gentlemen's Agreement between the United States and Japan in 1908 (Gutiérrez, 1995, pp. 43–44). In light of their treatment of Chinese and Japanese immigrants, one wonders why even the most rabid race determinists did not feel threatened by Mexican immigrants. According to Cardoso (1980), Mexican immigrants were tolerated because, in addition to possessing what American nativists considered a "homing pigeon" instinct, they "did not have to cross vast oceans to secure employment . . . and were never more than a short train ride away from their native land." Moreover, "what had proven to be a miserly wage for Europeans, Asians, and native laborers was an adequate income for the peon or campesino from rural Mexico" (p. 22).

Contrary to nativist expectations, contracted Mexican immigrant workers did not come to the United States for short periods of time and then return to their homes across the border. As a consequence and in the context of the depression of 1921–1922 that left more than six million men and women unemployed in the United States, nativists strongly urged the U.S. Congress to pass the National Origins Immigration Act of 1924, which simultaneously created the Border Patrol and, for the first time in history, represented undocumented Mexican workers as "illegal immigrants" (Portes & Rumbaut, 1990, p. 226). Although the U.S. economy improved significantly toward the end of 1922, the stock market crash of 1929 and the ensuing Great Depression again raised fears and concerns about the impact of immigrant labor on the employment opportunities of U.S. citizens. Because they could easily be cast as scapegoats, Mexican immigrants were rounded up and deported by the Border Patrol, the government agency created to monitor their flow into the country. While statistics involving Mexican immigration during this period in history are notoriously unreliable, most scholars estimate that "at least 350,000, and perhaps as many as 600,000" of the 1,422,533 Mexican-origin people living in the United States in 1930 were deported or forced to return to Mexico on their own between 1930 and 1940 (Gutiérrez, 1995, p. 72).

The second major wave of Mexican immigration to the United States began in 1942 with the U.S. government's creation of the Emergency Farm Labor Program, better known as the Bracero Program. Because the U.S. government's entry into World War II again resulted in the conscription and channeling of large numbers of men and women in support of the war effort, employers, especially in the Southwest's agricultural region, raised "a hue and cry about severe labor shortages" (Gutiérrez, 1995, p. 133). Concerned about the repeated exploitation of its citizens, the Mexican government remained reluctant to enter into a bilateral labor agreement until it received the U.S. government's assurance that "Mexican workers' interests would be protected" (p. 134). Desperate for unskilled labor, U.S. businessmen and landowners persuaded their government to grant work permits to 4.6 million Mexican laborers during the 22 years the Bracero Program was in place. It is important to remember, however, that during this same period, the Immigration and Naturalization Service (INS) apprehended and deported nearly 5 million undocumented Mexican immigrants, many of them as part of what the agency called "Operation Wetback." In the midst of this balancing routine, Congressional approval of the Immigration and Nationality Act (INA) of 1952, which exempted the spouses and minor children of U.S. citizens from numerical limits and the preference system, contributed to the steady growth in the number of Mexican immigrants entering the country legally (Durand & Massey, 1992, p. 6). By 1965, according to the U.S. Census Bureau, nearly 4 million persons of Mexican descent legally resided in the United States.

Because the Mexican economy could not generate enough jobs to support an exploding population and the economy in the United States was booming as a consequence of the Vietnam War, the ebb between the second and third waves of Mexican immigration was short-lived. A dramatic increase in the number of apprehensions reported by the INS signaled this shift. After exceeding the 100,000 mark in 1967 for the first time in several years, the number of apprehensions "approached five hundred thousand by 1970, exceeded six hundred eighty thousand in 1974, and neared the one million mark in fiscal 1977" (Gutiérrez, 1995, p. 188). In their attempt to place the blame for the shortage of jobs that resulted from a sharp recession in 1970 and 1971, the national print media published stories describing the influx of undocumented Mexican immigrant laborers "as a human flood or a silent invasion" (p. 188). Thus, while INS agents were engaged in an unprecedented series of neighborhood sweeps aimed at apprehending and returning so-called illegal aliens to Mexico, Congress initiated a debate about the best ways to bring the "silent invasion" to an end once and for all. The process, which began in 1972 with the introduction of legislation that would impose criminal sanctions against employers who knowingly hired undocumented immigrants and establish a new, counterfeit-proof national identification system, eventually culminated in the Simpson-Rodino bill that Congress enacted into law as the Immigration and Reform Control Act (IRCA) of 1986. While the criminal sanctions recommendation survived and a general amnesty for undocumented immigrants who could prove they had resided in the United States continuously for at least 8 years became part of the overall legislation, the identification system went down to bitter defeat. Despite all these efforts to curtail it, the Chicano/ Mexicano population in the United States more than tripled between 1965 and 1990 to 13.4 million. (Gutiérrez, 1995).

Although legislation aimed at immigration reform finally made it through Congress 14 years after it was first introduced, most research suggests that it has been generally ineffective in slowing the flow of undocumented Mexican immigrants into the United States (Durand & Massey, 1992). While some historians contend that the continuing immigration of Mexicans to the United States, both documented and undocumented, is caused primarily by Mexico's rapid industrialization and a tripling in its population growth since World War II (Kennedy, 1996), there is no doubt that one of the overriding factors responsible for this historic shift is "the central role that Americans of all walks of life have played" in encouraging the entry of undocumented immigrants during periods of extreme labor shortages in the United States (Gutiérrez, 1995, p. 211). Portes and Rumbaut (1990) highlight a second very important reason for the continuing flow of immigrants, Mexican and otherwise, into the United States:

> Contrary to the assertion that international labor migration is basically an outcome of individual decisions governed by the law of supply and demand, we argue that

the phenomenon is primarily socially embedded. Networks developed by the movement of people back and forth in space are at the core of the microstructures that sustain migration over time. More than individualistic calculations of gain, the insertion of people into such networks helps explain differential proclivities to move and the enduring character of migration flows. . . . Families apparently pass on their knowledge of the different aspects of the process and its expected rewards to younger generations. This mechanism helps explain the self-sustaining character of the flow as well as its selectivity of destinations. (p. 231)

THE SETTLEMENT PATTERNS
OF MEXICANOS IN CHICAGO

According to the U.S. Census, Chicago became the second-largest city in the United States in 1900, its unprecedented growth fueled by the internal migration of large numbers of people who left "the isolation and sterility of rural life for the cities" (García, 1996, p. 4) and the immigration of Central, Southern, and Eastern Europeans heavily recruited by employers to meet the demands of an increasingly industrial and rapidly expanding economy in the Midwest (Portes & Rumbaut, 1990). Because this massive movement of laborers helped fill the needs of Midwestern urban centers well into the beginning of the twentieth century, there was no expressed need for the Mexican immigrants who were pouring into the southwestern United States to fill the needs of an expansionist, agricultural economy in that region. The few Mexicans who made their way to Chicago and the Midwest often came as farm workers destined to labor in the sugar beet fields or "as members of railway construction and maintenance crews" (García, 1996, p. 5). Before long, however, the severe labor shortages caused by the outbreak of World War I and the passage of the Immigration Act of 1917, which restricted the immigration of Southern and Eastern Europeans to the United States, created a vacuum in the industrial Midwest that employers decided could be filled quickly through the importation of Chicano/Mexicano laborers from the southwestern United States and Mexico (García, p. 28).

The recruitment of 206 railroad track laborers at the Texas–Mexican border in 1916 signaled the beginning of large-scale Mexican immigration to Chicago (Año Nuevo Kerr, 1976). In 1919, employers in the steel mills of south Chicago and northwest Indiana contributed to the growing population by recruiting a large group of Mexicans as strikebreakers. Despite the fact that they eventually had to compete with personnel being discharged from the U.S. military, Mexicans established themselves as productive and hard-working members of the steel industry. By the mid-1920s, for example, nearly 25% of the work force at Inland Steel in South Chicago were Mexican (García, 1996, pp. 39–41). And by the late 1920s, large numbers of Mexicanos—"overwhelmingly young, male, unskilled, and unorganized" (Año Nuevo Kerr, 1976, p. 20)—were finding their way to Chicago and settling in the three neighborhoods closest to the jobs Chicago's major industries had to offer: railroad workers moved into the Near West Side, packing house workers into Back of the Yards, and steel workers into South Chicago. As García (1996) notes, Mexicanos "clustered around the industries that employed them, not only because they needed to be near work, but also because housing around the plants was cheap and accessible" (p. 58). While Mexicanos inadvertently contributed to the formation of segregated communities as a consequence of their initial work and settlement patterns, Betancur (1996) stresses the complicity of "slumlords" who "rented to Mexicans vacant, unhealthy, run-down property in pockets of deterioration where Europeans would not live" (p. 1303).

As profound an effect as the Great Depression of the 1930s had on the rest of the country, its impact on the, until then, growing Mexican-origin population in Chicago was devastating. Because nativists chose to blame Mexicanos for taking "the jobs of Americans" during the Depression (Rosales & Simon, 1987, cited in Betancur, 1996, p. 1318), most Mexicanos in Chicago lost their jobs and were repatriated to Mexico. By 1934, the Chicano/Mexicano population in Chicago, which had peaked at 20,000 in 1930, had shrunk to 12,500 (Año Nuevo Kerr, 1976). The downturn, however, was short-lived. Once the ill effects of the Depression waned and the United States entered World War II, the flow of Mexicans into the Midwest, especially the Chicago metropolitan area, began anew. Having learned that Mexicans were readily available to fill the low-end jobs that others refused to take, employers in the industrial Midwest persuaded the federal government to expand the Bracero Program to include the temporary migration of nonagricultural workers. The effects of the program on Chicago were quite pronounced, as more than 15,000 Mexican railroad workers were brought to Chicago as contract laborers between May 1943 and September 1945 (Año Nuevo Kerr, 1976). Before their contracts ended and they went back home, employers encouraged many of them to return and "to bring friends, relatives, and others they know" (Betancur, 1996, p. 1318) to ensure, as employers do to this day, that those who return are "poor, unskilled, [and] uneducated" (p. 1303). By 1950, the Mexican-origin population in Chicago surpassed its earlier peak in 1930 as it climbed steadily to 24,000 (Año Nuevo Kerr, 1976).

In the 1950s, as Mexicanos immigrating to Chicago began to extend their stays, viable social networks were established in the neighborhoods where they settled. In my conversations and interviews with members of Jaime and Rocío Durán's social network, for example, I learned that a handful of their fathers, uncles, and older siblings became part of the contract-labor flow to Chicago during this phase of Mexicano immigration. Like many of their compatriots, once they had established a household in the heart of existing Mexicano communities and a network of employment contacts, members of the group would pool their resources to help bring other residents from their ranchos to Chicago to work. Because they were not yet willing or able to put their wives and children through the long and dangerous journeys that they experienced as undocumented immigrants, most members of the group lived with other men from their ranchos and sent money back to support their families. Because they eventually hoped to rejoin their families and bring to an end the extreme isolation of their immigrant experience, few made plans to settle permanently in Chicago. In their hearts and minds, they imagined their present situation as temporary, something they would abandon as soon as their economic circumstances had improved and they could go home again.

By 1960, however, as more and more Mexicanos began to transform their temporary stays into semipermanent residency through their expanding social networks in the city, the Mexican-origin population of Chicago nearly quadrupled from its post-Depression low of 12,500 to 44,686. While many of the new immigrants continued to settle in the three original Chicano/Mexicano neighborhoods of the late 1920s (i.e., the Near West Side, Back of the Yards, and South Chicago), more and more of them moved into neighboring areas or created new "pocket" neighborhoods in other sites throughout the city (see Figure 2.1). At the time, no one could have anticipated the unprecedented wave of growth that was about to take place in Chicago's Mexican-origin population and the impact it would have on the city's racial and ethnic settlement patterns. While the lure of "minimum-wage jobs in sweatshop manufacturing" and an expanding service economy (Betancur, 1996, p. 1302) have been cited as central factors in the unprecedented growth of Chicago's Mexicano population, the continuing establishment and expansion of social networks like the one I examine in this book clearly contributed to the continuing growth of Chicago's Mexican-origin community.

At about the same time that the settlement of Mexicanos in the city's neighborhoods began its unprecedented expansion, the ramifications of the turbulent political, civil, and racial strife of the late 1960s began to make their impact felt in Chicago. As it had in most northern urban centers in the country, the groundwork for Chicago's racial and ethnic segregation was established at the end of World War II with an increase in the flight of white residents to the suburbs emerging on the periphery of northern cities and the continuing in-migration of African Americans from the southern United States (Frey, 1980; Massey & Denton, 1993). Because white flight was economically based, working- and lower-middle-class descendants of the Southern and Eastern European immigrants who had lived in ethnically mixed neighborhoods in Chicago for generations and could not afford to move to the suburbs crowded into the northwest and southwest corners of the city. With the help of unscrupu-

FIGURE 2.1 Census Tract Areas in Chicago with 250 or More Mexican-Origin Residents (1960)

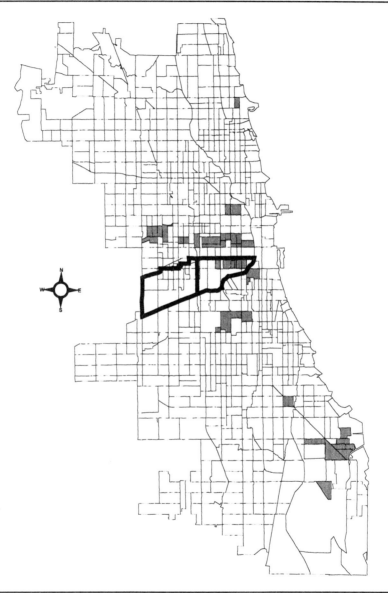

Sources: 1960 U.S. Census; Wessex Inc.

lous real estate agents and through the use of taunting and violence, many of them declared their neighborhoods White zones completely closed to African Americans (Massey & Denton, 1993). These tactics forced the thousands of African Americans still migrating to Chicago during this period to settle in their increasingly "hypersegregated" south and west side communities in Chicago (Massey & Denton, 1993). In the midst of a settlement process that transformed Chicago into the most segregated city in the United States (Massey & Denton, 1993), the expanding Chicano/Mexicano population in the city found itself also pushed into or contained in particular neighborhoods.

As the Chicano/Mexicano population of Chicago doubled to 82,097 between 1960 and 1970, Mexican-origin migrants and immigrants relocating to the city began to settle in increasing numbers in the relatively new Chicano/Mexicano community of Pilsen,[1] an area in transition predominantly occupied since the turn of the century by a mixture of Southern and Eastern European ethnics.[2] Because of the group's unprecedented growth, Chicanos/Mexicanos quickly "achieved majority in Pilsen" and started moving southwest into the adjacent and contiguous community of Little Village[3] (Betancur, 1996, p. 1319). By the time the Mexican-origin population of Chicago tripled to 255,793 between 1970 and 1980, Pilsen and Little Village became so densely populated that Chicanos/Mexicanos began to settle in adjacent communities often occupied by the members of European ethnic groups who were increasingly moving into affordable suburbs. At the same time, as the settlement of Mexicans in the north and northwest regions of the city continued to increase, a new Mexicano neighborhood emerged from within the Puerto Rican community in the Near Northwest Side of the city (Betancur, 1996). While the South Chicago community continued to grow steadily during this period, it remained relatively isolated from the more rapidly growing and highly congested Mexican neighborhoods to the north.

By the time the Mexican-origin population of Chicago passed the 350,000 mark in 1990, the ongoing settlement patterns were clear-cut. While racial prejudice and hypersegregation conspired to contain most African American residents within their all-black communities on the south and west sides of the city, Mexicanos continued to infiltrate the once all-White communities of the Northwest and Southwest Sides. As a consequence, Chicago today has three well-defined Mexicano "meganeighborhoods"[4] in the north, central, and south sides of the city (see Figure 2.2). Each continues to burgeon at the seams to such an extent that the Mexicano population has spilled over the city's borders into nearby suburbs. In the case of Cicero, a suburb that lies at the western end of a corridor of contiguous communities that includes Pilsen and Little Village, for example, Mexican-origin people now comprise 37% of its population.[5] With a combined 1990 population of 102,069 Mexican-origin residents and a saturation rate approaching 90% (Betancur, 1996), Pilsen and Little

FIGURE 2.2 Census Tract Areas in Chicago with 250 or More Mexican-Origin Residents (1990)

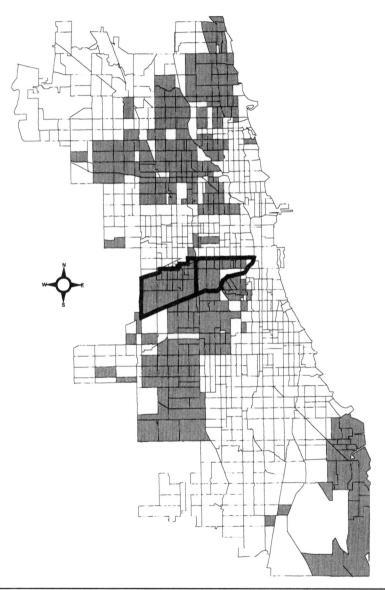

Sources: 1990 U.S. Census; Wessex Inc.

Village remain the largest, the most concentrated, and the most segregated Mexicano communities in the entire Chicago metropolitan area.

TIES THAT BIND, NEEDS THAT CALL:
NEGOTIATING THE TRANSITION BETWEEN HOME FRONTS

It is the evening of October 26, 1988. As I have done every day for the preceding two months in an effort to identify a Mexicano or Mexicana willing to serve as the initial contact person for a social network with which we can work,[6] I visit an advanced ESL class at *La Casa de Unidad* (The House of Unity). Because a new six-week session is beginning that night, the teachers and the students spend the first part of the period introducing themselves to one another. I listen as class members talk about their life experiences and their reasons for taking ESL classes. First and foremost, they are there because they want to learn enough English to prepare for the amnesty program that the federal government established through IRCA in 1986. Many of them also know that La Casa de Unidad will soon be offering amnesty classes and want to ensure a place for themselves by registering for English classes. When it's my turn to introduce myself, I speak briefly about my own family's immigration from Mexico, my youth in south Texas, my educational experiences in Chicago, and the research that has brought me to their classroom. After the introductions, their teacher, Monica, spends the rest of the first hour of class talking about what she hopes they will be able to accomplish during the coming six weeks.

After Monica announces a ten-minute break, we all step out into the hallway to stretch our legs and chat. One of the students, Jaime Durán, comes over to me, introduces himself, and asks me if I'd care to join him for a cup of coffee at a nearby restaurant. I accept his invitation, and we walk in the rain to a Mexican restaurant about two blocks from La Casa de Unidad. Before I know it, we have ordered dinner with our cups of coffee and have spent almost two hours talking about our lives. Jaime is not only interested in telling me about his experiences as an undocumented immigrant in Chicago; he is also curious about my own work and asks me a number of questions about what I expect our research to accomplish. I learn that Jaime first traveled from his rancho in the state of Guanajuato to Chicago in 1970 at the age of 17. A couple of years later he met his wife, Rocío, who had moved to Chicago in 1973 from her rancho in the state of Michoacán. While they have had three children, all of whom were born in Chicago over the preceding thirteen years, Jaime and his wife are still without legal documents. In addition to telling me about his work as the foreman of a railroad track repair crew composed completely of *"paisanos"* from his rancho of origin, Jaime tells me that he is a recovering alcoholic who hasn't had a drink in more than six years. I tell him that my colleagues and I are interested in establishing a relationship with members of a Mexicano social network so that we can spend time "hanging out" with them to learn about how they use oral and written language in their everyday lives. In the long run, I tell him, we hope to be able to educate others, especially the teachers in the schools, about the similarities and differences between how language is used in the home, community, and school.

When I return to Monica's class a few days later, she is interviewing her students as part of a role-playing activity and asking them questions related to their work. Of the nine students in her class,[7] two work in restaurants, one as a busboy and the other as a salad maker; two work in construction, one in cement and roadwork and the other in railroad construction; and the other five work in factories cutting ice, making screws, working with plastic sheeting, and making men's wallets. All of them say they work almost exclusively among other Mexicanos and rarely have any occasion to interact with English speakers. When break time comes, Jaime again invites me to join him for a cup of coffee. *"Esta vez"* (This time), he says, *"te quiero llevar a un restaurantito muy privado"* (I want to take you to a very private little restaurant). As we walk the three blocks from the community center to the "restaurantito," I begin to feel a bit disoriented. The place he is taking me to is not located on 18th Street, the principal business strip in the neighborhood, and I'm not aware of any small out-of-the-way cafes in the area. As we walk up to a two-story building squeezed tightly between two other buildings, I notice that the entrance to the first floor has store-like display windows on either side with heavy, drawn drapes that hide the interior. Jaime knocks lightly on the door and waits for the click of a lock being unlatched. After he grasps and turns the doorknob and pushes open the door with his shoulder, we walk in.

As soon as I step inside, I realize that we have just walked into Jaime's home. "Hi, *papi* [daddy]," a girl of about thirteen says to Jaime. "Hi, *m'ija* [my daughter]," Jaime responds. After he introduces me to his oldest daughter, Rosa María, and his two younger children, Yolanda and Juan Carlos, Jaime and I sit down in the living room while Rosa María goes to the kitchen to fix us some coffee. As I look around the apartment, I sense a coming home of sorts. While my colleagues and I have not yet met to decide who we are going to select as a contact person for our research project, intuitively, I sense that I will be working with Jaime and members of his social network. I am already imagining myself spending days on end with them over the next several years. Jaime and I chat for the next couple of hours about his love of traditional Mexican music, about problems with gangs in the neighborhood, about conditions in the schools his children attend, about how difficult it is, albeit not impossible, for the many who don't speak English to survive in this country.

After his wife Rocío comes home and I have a chance to meet her, we share a late supper, sit down to chat and watch television, and begin the slow but pleasant process of getting to know one another.

Before I leave their home that evening, I reflect on the historical circumstances that have brought Jaime and Rocío to this northern city so far away from their beloved ranchos in central Mexico. I suspect that many of the transitions they and members of their social network have experienced have been unsettling at best. True, their economic lives are probably much better than they would have been otherwise, but certain social and cultural aspects of those same lives remain unfulfilled. In the course of the days, months, and years I eventually end up spending with members of their social network in Chicago and Mexico, I learn through conversation, observation, and research about the ways in which they make use of oral and written language, not only to survive but to enrich their lives. I also learn something about how the transnational community that they have created for themselves—a complex, multidimensional social space that includes the home fronts they left behind in Mexico and the one where they have settled in Chicago—has changed over the years and what this means for them in terms of the social, cultural, educational, political, and economic options available to them now and in the future.

Paradise Lost, or The Great Escape?

Rancho Verde,[8] a hamlet of 106 dwellings crowded together on the edge of a bluff located at the southern end of the state of Guanajuato, is Jaime Durán's ancestral home. Here, in the rugged land that the community's ancestors settled more than 100 years ago, dozens of families share their lives, raising their few chickens, pigs, goats, cows, and oxen, toiling in the summer sun to grow their subsistence crops of beans and corn in the plots of land that they own in the surrounding area. The rancho is part of *el municipio de Textilpa y sus comunidades* (the municipality of Textilpa and its communities). Textilpa, a bustling city of 50,000 people known throughout the region for the manufacturing of clothing, is located some fifteen kilometers northeast of Rancho Verde (see Figure 2.3). Scattered throughout the municipio de Textilpa are the small town of *Pinicundo*, located about 3 kilometers from Rancho Verde, and 16 other ranchos. All of the ranchos lie on roads that stretch out like the spokes of a wheel to the south and the west of Textilpa. Most of them are no larger than Rancho Verde itself. Like Rancho Verde, most of them also have lost residents to Chicago and the other great urban centers in the United States that beckon them with their siren call of economic prosperity.

In the past few years, Rancho Verde has changed dramatically. Except for the electricity that came to the rancho in 1957 and supplanted their regular

FIGURE 2.3 Municipality of Textilpa, Guanajuato, Mexico, and Its Communities (1995)

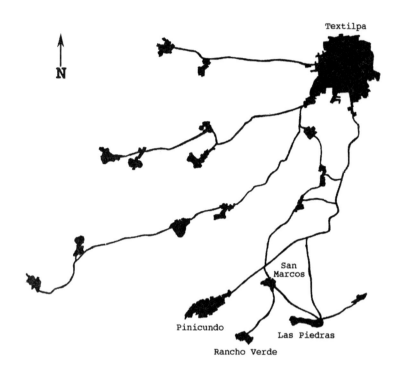

Source: Textilpa's Office of Public Works

use of candles and lanterns, all of the modern conveniences that most of us in the United States take for granted have been introduced in the past 10 years. In 1986, a pipeline carrying potable water to the rancho was installed. The 3-inch galvanized pipe runs along the front of each home, sometimes slightly hidden under the dirt, but usually exposed on the rock-laden ground. The introduction of running water has probably changed social relations in the rancho as much as any other recent development. The young women, especially, lament the water well's passing. "There," one of them said in Spanish during my first impromptu tour of the community, pointing down to the abandoned and dried-up well located at the foot of the bluff, "we used to gather and gossip, talk about boys, about our hopes and dreams. It was also one of the best places to flirt and talk with our boyfriends. From there," she continued, "we would carry the water containers up the steep incline back to our homes."

The gossip and flirting may continue, integrated into other social activities, but the water-gathering ritual is gone.

Rancho life has also changed in other dramatic ways. With the availability of running water came indoor plumbing and the sinks, toilets, and showers that this act of modernization made possible. Like everyone else in the rancho, during our first visit in 1989, my wife, Diane, and I had to go out into the woods to relieve ourselves, an unpleasant task for most of us who have been spoiled by the many conveniences that we take for granted. By our second visit in 1990, several families had installed toilets and showers that transformed another ritual activity. In 1990 we also traveled most of the 15 kilometers between Textilpa and Rancho Verde on a paved road that replaced the dirt road that used to connect Textilpa and Pinicundo. In 1997, only the last three and a half kilometers from Rancho Verde to the main road that connects Textilpa and Pinicundo (see Figure 2.3) remain unpaved. Aside from the bus that comes to the rancho at 8:30 every morning and again at 12:30 every afternoon, local residents and the salespeople who deliver goods to the grocery store or sell them door-to-door make up most of the traffic between the rancho and other communities in the surrounding area.

The telephone, another tool of modern life that we all take for granted in the United States, arrived shortly after the pipeline was installed and the roadway between Pinicundo and Textilpa was paved. At first, the single, public telephone was housed in a private home. After extensive discussion by the residents in 1994, the telephone was relocated to a small room conveniently built adjacent to *la capilla*, the chapel located in the rancho. Like all of the other conveniences, the telephone also has changed another ritual in the rancho: the frequency of letter-writing. Still, because of the expense and continuing unavailability of multiple, private telephones, the art of personal letter-writing as a form of communication has not disappeared to the degree that it probably has in our own cellularized lives.

Although the rancho has an elected representative who negotiates the needs of the rancho with government officials at the municipal level, most of residents' interactions with government representatives take place in Pinicundo or Textilpa. As a consequence, the two institutions that have the most direct influence on daily life in Rancho Verde are la capilla and the local elementary school. Located in front of a small concrete plaza built in 1994 to provide a paved area in which children could play and a few benches in which residents could sit, the whitewashed capilla with its oversized front doors and small steeple serves as the center of rancho life in spatial and social terms (see Figure 2.4). The adult men whom I've met at the rancho in the course of my fieldwork—most of them either temporary visitors from Chicago or elders who decided to spend the rest of their lives in the rancho—mind their livestock, tend their fields, or sit and chat outside the grocery store located near la capilla,

FIGURE 2.4 Rancho Verde, 1995

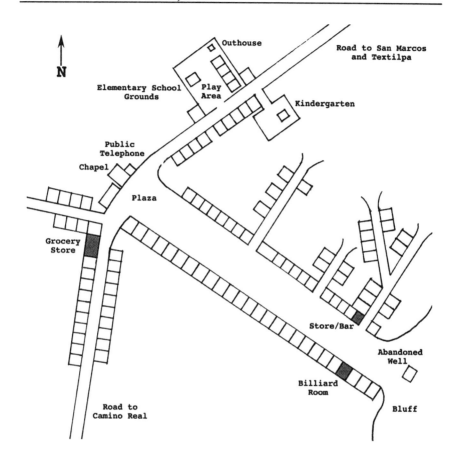

Unless otherwise noted, each square/rectangle represents a private home or dwelling.

sipping soft drinks, or outside the liquor store down at the other end of the rancho near the edge of the bluff, sharing a beer or two. It is the women and children who are more likely to visit la capilla on a regular basis. While mass is given on Sundays by a priest who visits from nearby Pinicundo, the women of the rancho have organized themselves so that a couple of them are at la capilla every day, helping to clean and maintain it, saying the rosary as part of their devotion to *la Virgen de Guadalupe* (the Virgin of Guadalupe), and praying for the well-being of members of the community who are in need of spiritual intervention.

In recent years, the elementary school located at the northern entrance to the rancho (see Figure 2.4) has become a second institutional focal point in the community. In 1995, the elementary school (the kindergarten across the street had an enrollment of 19) served the educational needs of about 96 children living in the rancho. The school, which now consists of five classrooms, an outhouse, a small plaza, and a playground area, was originally built as a one-room schoolhouse in the late 1970s. At the time, only one teacher was available to teach first grade. Students beyond that grade level had the choice of leaving school or walking to Pinicundo, where they could continue their elementary schooling. Because they were often stoned or bullied by the children of Pinicundo, very few children from Rancho Verde chose that option. In the 1980s, the women of the rancho petitioned the government and were granted two additional teachers. As a consequence of follow-up campaigns, the rancho now has five teachers serving its children's educational needs. All of the teachers live in Textilpa and travel to the rancho on the bus that comes and goes twice a day. Besides the 96 children who attend *primaria* (elementary school), five older children attend *secundaria* (middle school) in San Marcos, a rancho located two and a half kilometers away, and three young adults attend *preparatoria* (high school) in Textilpa. Because work opportunities related to school are relatively limited, most children in Rancho Verde terminate their studies after they complete primaria and then either move to Chicago to live and work with relatives or stay and work at home and in the fields until they get married.

Without a doubt, the event that has had the greatest impact on rancho life has been the departure of a large group of adult men and a number of traditional families (as defined by Rancho Verdeans) consisting of one or both parents and their children, most of whom have immigrated to and settled in the United States, mainly in Chicago, over the past 25 years. In trying to understand the extent to which people have left the rancho and the effects of their departure on the remaining inhabitants of the rancho, I asked Jaime Durán's cousins, Sandra Rodríguez and her sister, Amelia, to help me undertake an unofficial demographic survey of Rancho Verde in the early fall of 1995. The information we collected illustrates the devastating effects that the immigration of Rancho Verdeans, especially adult males, has had on family and rancho life.

According to the data, 32 (or 30%) of the 106 homes in Rancho Verde that have been shared by the 116 traditional families who have lived in them at one time or another sit empty for most of the year. The 41 families (35%) that have abandoned these homes have settled, at least semipermanently, in other communities. Aside from major repairs undertaken by family members who visit the rancho for the holidays or for an extended stay in the winter and the minimal upkeep that relatives or friends provide during the rest of the year, the vacant homes sit there slowly decaying from lack of use. Still, they provide many of the families that have left the rancho with the continuing hope or illusion that they have a home they may one day return to for good. Another 36 (34%) of the 106 homes are partially occupied because a husband/ father left his wife and children behind to go work in the United States. In some cases, older children in the family, usually—but not always—male, also have moved north to join their fathers or other relatives because there is no employment for them in the rancho or the surrounding area. That means, then, that only 32 (30%) of the 106 homes in Rancho Verde are fully occupied by families consisting of a father, a mother, and their children. An additional six homes (6%) are occupied by families that include widows and their children.

Of the 41 families that have left Rancho Verde, six have settled in Mexico: 4 in Textilpa, 1 in Mexico City, and 1 in Pinicundo. The other 35 families have settled in different parts of the United States: 2 in California, 1 in Colorado, 1 in North Carolina, and the remaining 31 in Chicago. Of the 36 fathers/ husbands who have left their wives and younger children behind in their search for employment, 11 have moved to California, North Carolina, Colorado, and Florida; the remaining 25 have settled in the Chicago area. Thus, out of a total of 565 potential Rancho Verde residents, 250 (118 adults and 132 children), or 44%, have moved and settled elsewhere, usually in Chicago. Only 315 (129 adults, including several elders who are members of extended families, and 186 children), or 56%, then, continue to reside in the rancho's 74 partially or fully occupied homes. As helpful as the economic impact of those who have left and send money home has been on those who stayed behind, there is no question that members of both groups face a plethora of emotional and psychological difficulties created by the renting of the community's social fabric.[9]

Despite the obvious social fragmentation that Rancho Verdeans have experienced, most of them appear to have come to terms with the current circumstances of their lives. Those who have remained behind in the rancho often comment on how they wish that the relatives and friends who have left could come back permanently; those who have left, in turn, also comment on how they wish they could return to the rancho and make their lives there. Some have tried to move back, taking their meager savings and investing them in tools, equipment, or a start-up business of one sort or another. Very few have been successful in the long run, and most have had to return to Chicago to earn a wage that makes it possible for them to try again. For the most part, their need to be with one another is temporarily fulfilled via occasional telephone calls, the letters they write to one another, and the recurring visits they make between the two home fronts. At least once a year, most of the adults residing in Chicago take a vacation or a leave of absence from their jobs to spend a month or two, sometimes a whole winter, in Rancho Verde. This gives them the time they need to reinforce their connections, to oversee their property, and to look into other concerns in preparation for what some hope will be their eventual and permanent return to the place they will always think of as home. Life being what it is, however, most, if not all, of them are destined to live out their lives far away from their rancho. If nothing else they are comfortable in the realization that a number of family members have settled with them in Chicago and have an opportunity to share in their daily lives.

Urban Nightmare, or The Promised Land of Rural Dreams?

Although Pilsen is sometimes inaccurately referred to as "one of the oldest Mexican neighborhoods in Chicago" (Garza, 1994a, p. 1), in reality, it is a relatively young community in comparison to the original three (the Near West Side, Back of the Yards, South Chicago), which were well-established by 1930. As a matter of fact, according to the U.S. Census Bureau, Pilsen's and Little Village's Mexican-origin populations have exploded since 1940 when, respectively, they were a mere 114 and 34.[10] The end of World War II didn't do much to change these numbers. By 1950, for example, Pilsen's Mexican population had increased 239% to 272, while Little Village's had climbed 165% to 56. Between 1950 and 1960, the Mexican-origin population in the two communities began to show signs of an approaching trend as Pilsen's increased an astounding 2,153% to 6,129 and Little Village's shot up 1,768% to 1,046. (The bold outline in the middle of the map of Chicago in Figure 2.1 highlights the contiguous neighborhoods of Pilsen, located on the right, and Little Village, located on the left.)

By the time the University of Illinois at Chicago opened its doors in the Near West Side in 1965, most Chicanos/Mexicanos had already been pushed south into Pilsen and out of one of their oldest neighborhoods in the city.[11] Thereafter, the Near West Side became known as Little Italy, home of the largest Italian-American community in Chicago. And because Chicago was still in the process of becoming the most segregated city in the United States—a status it maintains to this day (Massey & Denton, 1989, 1993)—the movement of African Americans into the East Garfield Park and North Lawndale communities also forced Chicanos/Mexicanos south, this time into Little Village. As a consequence of these momentous changes and the continuing growth of the Mexican-origin population in the region, the contiguous communities of Pilsen and Little Village merged and emerged as the newest and largest Mexican neighborhood in Chicago at about the same time that Jaime Durán and his wife-to-be, Rocío Valadez, immigrated to Chicago from their respective ranchos in Mexico in the early 1970s.

Life in Rancho Verde was not only difficult, but provided Jaime Durán with limited opportunities for the future. While he was growing up, for example, an itinerant teacher would occasionally provide classes for rancho children.

Even so, he, like many of his contemporaries, rarely had a chance to attend them because he had to work in the fields and care for the few goats and chickens that provided his family with some of its most basic necessities. Since Jaime's mother had died when he was five years old and his father had remarried, Jaime's father and his new wife were now busily trying to raise their five children in addition to the three to whom Jaime's own mother had given birth. With no income-generating employment available in the region and dependent on the few crops they grew and the few farm animals they owned, Jaime's family and friends lived in extreme poverty, barely able to eke out a subsistence level of existence. In the summer of 1970, with few options in sight, Jaime decided to follow in the footsteps of several of his male relatives and friends. At the age of 17, Jaime left Rancho Verde for Chicago hoping to find the kind of work that would help him support himself and the family members he had left behind.

Like so many Mexican immigrants before him, Jaime traveled by bus to the U.S.–Mexican border and crossed over with the help of a *coyote* (an individual who for a substantial fee engages in the unlawful practice of sneaking undocumented immigrants across the border). Once he was safely across, Jaime crammed himself into the covered flatbed of a pickup truck with a dozen other undocumented immigrants for the duration of the 1,500-mile journey from the border to Chicago. Jaime's trip was by no means unique. When Jaime told me about his first trip to Chicago, his *compadre* and brother-in-law, Arturo Ramírez, described a similar first trip in the company of 10 other undocumented immigrants, all of whom were jammed into the rear seat and trunk of a passenger car. Arturo told us how he spent the length of the trip lying on the rear floorboards of the car with several other men's legs draped over his body.

As soon as he arrived, Jaime integrated himself into the social network that his relatives and friends from Rancho Verde were in the process of establishing in Pilsen. Although he did not speak any English, his chances of finding work were greatly improved because of his connection to members of the social network, many of whom had been in Chicago for several years and had established relationships with employers desperate to hire Mexican immigrants. After working as a busboy and dishwasher in a restaurant, Jaime obtained a job working with a railroad track repair crew. While the hours were long and the work was hard, Jaime earned considerably more than most of his compatriots earned at their equally demanding and difficult jobs in factories, sweatshops, and the service industry. Over the years, Jaime learned the intricacies of building and repairing railroad track lines and became fluent enough in English to get promoted to the rank of foreman of a railroad construction crew, a job he held for many years.

Once he established himself in Pilsen, Jaime helped other male friends and family members make their way from Rancho Verde to Chicago. As soon as they arrived, Jaime would do his part to help them locate housing and find jobs. After he met and married Rocío in Chicago, Jaime became one of a handful of men from his rancho who had intact families in the city. Most of the men from his rancho, both married and single, lived together in groups to pool their meager earnings and to fill each other's need for the company of others. As late as the early 1990s, many of them were still living apart from the families they'd left behind in Rancho Verde. In 1989, after Jaime and a number of his fellow Rancho Verdeans were granted permanent residency through the 1986 amnesty program, several of them petitioned the U.S. government for permission to relocate their wives and children to Chicago. After they arrived in 1992 and survived a difficult period of adjustment and transition, members of their families integrated themselves into the smaller social networks affiliated with their ranchos, the transnational community composed of Jaime and Rocío Durán's social network, and the larger Mexicano community in Pilsen and Little Village.

Rocío Valadez's journey to Chicago followed a slightly different path than Jaime Durán's. In 1963, when Rocío was 9 years old, an agent for the Mexican government visited Rocío's rancho in Michoacán and asked if any of the men in San Jacinto were interested in participating in the Bracero Program, the contracting system established by the U.S. government to recruit Mexican laborers willing to engage in agricultural labor. So many men volunteered that the agent held a lottery to draw the names of the 15 men who would get to participate. Rocío's two older brothers, Pedro and Carlos Valadez, had their names drawn and went off to South Texas to work in the cotton fields to help provide for a family in desperate economic need back in San Jacinto. After the Bracero Program ended the following year, Pedro and Carlos went back to their rancho knowing that they would never again return to the United States as contract workers.

Three years later, Pedro decided to go and visit an uncle in Chicago who had told him about job possibilities there. He traveled from San Jacinto to the border city of Reynosa, Tamaulipas by bus, where he found a coyote willing to help him get across the river and provide him with transportation to Chicago. After getting a job with his uncle's help and working as a member of a railroad track repair crew for about six months, Pedro returned to San Jacinto and convinced his brother Carlos to travel with him to Chicago the following year. As soon as they got there, Pedro and Carlos managed to find steady jobs through the connections that Pedro had established, but they became so lonely living in the city by themselves that within the year, they headed back home. When the two brothers returned to Chicago on separate occasions in 1969, Carlos took 13 men from San Jacinto with him and Pedro took 7. A couple of years later, at the urging of the uncle that Pedro had stayed with during his first visit to Chicago, Pedro and Carlos decided to take their wives and children with them. Because of their reputations as diligent workers, Pedro and Carlos got their old jobs back as members of a railroad track repair crew and settled down with their families among the many other Mexican immigrant families that had settled there before them.

Once they established a stable social network in Chicago, Pedro and Carlos encouraged their younger siblings to move north to live with them in the Pilsen area. In 1972, Juan and Olga, Pedro and Carlos's younger brother and sister, acquired tourist visas and flew from Guadalajara to visit their brothers. When their visas expired, they stayed and found jobs. The following year, Rocío and her younger sister Teresa obtained student visas with the help of an uncle who had moved to Mexico City to become a teacher and flew directly from Mexico City to Chicago to visit their brothers and sister. Like Juan and Olga before them, Rocío and Teresa stayed after their travel visas expired and found factory jobs. Before long, their other sister, Diana, two brothers, Felipe and Moisés, and a number of other relatives and friends followed and integrated themselves into the complex social network that was by then firmly entrenched in Chicago.

By the time Jaime Durán and Rocío Valadez arrived and settled in with help from members of their respective social networks, the Pilsen community's Mexican-origin population had mushroomed from the mere 114 who resided there in 1940 to the 16,123 who lived there in 1970. Little Village, which itself was destined to surpass Pilsen in the coming decade in terms of its Mexican-origin population, had increased from 34 residents to 13,321 during that same 30-year period. When Jaime and Rocío arrived in Pilsen, they entered a world remarkably similar to the one they had left behind. As was true in the cities near their respective ranchos, the area's major thoroughfares, 18th Street in Pilsen and Cermak and 26th Street in Little Village, were bustling with Mexican-owned businesses. Everywhere Jaime and Rocío turned, they saw storefronts with Spanish names emblazoned on them. The faces and voices on the streets, the music emanating from record stores, and the Mexican pushcart vendors they encountered at street intersections literally brought a number of aspects of their home regions to their current lives. But while most of their compatriots had traveled before them via the railroad decades earlier, when Chicago was undeniably "the railway hub of the nation" (Puente, 1995, p. 12), Jaime, Rocío, and the many Mexican immigrants who joined them on their trek arrived by railroad, private automobile, pickup truck, bus, and airplane. Clearly, the circumstances surrounding Jaime's and Rocío's experiences in Pilsen exemplify the role that well-established social networks have played in the decision of Mexicanos in general to settle permanently in Chicago.

Between 1970 and 1980, the decade when Jaime and Rocío got married and started a family, Pilsen's and Little Village's Chicano/Mexicano populations continued to grow at a phenomenal rate. In that time period, Pilsen's Mexican-origin population increased another 99.6% to 32,173 and Little Village's increased a dramatic 290% to 51,973. Because they began to reach the saturation point in terms of how many Chicanos/Mexicanos they could house, the two communities burst at the seams and newly arrived Chicanos/Mexicanos began to settle in communities at their western and southern borders. As a result, during the following 10-year period (1980 to 1990), Pilsen's Mexican-origin population increased only 15.6% to 37,184 and Little Village's increased slightly more, 24.8% to 64,885. (The bold outline in the middle of the map of Chicago in Figure 2.2 highlights the contiguous neighborhoods of Pilsen, located on the right, and Little Village, located on the left. The unshaded census tracts in Pilsen represent commercial and industrial areas in the neighborhood.) In its continued expansion to the south, the overflow eventually swallowed the Back of the Yards, one of the three original Mexican-origin settlements in Chicago, as well as Brighton Park, McKinley Park, New City, Gage Park, and Chicago Lawn, and made them part of the largest Mexican-origin meganeighborhood in the city.

Over the next two or three decades, the conglomeration of neighborhoods listed above may well undergo the kind of growth in their Mexican-origin populations that Pilsen and Little Village experienced between 1960 and 1990. To the west, as I noted earlier, Little Village spilled its Mexican-origin population over the city limits into the suburb of Cicero, which is today considered the largest Latino suburb in the Chicago metropolitan area. In light of the continuing Mexicanization of the Chicago metropolitan area, the region is likely to provide researchers interested in understanding the lived experience of Chicanos and Mexicanos in the United States with valuable information for some time to come.

MEXICANO DISCOURSE IN THE
CONTEXT OF LIVED EXPERIENCE

I'm standing in Jaime and Rocío Durán's living room in Pilsen, where another adult literacy class is about to begin. As I look around, I notice several children playing together on the floor and a dozen adults in their twenties, thirties, and forties sitting around, chatting and waiting patiently for me to begin our first lesson. The adults in the room, the media and the government tell us, are illegal aliens—foreigners. Possibly, as far as some are concerned, strangers from another planet. Unwanted, in most cases, except for the cheap labor they provide. My colleagues and I call them undocumented immigrants. They are here in this room because they are participating in an amnesty program that in a matter of months will grant them permanent resident status and will for the first time in their lives allow them to move about in this country without the fear of being deported. There will be other fears, but this one will be banished. It will change their lives.

Because he's restless and ready to get started, Jaime calls out to me: "*¿Empezamos, maestro?*" (Shall we get started, teacher?) I smile and nod my head. Jaime calls out to his son Juan Carlos: "*¡M'ijo, tráeme mis armas!*" (My son, bring me my weapons!) Juan Carlos runs out of the room and returns with some paper and a pencil, which he hands to his father. Jaime then waits a moment while the other adult members in the group finish their individual conversations and prepare themselves to take notes, then looks toward me and signals the beginning of the lesson: "*Bueno, maestro*" (Okay, teacher), he says to me, "*parece que estamos listos*" (it looks like we're ready). I nod to Jaime, glance about the room again, surprised to see that even the children in the room, with paper and pencil in hand, are prepared to participate and begin the first battle in what I hope will become a war of words, both spoken and written, that will eventually help Jaime and members of his social network achieve their goal of becoming legal residents of this country.

The four months of private tutoring and classes that my colleagues and I provided Jaime and the rest of the adults in the setting that I've just described were part of the most intense formalized schooling that many of them had experienced in years or in their entire lives. Among the dozen adults in the group that day, one had finished the sixth grade, seven had reached only the third grade, and the rest had never had any formal schooling in Mexico. More recently, many of them had been attending adult literacy classes at La Casa del Pueblo, but because of the high demand for those classes and the large class sizes, most had received minimal individualized attention. And despite their ability to handle the material that we presented, in English and Spanish, orally and in writing, most of them also considered themselves semiliterate at best and not very articulate speakers. In short, how they described themselves in casual conversation or formal interview situations was very different from how they represented themselves when they were engaged in the purposeful use of oral or written language.

In the course of the nine years that I've worked with members of Jaime and Rocío Durán's social network, I've noticed the degree to which they enjoy their lives and their discursive interchanges. Although some of them, especially the older men from Jaime's rancho, seem unusually quiet, even shy, in large group gatherings, all of them share an affinity for sitting around and talking about their lives and the world around them. And while jokes, riddles, and traditional stories are often woven into the fabric of their conversations, the larger part is composed of narratives about their daily lives and expository observations on the social, economic, religious, and political issues that often catch their attention. In terms of reading and writing, a number of adult members in the group have told me that at worst, they engage in very little of either and at best, in moderate amounts of both. My extensive observations in the field have generally verified this position. Besides the reading and writing they do in connection with religious rites and the personal letters they exchange, members also engage in these two activities in relation to the commercial and legal transactions in which we all engage as a consequence of our participation in a document-oriented society.

Within the broad social, cultural, historical, political, and economic contexts that I have presented in this chapter, it is clear that members of Jaime and Rocío's social network participate in a variety of sophisticated and meaningful oral and literate activities. Because it is impossible to survey them all and because some of them have already been discussed elsewhere (Farr, 1993; Farr, 1994a, 1994b; Farr & Guerra, 1995; Guerra & Farr, in preparation), the rest of this book will focus on the major genres of oral and written practices that I have identified and to which I have gained access. While this partial view will provide us with partial insights, it is my hope that they will help us understand an aspect of Mexicano life that we still need to learn more about— the kinds of oral and written language practices that adult Mexicanos and their children bring into the adult literacy and public school classrooms where many of us first encounter them.

For example, in the metaphor LOVE IS A COLLABORATIVE WORK OF ART,[1] LOVE is considered the target domain because it represents an abstraction of "the internal mental or emotional world, sometimes of the social world" (Quinn, 1991, p. 57) that one is attempting to comprehend. A COLLABORATIVE WORK OF ART, on the other hand, is considered the source domain because it is more familiar and can be used to "readily conceptualize the relations among elements in such [a domain] and changes in these relations that result when these elements are set in motion conceptually" (p. 57).

Lakoff and Johnson (1980) believe that the three kinds of conventional metaphors they have identified—structural, orientational, and ontological—"are often based on correlations we perceive in our experience" (p. 151). In a structural metaphor, Lakoff and Johnson contend, "one concept is metaphorically structured in terms of another" (p. 14). The metaphor LOVE IS A COLLABORATIVE WORK OF ART, for instance, "picks out a certain range of our love experiences and defines a *structural* similarity between the *entire range* of highlighted experiences and the range of experiences involved in producing collaborative works of art" (p. 152). An orientational metaphor organizes "a whole system of concepts with respect to one another" (p. 141), usually in spatial terms. Orientational metaphors often operate in terms of such polar oppositions as up–down, front–back, on–off, and near–far. While they are usually physical in nature, Lakoff and Johnson note that they can vary from culture to culture. Finally, an ontological metaphor provides "ways of viewing events, activities, emotions, ideas, etc., as entities, substances, [containers, and persons]" (p. 25). Such metaphors as THE MIND IS AN ENTITY, INFLATION IS AN ADVERSARY, and THEORIES ARE BUILDINGS all fall into this category. In opposition to conventional metaphors, Lakoff and Johnson posit the existence of what they call "new metaphors." These metaphors "are capable of giving us a new understanding of our experience. Thus, they can give new meaning to our pasts, to our daily activity, and to what we know and believe" (p. 139).

While metaphors possess a number of useful characteristics for conceptualizing understanding, the most salient aspect for our purposes is their ability to carry over details of the extensive knowledge that we have about a source domain (A COLLABORATIVE WORK OF ART) to the target domain (LOVE), what Lakoff and Johnson call "metaphorical entailments" (Lakoff, 1987, p. 384). In Johnson's (1987) view, an entailment consists of "the perceptions, discriminations, interests, values, beliefs, practices, and commitments tied up with the metaphorical understanding" (p. 132). Each entailment, in turn, may include "other metaphors and literal statements as well" (Lakoff & Johnson, 1980, p. 140). The "large and coherent network of entailments" that emerges, especially with the use of new metaphors, can lead a "thinker to reorganize a target domain in its terms and to reason to new conclusions by following out the entailments of the new metaphor" (Quinn, 1991, p. 77). It is important to keep in mind that while the entailments of any metaphor, especially a new one, pick out and highlight a range of experiences, they also downplay and hide different aspects of the concept being examined.

Because the connections between varied conceptions of orality and literacy and the role that metaphor plays in them are socially, culturally, and politically constituted, ideology inevitably occupies a central place in their analysis. Ideology as a concept is, of course, highly contested and very difficult to define. There is, however, a perspective that I believe provides a meaningful way to interpret the entailments related to the various metaphors I will be examining. In their work, Berlin (1988) and Therborn (1980) champion a perspective that moves beyond Althusser's inclination to, as Berlin puts it, take a stance "in which ideology is always false consciousness while a particular version of Marxism is defined as its scientific alternative in possession of objective truth" (p. 478). No position, Berlin contends,

> can lay claim to absolute, timeless truth, because finally all formulations are historically specific, arising out of the material conditions of a particular time and place. Choices in the economic, social, political, and cultural are thus always based on discursive practices that are interpretations, not mere transcriptions of some external, verifiable certainty. The choice for Therborn then is never between scientific truth and ideology, but between competing ideologies, competing discursive interpretations. (p. 478)

According to Therborn (1980), ideology always addresses three specific questions: What exists? What is good? What is possible? The first question focuses on epistemological concerns: "*what exists*, and its corollary, what does not exist: that is, who we are, what the world is, what nature, society, men and women are like." The second responds to our need to establish ethical and aesthetic standards: "*what is good*, right, just, beautiful, attractive, enjoyable, and its opposites. In this way our desires become structured and normalized." Finally, ideology lets us know whether or not our expectations are reasonable: "*what is possible* and impossible; our sense of the mutability of our being-in-the-world and the consequences of change are hereby patterned, and our hopes, ambitions, and fears given shape" (p. 18). In order "to become committed to changing something," Therborn argues, "one must first get to know that it exists, then make up one's mind whether it is good that it exists. And before deciding to do something about a bad state of affairs, one must first be convinced that there is some chance of actually changing it" (p. 19).

In undertaking the conceptual/metaphorical analysis that follows, I borrow Lakoff and Johnson's (1980) ideas about how the entailments that a source domain introduces to a target domain can help us understand the very features

As a consequence of recent anthropological research on the relationship between orality and literacy, most scholars in the field are uncomfortable with the notion of a "great divide" between so-called literate and nonliterate societies.[3] Such a position is made even more difficult by the fact that literacy has become so widespread that it is virtually impossible to find a society untouched by it. To complicate matters, Finnegan's (1988) work on orality demonstrates how it can be used to fulfill many of the same functions that Goody and Watt (1968) believe are restricted to literacy. Like literacy, for example, orality can be used to preserve and challenge the status quo *and* for reflection and detachment. It may also, Finnegan speculates, "involve the kind of insight and comment on the human condition that we associate with literary expression more generally" (p. 165). "In practice," Finnegan contends,

> all cultures recognize differing forms of discourse which people can manipulate and switch between for various purposes, no one any more "natural" than the other. . . . Which medium and which form of discourse is going to be used for what purpose and in what context cannot be predicted *a priori*. (pp. 167–168)

As a matter of fact, on the basis of their work among the Vai of Liberia and the growing body of data concerning the problematic relationship between orality and literacy, Scribner and Cole declared in 1981 that "the metaphor of a great divide may not be appropriate for specifying differences among literates and non-literates under contemporary conditions" (p. 86).

In an effort to fill the theoretical vacuum created after the great divide perspective was discredited (see in particular Walters, 1990, and Williams, 1992), Tannen (1982) recommended the continuum as a viable substitute. What happens instead, Tannen proposed, is that "the two are superimposed upon and intertwined with each other" (p. 3) and form an oral/literate continuum. Like Tannen, several other scholars developed variations on the oral/ literate continuum model to illustrate how features that are considered "literary" can be found in spoken discourse (Green, 1982; Polanyi, 1982) and features of oral discourse can be found in writing (Rader, 1982; Lakoff, 1982). One investigator in particular (Heath, 1982), however, expressed concern about what she considered the inherent limitations of the oral/literate continuum. Because her work in a community she called "Trackton" in the Piedmont Carolinas suggested that it is impossible to "place the community somewhere on a continuum from full literacy to restricted literacy or non-literacy" (p. 111), Heath recommended the use of two continua, the oral and the written, and urged us to think of their relationship in dialectical terms.[4] In her view, the points and extent of overlap and the similarities in structure and function of the literacy events and their patterns of use in Trackton may follow one pattern, but will most likely follow other patterns in communities with different cultural features (p. 111). Therefore, Heath concluded, we must move away "from current tendencies to classify communities as being at one or another point along a hypothetical continuum which has no societal reality" (p. 116). There is always the danger, Heath declared, that in the context of the continuum model, a speech community (or the individual, in Tannen's case) will be placed toward the oral end of such a continuum and as a consequence will be said to be nonliterate, even when its members (or the individual) have demonstrated the ability to read and write to one degree or another and in one context or another.

More recently, Street (1984, 1993, 1995) and Grillo (1989) have introduced an approach that self-consciously downplays the differences and highlights the similarities between orality and literacy. In his work, Street is sharply critical of academic research that has focused on the cognitive consequences of literacy acquisition. In his view, there is very little to be gained from focusing on the differences between speech and writing because their relationship changes and/or differs so much from one context to another. Street's "ideological" model of literacy provides an alternative approach to the "autonomous" model used by supporters of a dichotomous and some supporters of a continuous perspective; it disrupts the existing binary and subsumes rather than excludes the work undertaken by the oppositional models. Street's model, then, acknowledges but still attempts to move beyond the dialectical relationship that results in what he calls "an oral/literate mix" (p. 9). Because he is highly critical of theoretical perspectives that confine debates about literacy to the issues of rationality, cognition, and relativism and that limit their analysis to the discontinuity between home and school languages and literacies, Street radically shifts the discussion away from what he considers the affiliated notions that there is a dichotomous split or a continuum between oral and written language.

In place of dichotomous, continuous, and dialectical models, Street proposes an alternative that encourages the analysis of oral and written language in the context of what he calls communicative practices. Communicative practices, according to Grillo (1989), can be described and studied within an interpretive framework that acknowledges "the social activities through which language or communication are produced." Such a framework also recognizes the varied ways "in which these activities are embedded in institutions, settings, or domains which in turn are implicated in other, wider, social, economic, political and cultural processes." Finally, Grillo contends, this particular interpretive framework encourages researchers to pay careful attention to the organization and labeling of the communicative practices themselves: the ideologies, linguistic or otherwise, that "guide processes of communicative production" as well as the utterances and texts, both individual and sequential, that result from them (p. 15).

Because members of Jaime and Rocío's social network cannot be said to be exclusively oral or literate and cannot be placed on some universal or imaginary continuum or continua that measure their varying degrees of orality and literacy, I also try to avoid placing orality and literacy in a binary relationship that demands that I discuss them in dichotomous or continuous terms. At the same time, while I believe that the two may be dialectically related—individuals sometimes use both simultaneously and one practice tends to inform the other—in practical terms, analysis along these lines would require that I speculate about such an interactive relationship on the basis of very limited data. Like Street (1993), I believe that research on literacy must make use of Grillo's concept of communicative practices in order to ensure that the uses to which a group of people put oral and written language are understood within the context of their personal and cultural lives. It is only by engaging in research that values and appreciates the circumstances under which different groups of people use oral and written language that we can begin to move beyond the inherent limitations of a perspective that identifies discontinuities among different kinds of discourses and inadvertently blames groups of people with so-called nonstandard forms of language for the educational and economic circumstances of their lives.

INTERROGATING THE IDEOLOGIES
OF CONSTITUTIVE METAPHORS IN LITERACY STUDIES

If we temporarily disentangle literacy from its symbiotic relationship with orality and examine it as an individually tropicalized entity, as so many scholars in literacy studies do, we discover that the figurative language they use not only describes some of the characteristics they find most salient but also implies a particular ideological position. While the binary relationship between orality and literacy is best illustrated through the use of the three orientational metaphors that have been popularized in the field (ORALITY/LITERACY AS A DICHOTOMY, ORALITY/LITERACY AS A CONTINUUM, and ORALITY/ LITERACY AS A DIALECTIC), I believe that our analysis of literacy will be better served through the use of ontological metaphors. As you may recall, Lakoff and Johnson (1980) contend that an ontological metaphor "allows us to pick out parts of our experience and treat them as discrete entities or substances" bounded by a surface in the same way that our bodies are (p. 25). As Lakoff and Johnson note, however, "merely viewing a nonphysical thing as an entity or substance does not allow us to comprehend very much about it" (p. 27). It is crucial, therefore, that we also examine the entailments that emerge from the use of an ontological metaphor in a particular context and provide us with detailed insights about its conceptual characteristics.

One way to understand the relationship between the ontological metaphors used to conceptualize literacy and their entailments is to refer to the former as principal or constitutive metaphors and to the latter as minor or basic-level metaphors (see Lakoff, 1987, pp. 380–415; and Quinn, 1991, pp. 60–65). While constitutive metaphors are considered "abstract, superordinate concepts . . . that 'provide the structures used' in complex cognitive models" (Quinn, p. 64), basic-level metaphors are those used in everyday and scholarly life to explain or define concepts in figurative terms which, when grouped together in varied configurations, comprise the principal metaphors of a particular analysis. Schön (1979) recommends a very similar analytical framework for examining what he calls the generative metaphors used in relation to social policy issues. Like constitutive metaphors, generative metaphors refer to "a certain kind of product—a perspective or frame, a way of looking at things—and a certain process— . . . a special version of SEEING-AS by which we gain new perspectives on the world" (pp. 254–255). Moreover, each story, as it is reflected in a generative metaphor,

> constructs its view of social reality through a complementary process of *naming* and *framing*. Things are selected for attention and named in such a way as to fit the frame constructed for the situation. . . . They select for attention a few salient features and relations from what would otherwise be an overwhelmingly complex reality. (p. 265)

It behooves those of us engaged in examining social policy issues such as literacy, then, to understand how these constitutive, or generative, metaphors are framed and how they shape the way we structure our understanding of the phenomenon at hand.

In the course of my search for metaphors used in the field, I identified 62 basic-level metaphors[5] used by scholars in their attempts to describe or define the concept of literacy.[6] As I worked through the process of finding different ways to group the basic-level metaphors as sets of entailments related to different constitutive metaphors, I tried to keep in mind Harvey's (1987) observation about Foucault's (1982) own attempt to identify the four dominant metaphors of the ages in his classic work on the "archaeology of language":

> thought and understanding never begin in a vacuum . . . , and never fully clear the decks to begin an "objective" analysis. Rather, the foreconceptions, preunderstandings, unthematized yet orienting structures, inhabit an analysis to begin with. Indeed, what is *found* by an analysis tends to be the realization, manifestation, of those foreconceptions. What this means is that . . . metaphors . . . do not simply arrive on the scene after the fact. Rather, they prefigure what will become visible or invisible, significant or insignificant, dominant or subordinate, representative or not. . . . (p. 200)

In light of my assumption that the basic-level metaphors used in the field reflect competing ideological positions, all of which overlap to one degree or another and can be consolidated, I have identified four constitutive metaphors that I believe best illustrate the major ideological perspectives operating in literacy studies: LITERACY AS ENTITY, LITERACY AS SELF, LITERACY AS INSTITUTION, and LITERACY AS PRACTICE.

Literacy as Entity

Of the 62 basic-level metaphors I identified, 9 describe literacy as something autonomous, as something that exists completely outside of the individual self and bureaucratic institutions. As the list below indicates, I have subdivided the nine into three sets (and labeled each with a phrase that captures its essence) because of the slightly different perspective each group represents:

Set 1—"The Power of the Unknown"

OBJECT[7]
MAGIC
VOODOO
TECHNOLOGY

Set 2—"Reading [between] the Lines"

AUTONOMOUS TEXT
LITERALISM
WAY OF TEXT

Set 3—"Going for the Gold"

KEY TO OPPORTUNITY
TOOL FOR ADVANCEMENT

All three sets are based on a dichotomous perspective of the world whereby literacy is set apart not only from orality but from all else, too. The first set suggests that literacy is positivistically constructed as an object that exists apart from and beyond any social or individual constraints. It also suggests that literacy has magical qualities that can transform an individual or a culture and bestow upon it special powers not available to the illiterate other. Within the perspective popularized by Goody and Watt (1968), for example, the introduction of alphabetic literacy magically transforms a culture from an illiterate into a literate one, from one trapped in the inconsistencies of a mythical past to one freed by its "sense of the *logos*, of the common and all-encompassing truth which reconciles apparent contradictions" (p. 46). The second set of terms more closely describes the way in which scholars like Olson (1977) conceptualize notions of literacy. According to Olson, the highest form of literacy is represented in the British essayist's ability to minimize "the possible interpretations of statements," which in turn makes it possible for meaning to reside objectively in the text (p. 268). For scholars who take this position, the written text becomes an inviolable and autonomous entity that best demonstrates the consequences of literacy. Moreover, under these conditions a literate individual cannot participate in the construction of text-based meaning; at best, she can only access it—literally lift it out whole and undisturbed from the text—and examine it as though it were an actual physical object. Finally, the third set of basic-level metaphors posits the notion that literacy is like a key or a tool, an actual artifact that one can hold in her hand and use to interact with and succeed in the world-at-large. This position implies that any person who is not able to locate such an instrument and make appropriate use of it will not be able to enact literacy in any meaningful way.

In Therbornean terms,[8] literacy exists as an entity set apart from individuals who may long to possess it, or be possessed by it, and from the institutions (e.g., schools and social service agencies) that want to help individuals acquire and use it to interact with others, especially those who are an integral part of social, cultural, legal, economic, religious, and political institutions that cannot function without it. In this context, the mutual goal of isolated individuals and integrated institutions is to find ways that will enable the society to function most efficiently for its own sake and, one hopes, for the good of all. In such an idealized state, of course, issues of poverty and injustice do not exist or are simply ignored. Because of the objectified nature of this construct, equality of opportunity and outcome is also assumed. While this ideological perspective is on the wane and has been broadly criticized within the academy, many of the assumptions underlying it still operate tacitly in notions about how literacy is conceived and how it is institutionally possible to help people become literate. These assumptions, however, are no longer isolated and objectified; instead, the "thingness of . . . literacy" has been converted into a conceptual idea (Stuckey, 1991, p. 29) and has migrated to the other principal metaphors described in this section: LITERACY AS SELF, LITERACY AS INSTITUTION, and LITERACY AS PRACTICE.

Literacy as Self

Because some scholars understandably conceptualize literacy as a characteristic a person acquires or possesses as an integral part of his individual self, it is not surprising that 16 of the basic-level metaphors I identified are related to the principal metaphor of LITERACY AS SELF. These can be divided into the following three sets, each of which reflects a different but related ideological position:

Set 1—"Measuring Up"

> SKILL
> ABILITY
> REGISTER
> INFORMATION
> KNOWLEDGE
> COMPETENCE
> WAY OF THINKING AND SPEAKING

Set 2—"Blessed are the Chosen"

> GOODNESS
> VALUE
> STATE OF GRACE
> RIGHT
> POWER

Set 3—"It's All in Your Mind"

> COGNITION
> CONSCIOUSNESS
> KNOWLEDGE-MAKING
> ATTITUDES AND MENTALITIES

All of the basic-level metaphors listed under this second category represent positions that are heavily influenced by the romantic notion that meaning is embedded in the mind or being of the individual and reflects the unique circumstances that he occupies. Although these metaphors tend to privilege the individual self, they also make the individual solely responsible for acquiring a certain level of literacy skills or abilities. Many of these basic-level metaphors can thereby be manipulated to victimize these same individuals and hold them responsible for their illiterate or semiliterate condition. While the first set of basic-level metaphors focuses on the more traditional notion of what an individual must acquire to be literate and successful in the society-at-large, the latter two, respectively, imply that literacy is determined by an individual's possession and exercise of a particular kind of social/political power or cognitive/mental state.

In ideological terms, the first set of basic-level metaphors intimates that the individual is responsible for striving to obtain a set of predetermined skills that will provide him with opportunities for advancement in personal and professional terms. It implies that if a person works hard and makes use of certain talents possessed equally by every person, nothing or no one will stand in the way of his success. In a capitalist society that glorifies the individual and supposedly provides unlimited opportunities for those willing to work hard, any person who does not develop the kinds of skills or abilities necessary for success is assumed not to be taking advantage of those opportunities.

The second set of basic-level metaphors imbues the individual who possesses or is possessed by these particular qualities with an aura of achievement. To be literate is to be blessed, to be empowered, to be capable of individually striving for "life, liberty and the pursuit of happiness." In contrast, this set implies that a person who is illiterate is bad, sinful, powerless, and incapable of exercising the rights bestowed on the literate. While the first set describes the kinds of objective strategies an individual must strive for to succeed, this set suggests that literacy is a mystical state that one can readily achieve by behaving in a certain way.

Finally, the cognitive-based or mind-oriented perspective reflected in the third set establishes the notion that the individual mind, our consciousness, is the center of being. From this point of view, our success is not measured by what we are capable of doing or by how blessed or fortunate we are, but by what we think and who we are. It reflects Descartes's famous adage, "I think, therefore I am." Because of the implied split between the mind and the body, literacy is conceived as one's ability to examine and interpret the world in objective and dispassionate terms.

Literacy as Institution

While the basic-level metaphors associated with LITERACY AS SELF focus on the qualities an individual must acquire or possess to be considered literate, LITERACY AS INSTITUTION conceptualizes literacy as something conceived or undertaken by others for the greater good of the individual and of the society of which she is a member. The 17 basic-level metaphors I identified in connection with this constitutive metaphor reflect four different perspectives on how literacy operates as a highly institutionalized apparatus.

Set 1—"Playing the Money Game"

COMMODITY
COMMON CURRENCY

CONSUMERISM
ECONOMY

Set 2—"Engaging a Faceless Enemy"

CURE
WEAPON
BATTLE
WAR

Set 3—"Learning to Follow the Rules"

LEARNING
ADAPTATION
CONVENTION
CONVERSION
CULTURE
SCAFFOLDING

Set 4—"Holding a Gun to Your Head"

EXPLOITATION
VIOLENCE
SYSTEM OF OPPRESSION

The first two sets of basic-level metaphors position literacy as an institutional artifact that circulates throughout the society-at-large in both positive and negative terms. The more capitalist-oriented approaches recommend literacy as a currency that makes it possible for members of the society to buy their way to success. The more literate one is, the richer one is and the more material goods one can acquire. This perspective is reflected in the widely accepted adage that "To get a good job, you need a good education." The second set actually posits literacy's opposite, illiteracy, as the disease or the enemy that we as a society must fight against using the institutional means available to us. If illiteracy is seen as a disease that leads to poverty, ignorance, and injustice, then literacy is seen as the cure for these particular ailments. If, on the other hand, illiteracy is conceived of as an enemy against which all of society must be mobilized, then it becomes necessary for everyone from the neighborhood community organizer to the President of the United States to rally the troops and send them into the war zone. Kozol's *Illiterate America* (1985) and former first lady Barbara Bush's literacy campaign are typical cries raised in the wilderness against an enemy that threatens our way of life.

Less strident and more academic in tone are the basic-level metaphors in the third set. Here we encounter E. D. Hirsch's (1987) recommendations that literacy be conceptualized as a body of information that any member of our society must know and be able to manipulate. Culture as canon becomes the rallying cry. Early attempts in composition studies to develop the notion that college students must learn academic discourse conventions to be successful is another aspect of this perspective. While critics have recently challenged the more static, insider/outsider conceptions of the cultural literacy and academic discourse community perspectives, the view that students have to operate within existing institutional constraints in order to demonstrate their literacy survives as a cornerstone of this position. In both cases, learners have to be provided with the necessary scaffolding and are judged on their ability to meet certain institutional expectations.

Unlike the perspectives that emerge in the other three principal metaphors, one perspective in this category clashes violently with all others. Manifested in Set 4 is a view of literacy that, based on Stuckey's *The Violence of Literacy* (1991), questions all current academic, social, and institutional approaches to it. Stuckey uses the basic-level metaphors in the final set to attack academically and institutionally based arguments that suggest that poor and working-class people can overcome the social and economic oppression they face in their lives simply by becoming literate and joining the mainstream or middle class. "The theory of this study," Stuckey says of her book, is that

> literacy is a system of oppression that works against entire societies as well as against certain groups within given populations and against individual people. . . . Literacy oppresses, and it is less important whether or not the oppression is systematic and intentional, though often it is both, than that it works against freedom. Thus, the questions of literacy are questions of oppression, they are matters of enforcement, maintenance, acquiescence, internalization, revolution. . . . Only when the forms of oppression are undermined can the question of what to do with one's life become central. (p. 64)

In short, until those in control of an economic system that determines who will have power and who will not are replaced and the economic system itself is transformed, any attempt to deal with the so-called literacy crisis is bound to fail miserably.

Literacy as Practice

Of the four constitutive metaphors presented here, LITERACY AS PRACTICE is currently the most popular among scholars, primarily because it reflects the now widely acknowledged view that literacy is a socially constructed and highly contextualized activity. Literacy is no longer considered a singular, monolithic, or universal entity; instead, scholars who take a practice-oriented perspective contend that there are many literacies in any society serving multiple and culturally specific purposes. The 20 basic-level metaphors associated with this constitutive metaphor fall into the following four sets:

Set 1—"Tellin' It Like It Is"

    CRAFT
    TECHNIQUE
    PERFORMANCE
    STORYTELLING
    RHETORICAL ACT
    PURPOSEFUL ACT

Set 2—"Working It Out Together"

    DIALOGUE
    PARTICIPATION
    INVOLVEMENT
    ENGAGEMENT

Set 3—"The Food and Fabric of Our Lives"

    QUILT
    WEAVING
    SMORGASBORD

Set 4—"Caught in the Act"

    SOCIAL PRACTICE
    SOCIAL CONSTRUCT
    SOCIAL EXCHANGE
    SOCIOCULTURAL PROCESS
    SOCIOCULTURALLY CONSTRUCTED ACTIVITY
    COMMUNITY PRACTICE
    IDEOLOGY

Scholars who use the basic-level metaphors in Set 1 conceive of literacy as a rhetorical activity that requires individuals to use language to negotiate a meaningful relationship with others. While the items included in Set 1 are in some ways similar to the skills and abilities mentioned in LITERACY AS SELF, they differ in that the former are more interactive and socially outward-looking. It is true that the point of departure for these activities is also the individual, but they tend to be more sophisticated and require a greater degree of intention on the part of the individual. While the basic-level metaphors in Set 1 take the individual as the key agent, those in Set 2 are dialogically oriented and require the active participation of more than one agent. Whether the practice being engaged in is rhetorical or dialogical, the bottom line is that the individual is involved in a complex social activity that requires an understanding of the self and the anticipated audience. Unless both participate in the social activity, it loses its value as a clearly identifiable practice.

Although the basic-level metaphors in Set 3 appear as though they could easily be listed under LITERACY AS ENTITY, the crucial difference that separates them from the items listed in that category is their inherent multiplic-ity. Each of the terms in this set implies an activity in which a variety of items are blended together to create something original. At the same time that they signal the involvement of more than one individual in a process, they also highlight the fact that a multiplicity of each is possible. The items in Set 4 are the most direct indicators of this position's interpretation of literacy. All of them indicate that literacy is both multiple and highly contextualized. They also highlight the important role that social and cultural factors play in this particular conception of literacy.

Because it suggests that literacy involves the manipulation of a particular entity by a particular individual or individuals interacting with another or others in a particular institutional setting, this perspective is the most flexible of the four. And because all of these variables must come into play, it makes it impossible to conceive of literacy in singular terms. Thus, in the end, there is no way to escape the realization that all of these factors will inevitably give rise to a multitude of literacies. Under these circumstances, it is clear that an individual's literacies vary according to the personal and social circumstances of his or her life, so everyone is considered literate in certain situations and not in others. The goal, from this perspective, is not to master a particular form of literacy, but to develop one's ability to engage in a variety of social practices that require us to operate in a plethora of settings and genres to fulfill different needs and goals. In academic terms, it means that identifying and understanding a set of assumed universal standards is not only no longer possible, but no longer meaningful. As scholars, it becomes our responsibility to identify and understand the varied ways in which different groups of people make use of literacy in their lives and to assist everyone in becoming more adept at making use of whatever literacies they deem important in their present and future lives.

INTEGRATING METAPHORICAL FRAMES AND IDEOLOGIES

Scholars who have specifically looked at the ways in which literacy has been represented in definitional or conceptual terms have taken different positions in relation to the four constitutive metaphors I have discussed here. In "Tropics of Literacy," for example, Brodkey (1991) limits her analysis to a comparison of conventional/functional literacy, on the one hand, and critical/dialogical literacy, on the other. In the course of deconstructing the ideological foundations of the two positions, she argues against the limitations of the former and the possibilities likely to emerge from the latter. In her examination, Novek (1992) engages in the kind of critique that I do in this section. She examines a wide variety of metaphors found in the promotional literature of adult learning programs, the popular press, and scholarly work. Her goal, as she describes it, is to identify the "negative effects associated with certain language uses and frames associated with the practices of reading and writing." While Novek does not take as strong a position as Brodkey, she concludes by noting that in "a different framework, language may enable alternative constructions of literacy which are grounded in social context and place no value judgments on the selected modes of communication individuals choose to use" (p. 231).

Finally, in "Literacy in Three Metaphors," Scribner (1988) provides a schematic overview of three metaphors—LITERACY AS ADAPTATION, LITERACY AS POWER, and LITERACY AS A STATE OF GRACE—and argues "that any of the metaphors, taken by itself, gives us only a partial grasp of the many and varied utilities of literacy and of the complex social and psychological factors sustaining aspirations for and achievement of individual literacy" (p. 73). It comes as no surprise that at the end of her essay, Scribner argues that we need to value all three positions equally because, while they raise different issues, all of them are legitimate: "Ideal literacy," she concludes, "is simultaneously adaptive, socially empowering, and self-enhancing" (p. 81).

While at first reflection Scribner's (1988) position appears untenable because it embraces conflicting ideological perspectives as equally valid, recent theoretical work in the field suggests that it may actually be the most reasonable one for us to take. The current position, however, is framed differently and takes into consideration much of what we have learned about literacy since Scribner's essay was first published. Schön (1979), I believe, provides us with a framework that explains the position most effectively. In the course of examining social policy debates, Schön contends, we become aware that they "reflect multiple, conflicting stories about social phenomena"—"stories which embody different generative metaphors, different frames for making sense of experience, different meanings and values" (p. 269). While we may be tempted to accept only one of the many stories as the best response to the dilemma at hand, Schön believes this would be inappropriate because in most of these cases, "adversaries do not disagree about the facts; they simply turn their attention to *different* facts" (p. 269). In Schön's view, a more constructive response is to engage in a type of inquiry he calls *frame restructuring*:

> we respond to frame conflict by constructing a new problem-setting story, one in which we attempt to integrate conflicting frames by including features and relations drawn from earlier stories, yet without sacrificing internal coherence or the degree of simplicity required for action. We do this, I believe, in the context of particular situations whose information-richness gives us access to many different combinations of features and relations, countering our Procrustean tendency to notice only what fits our ready-made category schemes. (p. 270)

Of the four constitutive metaphors I have identified, LITERACY AS PRACTICE, I would argue, best reflects Schön's (1979) notion of frame restructuring. A careful examination of this particular constitutive metaphor reveals that it subsumes and integrates all of the other conflicting frames in a way that simultaneously creates a new perspective and maintains an "internal coherence or the degree of simplicity required for action" (p. 270). Equally important, this position is self-reflective enough that it self-consciously addresses the issue of ideology. Like Street's and Grillo's attempts to reformulate the binary relationship between orality and literacy, this position, which actually reflects Street's ideological model of literacy,

> does not attempt to deny technical skill or the cognitive aspects of reading and writing, but rather understands them as they are encapsulated within cultural wholes and within structures of power. In that sense the ideological model [represented in LITERACY AS PRACTICE] subsumes rather than excludes the work undertaken within the autonomous model [which I would argue is reflected in the other constitutive metaphors, especially in LITERACY AS ENTITY]. (Street, 1995, p. 161)

It is for this reason that the basic-level metaphor I have developed and that I will now describe and contextualize in terms of rhetoric emerges from the LITERACY AS PRACTICE perspective.

ORALITY AND LITERACY AS RHETORICAL PRACTICES

In the course of identifying and collecting examples from the communicative repertoire that I have heard and seen members of Jaime and Rocío Durán's social network enact over the past 9 years, I have struggled with the difficult task of constructing a metaphor that would reflect them as socially and culturally situated practices. In the process, I have tried to be mindful of the important role that rhetoric plays in how members of the group represent themselves and their culture to me and to one another in both oral and written language. I've learned that it's not enough to identify the places where they perform variations of their particular oral/literate mix; it's equally important to understand when and why they do it. As a consequence of the interplay among my concerns; my theoretical perspective as a scholar in language and literacy studies; and the Mexicano perspective that I have gleaned from the material I have collected, the interviews I have conducted, and my own observations of their daily lives, a particular basic-level, yet complex, metaphor that captures some of the key components of the group's communicative practices has emerged. As I see it, ORALITY AND LITERACY are interpreted by members AS RHETORICAL PRACTICES involving the representation of self and culture in conventional and inventive terms.

In "Arguing About Literacy," Bizzell (1988) contends that we need to "see the production of literacy [and orality, I would add emphatically] as a collaborative effort" by adopting "a rhetorical perspective on literacy, which dialectically relates means of persuasion to audience's canonical knowledge" (p. 150). Such a position, she suggests, "implies not only a notion of the provisionality of all arguments but also a view of literacy as something local, something shared in a social context" (p. 148). In other words, Bizzell argues, rhetorical acts can take place only within a discourse community, of which the rhetor may or may not be a member. While Bizzell (1982) originally conceptualized a discourse community as a dynamic environment in which rhetorical conventions change continuously over time, the notion has been criticized in recent years (Harris, 1989; Spellmeyer, 1993) because more often than not it has been presented as a static entity that requires anyone interested in becoming a member to engage in behavior constrained by the community's unchanging conventional practices. As a consequence of these critiques, some scholars have proposed alternative conceptions that allow for "divergence and multiplicity." Lyon (1992), for example, has suggested that it is not enough "just to read the community's texts" or "examine the text's community." If we wish to describe social groups, language, and reality as dynamic, Lyon argues, we must "delineate the aims, actions, and structures of association within specific discourse groups" (p. 285).

The metaphor, or conceptual definition, that I am proposing makes clear that members engage in rhetorical practices that will help them fulfill a specific set of aims by engaging in certain actions within the "structures of association" operating in their discourse community. To do so, however, members of the group must come to terms with the tension that results from their varied attempts to accommodate their practices to and challenge the constraints of the discourse community in which they operate. Stewart (1995), who believes that "cultural, ethnic, and family history help to define available meaning options, and individual experience helps frame interpretation," refers to it as "a continuing tension between the repeated and the unrepeatable, between law and surprise" (p. 119). Interestingly, this tension has been described in very similar terms by a number of other theorists and philosophers of language. Rorty (1979), for example, contends that this same tension is produced when what he calls "abnormal discourse" is introduced into settings where "normal discourse" is constraining what members of the community believe is appropriate discursive behavior. In *The Dialogic Imagination*, Bakhtin (1981) argues that the forces a speaker or writer encounters encourage her to make use of either "internally persuasive" or "authoritative" discourse. Finally, Foucault (1982) frames this same conflict as one produced by a battle of wits between the "voice of Inclination" and the "voice of Institution." In each case, a person is caught in the dialectical tension between the need to be conventional and the desire to be inventive.

While Bizzell's and Lyon's ideas provide a framework for understanding the place of rhetorical practices in a discourse community setting, they leave open the question of how someone who wishes to engage in a community's rhetorical practices is to be conceptualized. Berlin (1991) and a number of other scholars who have developed what is generally recognized in the field of composition studies as epistemic rhetoric provide a perspective that builds on and complicates Bizzell's and Lyon's position. According to epistemic rhetoric, what I am referring to as the self can no longer be conceived of as an "individual," as a "unified, coherent, autonomous, self-present subject of the Enlightenment" that possesses "a transcendent consciousness that functions unencumbered by social and material conditions of experience, acting as a free and rational agent who adjudicates competing claims for action" (Berlin, p. 18). To conceive of the self in these terms is to imagine a positivistic world where subject and object are dichotomous and isolated from one another rather than dialectical, even relational. For this reason, the self, as a problematized and socially constructed, postmodernist figure, is now conceived of as a "subject," "as the product of social and material conditions. Here the subject is considered the construction of the various signifying practices, the use of language, of a given historical moment . . . " (Berlin, p. 18).

While my original inclination as I developed the metaphor I am presenting here was to reverse the traditional juxtaposition of a colonizing self and an exotic other, Urban (1989) provides a much better option. In Urban's view, "It is discourse—specific instances of speaking and the types to which they are related—that is the fulcrum between self and culture, between individual and society" (p. 50). That, to me, seems to be what members are doing when they engage in the oral and written language practices that are part of their communicative economy. For the most part, then, they are not representing

their discursive selves in relation to some cultural other that exists in an oppositional context; if anything, their primary goal is to represent the relationship
between the self as they identify it (or of the "I" in Urban's terms) and the
shifting culture by which that "self" or "I" is partly formulated and in which it
is rhetorically situated. On occasion, of course, there are exceptions. A number
of the oral and written excerpts I include in Chapters 4 through 6 present
members of the group talking or writing about their personal experiences in
the contact zones where they meet cultural others outside the parameters of
their own home fronts.

Because the term "representation" was originally used by positivists who
posited a distinct separation between an autonomous subject and her attempts
to describe the world "out there" in objectivist terms, my use of the term here
is weighted down by many of the same problems inherent in the concept of
"self." We have to keep in mind, however, that positivists conceived of the
truth "corresponding to an objective reality that could be grasped and accurately
described," if only language itself could be "freed of bias, superstition, prejudice" (Greene, 1994, p. 208). My intended use of the term is much more
problematic than that.[9] As I am using it, "representation" is really a stand-in
for such implicitly fluid concepts as creation, constitution, construction, and
invention. For me, then, "a study of representation becomes, not a study of
mimetic mirroring or subjective projecting, but an exploration of the ways in
which narratives . . . structure how we see ourselves and how we construct our
notions of self, in the present and in the past" (Hutcheon, 1989, p. 7). Under
these circumstances, "past events [and present experiences] are given *meaning*,
not *existence*, by their representation . . . " (p. 83). My decision to use this
term, of course, begs the question: Why not use one of the others—creation,
constitution, or construction—in its place? In a word, the term seems more
politically loaded than any of the other terms. In a supposed democratic state
like ours, the concept of representation carries special connotations and implications that most of the other terms do not and cannot possess.

In "The Cultural Basis of Metaphor," Quinn (1991) takes Lakoff and
Johnson (1980; see also Johnson, 1987, and Lakoff, 1987) to task for making
the "seemingly unqualified claim that metaphor underlies and constitutes understanding" (p. 59). The narrower claim that she offers suggests that metaphors
"do not merely recast existing understanding in new terms, but supply the
understander with heretofore unconsidered entailments drawn from the metaphorical source domain" (p. 60). As I noted earlier, I agree with Quinn's
argument that instead of developing metaphors from scratch, most of us tend
to select or favor particular metaphors "just because they provide satisfactory
mappings onto already existing cultural understandings—that is, because elements and relations between elements in the source domain make a good
match with elements and relations among them in the cultural model" (p. 65).

In the context of Quinn's perspective, the metaphor that I present here is not new; it simply emerges from my many years of involvement in scholarly work on language and literacy and in the lives of social network members. If anything, it reflects my participation in the search for alternative constructions of orality and literacy that "are grounded in social context and place no value judgement on the selected modes of communication individuals choose to make" (Novek, 1992, p. 231).

CHAPTER 4

Oral Language Use
in Everyday Life

During the first three and a half years I visited Jaime and Rocío Durán's home,[1] it was almost always full of people participating in and recreating the vibrant communal life they had shared in their respective ranchos. The most active participants in their daily lives included extended family members who lived with Jaime, Rocío, and their three children in the largest of the six apartments in the two buildings that the couple owned on a single lot in the Pilsen community. At various times, the family shared their first floor apartment, which consisted of a living room, a kitchen, a dining room, four small bedrooms, and two bathrooms, with a male and two female cousins. At one point, Rocío's sister, Olga Ramírez, her husband, and their three children moved in and lived with them for almost a year. Jaime and Rocío's acceptance of communal living was accentuated further by the fact that they rented their other five apartments, each of which consisted of a living room, a kitchen, a bathroom, and one or two bedrooms, to relatives and close friends, most of whom also dropped by occasionally.

In addition to those who lived on their property, several of Jaime's cousins and compadres, his brother, and two sisters, as well as Rocío's three sisters, three brothers, two nieces, and her best friend, and members of all of their families, would come by to visit for a few hours from a few blocks away, from a suburb of or another neighborhood in Chicago, or from their ranchos in Mexico. Like most families in the social network, the Duráns regularly hosted a variety of formal gatherings to celebrate special occasions. What I found unusual, however, was the frequency with which as many as 20 people would gather informally on any given evening after work or during the weekend. While some guests would stop by for dinner, to pick up or drop off a personal item or a child someone in the family was babysitting, to listen to music or watch a television program, most of them usually stopped by to engage in casual conversation, to participate in a highly valued "secular ritual" (Moore & Myerhoff, 1977) that many of them refer to as *"echar plática"* (to chat).

While most research on Mexicano discourse has focused on various genres of folklore and oral literature, among them jokes, riddles, proverbs, and tales (Aiken, 1980; Briggs, 1988; Campa, 1976; Espinosa, 1985; Herrera-Sobek, 1982;

Miller, 1973; Paredes, 1956; West, 1988), in this chapter I want to focus on three genres of echar plática—"self-oriented" personal narratives, "other-oriented" personal narratives, and propositional statements—in which the narrator's point of view shifts along a continuum between humor and seriousness, on the one hand, and narration and exposition, on the other. The importance of understanding the form and function of these genres, I believe, is reinforced by a series of interviews with several group members that suggests a generational shift from the folklore and traditional stories that adult members heard while they were growing up in Mexico to the telling of stories in the United States based on personal experience and the construction of shared knowledge (Guerra, 1992). Just as folklore and oral literature used to do, genres based on lived experience now serve to reinforce the strong personal bonds that group members value and that make the social network possible in the first place.

To establish a context for my examination of the three genres of echar plática, as well as the personal letters and autobiographical narratives that I discuss in Chapters 5 and 6, I examine in the first section of this chapter the different ways in which rhetoric and ideology are implicated in the formation and maintenance of genres in general, especially in terms of how the point of view of the self or the "I" (Urban, 1989) is represented in a narrator's rhetorical stance and in the reported speech of others in the narratives themselves (Bakhtin, 1986). The second section reviews a set of strategies that members discussed during sociolinguistic interviews as essential elements in the successful presentation of a rhetorical self. Significantly, the strategies they mention emerge from their awareness of how good speakers develop their abilities in the first place and how language operates in a range of genres. Finally, the third and fourth sections provide sample texts of, and discuss the ways in which group members utilize, two narrative genres to lighten the human burden of daily living, and an expository genre to enlighten each other about the real and rhetorical options available to deal with the burden.[2]

THE RHETORIC AND IDEOLOGY OF GENRES

Just as rhetoric and ideology play key roles in a scholar's metaphorical representation of orality and literacy, they also inform how members of Jaime and Rocío's social network construct notions of self, both individually and communally, in the context of an array of oral and written genres available in the group's communicative economy. To understand their communicative practices, then, we need to understand how rhetoric, ideology, and genre interact with one another in the social spaces that members occupy. Because it is our job as scholars to ponder abstractions of this kind in our research on language and literacy, we often struggle mightily to find ways to conceptualize, analyze, and interpret them overtly at a metacognitive level. Not surprisingly, members of the social network breathe life into these abstract concepts "confidently and skillfully *in practice*," as Bakhtin (1986) says about everyone's "repertoire of oral (and written) speech genres," even though "it is quite possible for us not even to suspect their [abstract concepts'] existence *in theory*" (p. 78). In this and the following two chapters, I want to demonstrate the roles that rhetoric and ideology play in how members use these genres to transform their unacknowledged theories into practice. An understanding of the interactive nature of these three elements may help us appreciate the facility with which members use oral and written language (or at least my transcribed and translated representations of them) in the situated context of their transnational community.

According to Bakhtin (1986), speech genres are *"relatively stable types* of . . . utterances developed" in every sphere in which language is used (p. 60). To complicate matters further, Bakhtin contends that there is an "extreme *heterogeneity* of speech genres (oral and written)" (p. 60) available to members of any community. In view of the multiplicity of genres, it is impossible for any researcher to identify every genre in a group's communicative economy. On the other hand, the study of a group's most often used genres, as well as an examination of how members introduce and deal with new ones brought in by fellow members or outsiders from the borderlands they share with other communities, may provide some insight into what Galindo and Brown (1995) consider "the importance of genre for examining relationships among identity, cultural interpretation of experience, and reproduction of cultural values" (p. 147). In my estimation, the face-to-face gatherings and the letter exchanges[3] among members provide them with opportunities to enact some of their most highly valued genres to construct multiple points of view that are essential in reinforcing their commitment to one another.

In a communicative sense, one could argue that members of the group use the genres they value most highly as sanctioned occasions to engage in what Moore and Myerhoff (1977) refer to as "secular ritual." As McLaren (1986) notes, Myerhoff "distinguishes rituals from habits and customs by their utilization of symbols; rituals are said to possess a significance beyond the information transmitted" (p. 42). Moreover, as Myerhoff (1982) herself points out, "rituals are innately rhetorical" (p. 128) and, I would add, innately ideological. To understand how rhetoric and ideology function in the context of the genres I examine in the rest of this book, we first need to formulate a better sense of what genres are and how they interact with one another as part of a group's communicative repertoire.

According to Hanks (1987),

> genres can be defined as the historically specific conventions and ideals according to which authors compose discourse and audiences receive it. In this view, genres

consist of orienting frameworks, interpretive procedures, and sets of expectations that are not part of discourse structure, but of the ways actors relate to and use language.[4] (p. 670)

To better understand Hanks's definition, it may be useful at this point to invoke Lakoff and Johnson's (1980) metaphorical language and look at the concept of genre in ontological and orientational terms (see Chapter 2). Ontologically, we can think of a genre as a dynamic container whose form and content a group tries to hold in place through its conventions, ideals, and expectations, knowing full well that the task is all but impossible. After all, like Bizzell's (1982) conception of discourse communities, each container's form, function, and content are always open to revision, especially as a consequence of how actual group members interpret, relate, and use them in the course of their everyday lives. In orientational terms, we can imagine each genre connected to a vibrating web of other genres, both oral and written, that together comprise the group's communicative economy. Not unexpectedly, the available genres are influenced by the group's rhetorical and ideological practices, which, in turn, are constantly changing as individual and group beliefs and values are themselves influenced and changed by an array of social, cultural, political, economic, and linguistic forces.

Each genre that is part of the complex, fluctuating web and ontological/orientational framework that I've just described, I would argue, represents what Bourdieu (1991) calls a "field" in his theory of practice:

> there is a political space, there is a religious space, etc.: I call each of these a *field*, that is, an autonomous universe, a kind of arena in which people play a game which has certain rules, rules which are different from those of the game that is played in the adjacent space. (p. 215)

Thompson (1991) refers to these fields as "the specific social contexts . . . within which individuals act" (p. 14). As Bourdieu makes clear, individuals do not "play" in these fields without rhyme or reason, that is, without having learned the rules and having practiced them to the point where they become natural. Bourdieu calls the process by which one acquires these rules, the ability to act or react in certain ways, a *habitus*. While these rules, or "dispositions," are inculcated "through a gradual process . . . in which early childhood experiences are particularly important" (Thompson, p. 12), over time they become *structured, durable*, and eventually *"generative* and *transposable* in the sense that they are capable of generating a multiplicity of practices and perceptions in fields other than those in which they were originally acquired" (p. 13). Bakhtin (1986) says much the same thing about speech genres when he notes that "we are given . . . speech genres in almost the same way that we are given our native language, which we master fluently long before we begin to study grammar" (p. 78). In the context of the present discussion, two of the most critical elements of the habitus that influence the fields, or genres, present in the communicative economy are the rhetorical and ideological dispositions possessed by members of the group.

While the rhetorical perspective that members describe (see the next section) is grounded in the epistemic or new rhetoric view that "the external world is not a neat, well-ordered place with meaning, but an enigma requiring interpretation" (Young, Becker, & Pike, 1970, p. 25), the rhetorical strategies they discuss also bear an uncanny similarity to Aristotle's classical notion of the *pistis*. According to Lunsford and Ede (1984), Grimaldi defines pistis

> as source material, material which comes from the logical analysis of the subject [logos], from the study of the character of the speaker or audience [ethos], and from the study of the emotional context potentially present for this audience in this subject and situation [pathos]. (pp. 88–89)

In their discussion of the rhetorical strategies they admire in good speakers and in my analysis of how those strategies operate in the range of oral and written genres that I examine, members place a higher value on narration (pathos and ethos) than on exposition (logos). This tendency also manifests itself in the central role that point of view plays in the content, context, and function of the genres they prefer to practice.

While Hanks (1987) is correct in arguing that despite the "value-laden orientation" of every genre, a work "cannot be reduced to a reflection of ideology, since it is shaped by constructive principles specific to discourse" (p. 671), we cannot deny the fact that ideology plays at least a partial role in how genres are constructed and the process by which some are granted more value by members of any group. Ideology is certainly pertinent in helping us understand the choices that members make, especially in terms of the three questions that Therborn (1980) believes an ideology must answer: what exists, what is good, and what is possible? Because members of Jaime and Rocío's social network generally belong to the same racial/ethnic group and the same economic class, issues of power within the social network, that is, ideological issues about which genres are more important and who has the right to engage in them, tend to play themselves out in the context of three other social variables: age, gender, and status or prestige within the group. It comes as no surprise, then, that in terms of the generational and patriarchal biases present in the group's system of values and beliefs, older members, and men in particular, are more likely to be granted the right to speak. But we can't forget that ideology also manifests itself in terms of whether speaking or writing is more prestigious within the group, and why. Again, because members share a well-respected oral tradition, the ability or opportunity to engage in genres of "echar plática" (to voice one's words overtly in a social or public space) seems to be valued more highly than the ability to put words on paper (to voice one's words covertly in an individual or personal space). In short, the highest value appears to be placed on the public display of an individual's rhetorical and discursive power in the context of the social spaces in which members of the group are most likely to participate vigorously: their ethnically, culturally, politically, economically, and linguistically segregated home fronts.[5]

LANGUAGE AWARENESS AND RHETORICAL
SELF-FASHIONING AMONG MEXICANOS

How people position or represent themselves in rhetorical or discursive terms varies, not only with a group's language and culture, but also with the subject matter, the age, the gender, the status of speakers and members of their intended audience, and the genre in which they are operating. Members of Jaime and Rocío Durán's social network are no different. As is true in Chicago, both casual and intimate conversation are important characteristics of their social lives in Mexico. In view of their close-knit ties and the relatively small number of people who make up the home fronts that comprise their transnational community, not to engage others in conversation or to participate in some exchange of stories or ideas is generally considered antisocial. While participation in such activities as corn roasts, cookouts, card games, birthday parties, Tupperware parties, baptisms, first communions, *quinceañeras* (sweet 15 birthday parties), weddings, and funerals may provide a formal atmosphere where traditional and personal experience stories can be shared, a simple house visit is enough to create the necessary conditions for those who like to echar plática. And because oral language is such a central part of their daily lives, adult members of the group are sensitive to and aware of its abstract qualities and the ways in which it can be used to entertain, to enlighten, and to effect change. They also have a distinct sense of the kinds of people whose language use they admire, of the diversity and commonality of opinion and linguistic ability in their community, and of what it takes to influence the views and actions of individuals with whom they interact on a regular basis.

While it is easy to assume that members of a small, traditional, and tightly knit group all share a similar worldview and have achieved a high degree of consensus, the fact is that adult members of Jaime and Rocío's social network are clearly aware of the diversity of styles and points of view held by group members. *"Todos tenemos un pensamiento diferente"* (We all have a different way of thinking), Olga Ramírez (see Table 4.1)[6] contends, *"y en la forma de pensar a veces no salimos de acuerdo y no nos impresionamos uno al otro"*

TABLE 4.1 Background Information on Interviewees and Participants in Samples of Oral Discourse (1990)

Name	Age	FS*	Relationship**	Occupation
Antonio García	22	3	Edith's husband	Scavenger service crew member
Edith García	20	8	Rocío's niece	Meat processor
Enrique Rodríguez	33	10	Jaime's cousin	Short-order cook
Fernando Vásquez	40	6	Rocío's cousin	Railroad track repair crew member
Francisco Madera	39	9	Jaime's friend	House painter
Jaime Durán	37	0	Rocío's husband	Railroad track repair crew leader
Leticia León	24	9	Rocío's niece	Meat processor
Lucinda Cabrera	50	2	Rocío's friend	City street repair crew member
Marta Valadez	34	12	Roberto's wife	Supervisor at catalog shipment center
Olga Ramírez	40	3	Rocío's sister	Meat processor
Pedro Valadez	48	2	Rocío's brother	Farmer in Mexico
Roberto Valadez	39	6	Rocío's brother	Packer at catalog shipment center
Rocío Durán	35	2	Jaime's wife	Plastics factory laborer
Rosa Durán	15	10	Jaime & Rocío's daughter	Student
Salvador Durán	48	0	Jaime's cousin	Railroad track repair crew member
Susana Rodríguez	23	8	Rocío's niece	Packer at catalog shipment center
Teresa Pérez	34	6	Rocío's sister	Meat processor

*FS denotes years of formal schooling.
**All relationships are based on the eventual association between the person listed and Jaime and Rocío Durán, the core couple in the social network.
Note: For easier referencing, names are listed in alphabetical order according to first name.

(and we don't always agree in our way of thinking, and we don't influence one another). Moreover, as Enrique Rodríguez explains, *"Hay unos que interpretamos de una manera. Otros somos más desabridos, más incipios. . . . Y uno es más chistoso"* (There are some among us who interpret in a certain way. Some of us are ruder, more insipid. . . . And another is funnier). When it comes to the art of persuasion, Enrique believes that these different ways of looking at the world surface and make the task very difficult:

> *Muchas veces trata uno de convencer, pero como uno ve las cosas diferente. . . . Cada quien vemos las cosas a su modo de uno y de acuerdo a la conveniencia a cada quien.*

> (Quite often one tries to convince another, but since one sees things differently. . . . Each of us sees things the way he wants to see them and in keeping with what is convenient for each of us.)

In the end, if one wishes to influence another person, whether that person is a relative, friend, or fellow employee, one has to find common ground. In

Roberto Valadez's view, you have to make sure *"que ninguno de los dos se sienta dañado, ofendido tampoco, y que detengan un convencimiento ¿verdad? Bueno, para que no haiga problemas"* (that neither of the two feels hurt or offended, and that they share a conviction, right? That way there won't be any problems).

Most of the adults interviewed note that speakers who are respected for their ability to use language to entertain and to convince others possess *"una facilidad de palabras"* (a way with words). There is, however, some disagreement about whether an individual is born with this ability or develops it through formal education. On the one hand, Salvador Durán believes that a person with this capability

> *tiene muy buen estudio. Sabe hablar, sabe aplicar bien las cosas a como deben de ser, y ya convence a los demás a que se haga como él dice. . . . Como tienen estudio, son personas estudiadas, tienen una manera, tie-nen la manera de convencer a los demás porque hablan muy especial.*

> (has very good schooling. He knows how to speak, knows how to do things as they should be done, and so he convinces everyone else to do as he says. . . . Because they are well-educated, they are learned per-sons, they have a way of convincing everyone else because they have a special way of speaking.)

Jaime Durán, on the other hand, argues that individuals are more likely born with such an ability. Says Jaime:

> *Estas personas de por sí ya nacieron así porque no son personas que se prepararon. . . . Desde que nacieron les gustó hablar de ese modo y les fue quedando su manera de hablar.*

> (These persons without question were born that way because they are not persons who had schooling. . . . From the time they were born they liked to speak in that way and their way of speaking stayed with them.)

Enrique, however, speculates that both nature and nurture play a role in how good a speaker one becomes:

> *Es por la educación o nacieron así prácticamente. Tienen las facilidades porque yo me imagino que instruirse, por ejemplo, la educación, tiene mucho que ver. Pero se han dado casos, me imagino yo, [en que uno] no tiene ninguna educación, ni nada, y sin embargo tiene el poder de convencer.*

their lives. In her view, such stories "belong" to the tellers because they are responsible for recognizing that something is "story worthy" in their own experience and for "creating identifiable, self-contained narratives" that join their perceptions of those personal experiences and "the conventions of 'story' in appropriate contexts" (pp. 268–269). While personal experience stories also can be subdivided on the basis of context or content, Stahl prefers to distinguish two kinds on the basis of how storytellers use the "first person form." In the first kind, "self-oriented" tellers "delight in weaving fairly elaborate tales that build upon their own self-images and emphasize their own actions as either humorous or exemplary." In the second, "other-oriented" tellers "underplay their personal role in the story to emphasize the extraordinary nature of things that happen in the tale." In these, the person telling the story "serves mainly as witness and recorder of incidents in which other people are the primary participants" (p. 271). Although I find Stahl's framework useful for my own analysis, there is one very interesting difference that I need to point out in terms of what each of us discovers. While the sample texts of other-oriented personal narratives that Stahl examines follow "a dialogue pattern rather than [the] individual 'performance-piece' format" (p. 272) she sees in self-oriented ones, the sample texts of the two types of personal narratives that I examine suggest the exact opposite. This contrast probably has as much to do with how each of us conceptualizes notions of self and other as with the cultural and discursive differences of the respective narrators whose sample texts we examine.

"Self-Oriented" Narratives

When members of Jaime and Rocío's social network want to entertain or make other members laugh, they sometimes tell traditional jokes, riddles, or stories. While the personal style of the individual storyteller may result in degrees of variation, by their very nature, traditional pieces are constrained by the conventional form, language, or punch line inherent in them. As I noted earlier, however, there seems to be an increasing tendency among adult members to tell fewer traditional stories and more nontraditional ones based on personal experiences that involve playful forms of language. More often than not, these stories emerge in the context of the joking and teasing (Farr, 1990) rituals in which members participate. While some of these stories are told from a single, first-person point of view, most take on a dialogical character that encourages the mingling of multiple first-person perspectives. Instead of one person taking the floor for an extended period of time, as often happens with traditional stories and other-oriented personal narratives, members of the audience often become co-participants as the joking or teasing ritual unfolds. Finally, to joke, usually by poking fun at oneself, or to tease others successfully, group members also must know something about their own personal quirks and weaknesses and those of others. After all, individuals have to be careful to create humorous allusions or double entendres without becoming offensive. In either case, making people laugh is a difficult task that requires a speaker who has mastered key rhetorical strategies, has a good understanding of the genre, and possesses a good ear and a good sense of timing.

Probably because much of our time together was spent eating or sitting around the kitchen table, many of the personal jokes that people told involved food. Just as traditional jokes build on a misunderstanding or a double entendre, the personal jokes shared by members of the social network were based on spontaneous and intentional forms of miscommunication. The first sample text involves Lucinda Cabrera, one of the women in the group who spoke most freely as well as one of the group's most proficient rhetoricians. I suspect the fact that she was never intimidated by any of the people present—neither the few men who sometimes squelched a woman's desire to speak or those of us who because of our professional status as teachers, often intimidated them inadvertently—had something to do with it. In addition to manipulating easily the appropriate rhetorical strategies from the set that members of the group outlined earlier, Lucinda also used her squeaky, childlike voice in dramatic fashion to draw laughter from her audience. On one occasion, shortly after we had finished eating a very filling meal, Lucinda reported a conversation with a friend that contrasted the pleasure Lucinda felt while eating three hot stuffed peppers and the way she would feel once they had to be eliminated from the body:

> ¡Ai, bendito sea Dios! ¡Ai, que a gusto comí yo! Y luego le dije, "Sí, pero al ratito—" "Al ratito hay que ver," dice, "porque te comistes tres chiles rellenos [risa], a gusto no vas a estar."

> (Oh, blessed be the Lord! Oh, how pleasantly I ate! And then I said to her, "Yeah, but in a little while—" "In a little while we'll see," she said, "because you ate three stuffed peppers [laughter], comfortable you're not going to be.")

Here, Lucinda seduces her audience into listening by first reporting from a first-person point of view and in highly ecstatic terms how elated she felt during her meal. She immediately switches to what she began to tell her friend, who in turn interrupts her and tells her what every member of the audience expected—that a little later the pleasure she had enjoyed would be replaced by the discomfort she would experience. Paradoxically, in telling this personal joke, Lucinda raises her status in the eyes of others. By making fun of herself, she demonstrates her self-confidence, the pleasure she finds in humor, and a desire to bond with listeners who undoubtedly have had similar experiences.

Like personal jokes, teasing provides participants with opportunities to create utterances with a humorous twist to them. While personal jokes are often self-deprecating in nature, teasing can be both self-deprecating and directed by the speaker at someone she considers vulnerable, yet willing to serve as the brunt of the joke. Some of the best examples of adult teasing among members focus on the relationships of men and women in the group with real and imaginary *novias* (girlfriends) and *novios* (boyfriends). During one exchange, for example, Rocío and her younger sister, Teresa Pérez, are innocently talking about whether or not the back door was left unlocked the night before when Lucinda unexpectedly shifts the conversation in a new direction:

Rocío: *¿A qué hora saliste a tirar la basura?*
Teresa: *Salí como, como a las seis.*
Rocío: *Porque, ¿estaba la puerta cerrada, la de atrás?*
Teresa: *Cuando yo fui estaba abierta, pero yo la cerré.*
Rocío: *¡Dios mío! Ora en la mañana que me levanté estaba abierta otra vez.*
Lucinda: *Es mi novio cuando viene borracho de /?/ [Risa]*
Lucía: *¿Cuál novio?*
Lucinda: *A mí se me hace que anda ahí Pablito.*
Juan: *A la mejor Leticia es la que tiene el novio. Se ríe mucho, ¿verdad? Hasta coloradita se puso.*
Rocío: *Acá mi hermana [Lucinda] anda descubriendo los novios de Teresa y de Leticia. El mío no, ¿eh? ¡Ni lo mande María Santísima!*
Rosa: *Yo creo que sí es el mío.*
Rocío: *Ni el tuyo ni el mío, porque tu papá no está y orita tienes prohibido [tener un novio].*

(Rocío: At what time did you go to throw out the garbage?
Teresa: I went out about, at about six.
Rocío: Because, was the door closed, the back door?
Teresa: When I went out it was open, but I closed it.
Rocío: Oh, my God! This morning when I got up it was open again.
Lucinda: It's my boyfriend when he comes home drunk from /?/ [Laughter]
Lucía: What boyfriend?
Lucinda: I get the feeling that Pablito is around somewhere.
Juan: Maybe it's Leticia who's got the boyfriend. She's laughing a lot, you know? She's even turned a little red.
Rocío: Over here my sister [Lucinda] is discovering Teresa's and Leticia's boyfriends. Not mine, eh? May our very Holy Mary not command it!
Rosa: I think it's mine.
Rocío: Neither yours nor mine, because your dad's not here and right now you're prohibited [from having a boyfriend].)

As this conversation unfolds while we're sitting at the kitchen table, the dialogue is fairly innocuous. Rocío's goal is simply to solve a minor mystery: why the back door was left unlocked. Once Lucinda introduces the idea of a boyfriend, the conversation suddenly shifts as people pick up on her desire to turn the whole affair into a joking matter. After I tease Leticia by suggesting that it might have been her boyfriend and not Lucinda's who had left the door unlocked, Rocío's 15-year-old daughter, Rosa, teases Rocío by introducing the possibility that it might have been Rosa's boyfriend. Rocío quickly invokes her husband's mandate and denies that it's either of their boyfriends. Although the joke dissipates as quickly as it emerges, the shifts in who chooses to participate in constructing the joke reveal something about their sense of propriety in having a boyfriend visit them. For while Lucinda and Rosa challenge the assumption that neither married women nor young girls in the social network are supposed to have boyfriends, Rocío discloses her more conventional view by invoking the name of the Virgin Mary and her husband's prohibition. Thus, personal jokes not only reveal the pleasure group members have in entertaining one another with playful language and ideas; they also reveal the ideological principles that members of the group support or question.

The final example of teasing, which also took place at the kitchen table, consists of two excerpts from an extended 20-minute conversation. Just before Rosa decided to tease her mother, someone in the group had been talking about how different women looked in miniskirts. Remembering that the European American secretary who works for Jaime's boss and who had visited the family a few day's earlier was wearing a miniskirt, Rosa flawlessly shifts the subject to her:

Rosa: *Como los [vestidos] de la secre [secretaria].*
Leticia: *¿/?/ quieres que te manden?*
Rocío: *Rosa, déjame comer en paz.*
Leticia: *¡Ah!*
Rosa: *¿Yo qué dije? Yo no más dije los de la secre.*
Leticia: *Pos, hablando de la secre no significa nada.*
Rosa: *¿Verdad? Y no más dije secre.*
Jaime: *Aquí, aquí en esta casa yo creo que sí.*
Rosa: *Y no más dije secre, no dije Miriam.*
Jaime: *¿Verdad, hija?*
Rosa: *Sí. Hay de muchas secretarias.*
Jaime: *Ooo, hasta eso.*
Rocío: *Pero no más una secretaria es la que, la que. Yo mejor no digo nada.*
Rosa: *¡Eh, ándele!*

(Rosa: Like the ones [dresses] the secre [secretary] has.
Leticia: /?/ you want them to take you?
Rocío: Rosa, let me eat in peace.
Leticia: Ah!
Rosa: What did I say? I just said the secre's.
Leticia: Well, talking about the secre means nothing.
Rosa: Right? And I just said secre.
Jaime: Here, here in this house I think it does.
Rosa: And I just said secre, I didn't say Miriam.
Jaime: Right, daughter?
Rosa: Yes. There are many kinds of secretaries.
Jaime: Ooh, that's for sure.
Rocío: But only one secretary is the one that, the one that. I better not say
    anything.
Rosa: Ah, all right!)

In this first excerpt, we have two women (Rosa and Leticia) skillfully building an implicit case through teasing to prove Rocío's jealousy. When Jaime acknowledges the fact that "here in this house" talking about the secretary is indeed a significant act, it suggests that he may be prepared to come to his wife's defense. But Rosa's quick disavowal shifts his position and he decides to join Rosa and Leticia in the teasing ritual. By then, however, Rocío's attempts to distance herself from the teasing—"Let me eat in peace" followed by her later "I better not say anything"—let the others know (inadvertently or purposefully?) that she acknowledges her role in the ritual. Rosa's triumphant "Ah, all right" immediately after Rocío's second attempt to distance herself signals that Rosa now knows she has the upper hand in the teasing ritual.

Later in the exchange, Rosa proposes an implicit comparison between her mother and the secretary based not on physical appearance but on money. In this second excerpt, Rosa, Leticia, and Jaime increase the pressure on Rocío to the point where she threatens to retaliate violently to bring the teasing ritual to an end:

Rosa: *Papi, no más con que tenga mucho, mire, ¡mire pa!* [*Forma un círculo
    con el pulgar y el dedo índice para indicar una moneda del tamaño de
    un dólar.*]
Jaime: *¿Dinero?*
Rosa: *Uh-huh.*
Rocío: *Ya déjame. Está igual de pelangocha que nosotros.*
Rosa: *¡Ah, entonces no está buena, pa!*
Jaime: *No, tiene centavitos.*

Leticia: *Sí, ¿verdad?*
Rocío: *Ah, veo qué bien sabes.*
Rosa: *A mí, ya les digo, que me dé el dinero, está bueno.*
Leticia: *Tú, Jaime, aviéntatele, que al cabo—*
Rosa: */?/ ¿verdad, Leticia?*
Rocío: *Está bueno. No más esperando, ¿verdad, Leticia? A ver cómo /?/*
Leticia (a Jaime): *Si quieres yo te ayudo.*
Jaime: *A recibir los chingazos que me va a dar mi vieja, ¿o qué?*
Leticia: *¡Claro! [Risa]*
Rocío: *Leticia, estás muy cerquita de mí, Leticia.*
Leticia: *No, pos, eso no importa.*
Jaime: *Eres buena para correr, ¿verdad?*
Leticia: *Sí.*
Rosa: *Pero no alcanza. ¡Mire, agarró una botella! ¡Agarró una botella, Leticia!*

(Rosa: Daddy, as long as she has a lot of, look, look, Dad! [Forms a circle
   with the thumb and forefinger to indicate a dollar-sized coin.]
Jaime: Money?
Rosa: Uh-huh.
Rocío: Just leave me alone. She's just as dirt poor as we are.
Rosa: Oh, in that case she's no good, Dad.
Jaime: No, she has a little money.
Leticia: Yeah, right?
Rocío: Oh, I see you know that very well.
Rosa: As for myself, I'm telling you all, let her give me the money, it's all
   right.
Leticia: You, Jaime, throw yourself at her. Anyway—
Rosa: /? ?/ right, Leticia?
Rocío: It's all right. Just waiting, right, Leticia? To see how /? ? ?/
Leticia (to Jaime): If you like, I'll help you.
Jaime: To take the damn blows that my old lady is going to give me, or
   what?
Leticia: But of course! [Laughter]
Rocío: Leticia, you're real close to me, Leticia.
Leticia: No, well, that doesn't matter.
Jaime: You're fast on your feet, right?
Leticia: Yeah.
Rosa: But she won't catch up to you. Look, she picked up a bottle! She
   picked up a bottle, Leticia!)

Although Rocío's oral responses suggest that she is very upset about being
ganged up on by her niece, her daughter, and her husband, the occasional

smile that crosses her face suggests her complicity in the teasing ritual. Figuratively and ideologically speaking, Rocío is being forced to question her husband's monogamous commitment to her by the very people who should be reinforcing it. Interestingly, after Jaime acknowledges that Rocío is on the verge of becoming violent and Leticia agrees to help him deal with it, Rocío warns Leticia that she's close enough to be the first to experience her ire.[8]

In the end, the fact that Rosa, Jaime and Rocío's 15-year-old daughter, initiates this long exchange and knows exactly what to do to keep it going verifies Bakhtin's (1986) claim that we "are given these speech genres in almost the same way that we are given our native language, which we master fluently long before we begin to study grammar" (p. 78). Moreover, the other excerpts in this section vividly demonstrate the participants' awareness of the important role that joking and teasing play in helping members of the group bond more closely by mutually acknowledging the character weaknesses that we all possess. Thus, while joking about oneself may paradoxically empower the speaker, teasing does not necessarily weaken the person being teased. If anything, it shows that the person is strong enough and has enough faith in group members to bear the brunt momentarily for the humor and pleasure that others may enjoy.

"Other-Oriented" Narratives

Like traditional and self-oriented narratives, other-oriented personal narratives often relate events that provide fascinating character studies and alert members of the audience to the range of personal strengths and weaknesses that manifest themselves as part of the human condition. Unlike self-oriented narratives, however, other-oriented personal narratives do not usually involve or build on repartee. Instead, as Stahl (1983) notes, they "emphasize the extraordinary nature of things that happen in the tale" (p. 270). In the context of the lives of social network members, other-oriented narratives tend to focus on events or experiences that narrators have had outside the parameters of their home fronts. Because older adults in the group spend much of their time interacting with one another, they have fewer opportunities to enter the variety of contact zones that their children enter because of their greater acculturation to other cultural experiences. In the case of older adults, the work site, commercial or bureaucratic settings, and travel seem to provide the best opportunities for other-oriented experiences. Finally, although narrators always tell their stories as part of the face-to-face conversations that they value, their stories are more prone to follow the "individual 'performative-piece' format" (Stahl, 1983) because they need to provide extensive details to represent the drama of a personal experience that has provided a complex and meaningful lesson.

The first sample text presents a story that Rocío told several other participants and me one evening while we were chatting in her living room. The story is one of several prompted by informal inquiries that a colleague and I made about the difficult conditions that women in the social network, almost all of whom work full-time outside the home, face at their job sites. When her turn comes, Rocío tells the following story about a situation she faced at work involving Billy, her boss; Rose, her immediate supervisor; and a young woman having difficulty fitting in. Rocio's narrative illustrates her efforts to interact with a variety of cultural others as they struggle to come to terms with a problem that none of them has been able to resolve.

Y [en donde trabajo] hay una muchacha jovencita de como unos vein-
tidós años. Ya tiene una semana y [Rose] me dijo, dice, o sea, le gritó,
[Rose] le ha gritado feo a ella. Dice que pero no entiende que de ningún
modo que le diga. Yo hasta le pregunté qué [idioma] hablaba y dijo que
español, que era, venía de Virginia. Y sí, pues, es güera. Yo dije, no
vaya a ser polaca o algo, ¿verdad? Dijo, "¡No! ¡Sí, sí, sí, yo hablo in-
glés!" Pues ya le digo yo cómo acomodé la caja y todo eso y más o
menos lo poquito que le puedo decir, pero no, yo también veo que no
más no. Y dijo este Billy, "Dice [Rose] que ya no vayas a ayudarle."
Dice, "Ya le dijiste. Deja que Rose batalle con ella," dice, "porque ella
cada rato está gritando que no quieren más personal mexicano. ¡Pos
cómo batalla! Pues ahora que se espere." Pero me da lástima porque no
más anda atrás de ella y están /peleándose/. . . . Y Rose dice, "Yo ya es-
toy cansada. Ya tiene una semana y no aprende." Y luego le digo,
"Rose, pero es que necesita uno de decirles ¡hasta cómo agarren las bo-
tellas!" Dice, "Pero ¿tú crees que yo no le he dicho? ¿Tú crees que yo
no /?/ ?" Le digo, "Yo sé Rose." Dice, "¡Ora yo te he mirado que tú tam-
bién vas a decirle!" Le digo, "Rose, pero ella no me entiende. Yo sé que
no me entiende." Y dice, "Pues yo no sé qué [idioma] habla porque a mí
no me entiende, a ti no te entiende, a Billy no lo entiende, ¡a nadien en-
tiende!" Y pues [la muchacha jovencita] dice que tiene un niñito de cua-
tro meses y que quiere trabajar y ya yo le dije pues que tratara de por
lo menos moverse sus manos. Ora ella no se preocupa si ve que las botel-
las se caen. Y nosotros nunca dejamos que pase eso. Y ella en el trabajo
y las botellas cayéndose y ella no se preocupa.

(And [where I work] there's a young girl of about twenty-two. She's been there a week, and [Rose] told me, she says, that is to say, she screamed at her, [Rose] has screamed at her in an ugly way. She says that she doesn't understand no matter how she tells her. I even asked her what [language] she spoke, and she said Spanish, that she was from, came from Virginia. And yes, well, she's light-skinned. I said, she may be Polish or something, you know? She said, "No! Yes, yes, yes, I speak English!" Well, then, I tell her how I arranged the box and all that and more or less the little that I can tell her, but no, I can also see that there's no way. And then, Billy says to me, "[Rose] says that you shouldn't help her." He says, "You've already told her. Let Rose struggle with her," he says, "because she's constantly yelling that they don't want any more Mexican workers. And how she fights! Well, now, let her wait." But I feel sorry because she's always after her and they're /fighting/. . . . And Rose tells me, "I'm already tired. She's been here for a week and she doesn't learn." And then I tell her, "Rose, but it's just that someone has to tell them even how to hold the bottles!" She says, "But you don't think I haven't told her that? You don't think I haven't /?/ ?" I tell her, "I know, Rose." She says, "Now I've noticed that you also are going to tell her!" I tell her, "Rose, but she doesn't understand me. I know that she doesn't understand me." And she says, "Well, I don't know what [language] she speaks because she doesn't understand me, she doesn't understand you, she doesn't understand Billy, she doesn't understand anyone!" And so [the young girl] says that she has a four-month-old baby and that she wants to work and so I've already told her, well, to try to, at the very least move her hands. Now she doesn't even worry about it if she sees the bottles falling. And we never let that happen. And she's at work and the bottles are falling and she doesn't worry about it.)

Rocío's story reveals the overt power relationships that exist between bosses and workers, on the one hand, and between newer and more experienced workers, on the other. Despite varied attempts by her, her boss, and the supervisor to teach the young woman the appropriate technique involved in a job activity, their inability to communicate with her creates a situation that makes everybody else's job more difficult. As she reports the back-and-forth exchange among the different "characters" in her story, as listeners, we are given an opportunity to witness Rocío's self-represented valiant attempts to help Rose, her supervisor, and the young woman herself. At the same time, however, we get a sense from her telling about the potential point of view of a young woman who seems overwhelmed by linguistic and personal problems related to issues of self-identity and motherhood, who doesn't fit into Rocío's (and Rose's?) culturally and ideologically oriented expectations about an individual's responsibility at work. Curiously, the story has no explicit punch line, no closing moral about how people should resolve such a difficulty if it were to present itself to them. Instead, the situation is left unresolved and members of the audience have to evaluate it on the basis of their own related experiences and dispositions.

The second other-oriented narrative also operates within a performative-piece format, but it differs from the first in that it is a personal narrative based on a claim made by a speaker during a conversation where a number of different social issues are being discussed. In this sample text, Pedro Valadez, Rocío's older brother and a respected storyteller, is paying his sister's family a visit from his home in Mexico. He is part of a group of eight men who are passing the time *echando plática* (chatting) in Jaime and Rocío's living room. Pedro's tale is part of an hour-long conversation about political and economic problems in Mexico and the United States. More specifically, Pedro is responding to a question someone in the group raised about whether U.S. government officials are likely to let the Social Security system run out of money in light of its projected shortfalls. Unlike his sister, Rocío, whose story was open-ended both in how it began and ended, Pedro first states his position in what we typically call a thesis statement or topic sentence in academia and then proceeds to provide an extended narrative that makes use of description and dialogue in much the same way Rocío did:

> *Digo yo una cosa, que esto no lo cambian estos hombres tratándose ya de su vejez de uno. . . . Yo conocí un caso de un señor, hasta joven se veía todavía, yo ni creía que tenía 65 años. Pueda ser que ya represente yo más edad que él. Un indio de los de allá de México, que es más, ni la barba blanca, ni digamos la cabeza. Tenía un contrato de 1943, que vino a, que estaba en el estado de Nevada, pero del Rock Island. Cumplió 18 meses trabajando en el Rock Island para el ferrocarril. Traía un contrato, el hombre. ¿No le cree? No lo tira desde ese año y eso hace dos años que lo miré y [lo tenía] en una bolsita de hule. Pero quiero que sepan que está más sucio creo este papel [aquí] que el contrato que traía ese hombre. ¿Fíjese? Lo saqué y dije, "Oiga, esto parece hasta falso, como tiene 42 años que se lo hicieron." Y mire, limpiecito que no tenía ni una gota de tierra. (Juan: ¡Fíjese!) Y ya le empecé y le dije otra cosa: "Señor, mire, usted no representa 65 años." Dijo, "No, señor, pero aquí traigo mi acta de nacimiento. Mire." . . . Y ya te digo del hombre ese, parece que obtuvo su segura de la ayuda del seguro social. (Juan: ¿Y cuánto tiempo estuvo trabajando?) Diez y ocho meses, nada más. (Juan: ¿Diez y ocho meses, nada más?) Y no más contratado. No más volvió a Estados Unidos. Cumplió sus 65 años, y le regresaron su dinero para atrás. Lo están manteniendo.*

(I say one thing, that this is not going to be changed by these men when it has to do with one's old age. . . . I know the case of a man, he still looked young at the time, I couldn't believe that he was 65 years old. It's possible that I might look older than he did. One of those Indians from over there in Mexico, and what's more, not a grey beard, not even [a grey hair] on his head. He had a contract from 1943, that he came to, that he was in the state of Nevada, but on the Rock Island. He spent 18 months working on the Rock Island for the railroad. He had a contract, the man. Can you believe it? He hasn't thrown it away since that year, and it's been two years since I saw him, and [he had it] in a small rubber bag. But I want you to know that I think this piece of paper [here] is dirtier than the contract that that man had. Can you imagine? I took it out and I said, "Listen, this almost looks false, since it's been 42 years that they made it for you." And listen, so clean that it didn't have a drop of dirt on it. [Juan: You don't say!] And I started and I told him something else: "Listen, sir, you don't look like you're 65." He said, "No, sir, but I've got my birth certificate right here. Look." . . . And I tell you about that man, it seems he obtained his pension from the Social Security office. [Juan: And how long was he working?] Eighteen months, no more. [Juan: Eighteen months? No more?] And he was only contracted. He never returned to the United States. He turned 65 and they returned his money. They are supporting him.)

Instead of providing a series of logical arguments based on facts in support of his stated position, Pedro segues into a story about an older man he met in Mexico who has so much faith in the system that he carefully preserves the very document that will verify his eligibility for Social Security support. More than that, Pedro reports that the man used the document as evidence and was awarded a pension on the basis of it. Like Rocío's story about the troubled young woman at work, this narrative is performed in a lively fashion that provides Pedro with the opportunity to represent another person in terms that highlight Pedro's own implied self-representation as a sophisticated and inventive storyteller. By focusing on the care with which the man he met protects his documents, Pedro emphasizes what Stahl (1983) refers to as "the extraordinary nature of things that happen" (p. 270). From my perspective (as the only person who interrupts his narrative), I undoubtedly find the fact that the man is awarded a pension on the basis of 18 months of work incredulous and therefore question it. My attempt at dealing with what I consider a lack of logic in this element of the story is quickly set aside as Pedro concludes by reporting that the U.S. government is still "supporting him."

Self-oriented and other-oriented personal narratives make use of several rhetorical strategies that members of the social network identified as important elements in the arsenal of a good speaker. Both, for example, are unquestionably based on honesty and experience, key ethical concerns that undergird their demand for sinceridad (sincerity) on the speaker's part. And yet, because their goal is to humor and entertain members of the audience, stories told within these two genres—whether they are dialogically created as the discourse unfolds or extended monologues that highlight the other rather than the self—also make important use of such other rhetorical qualities as gracia (grace or wit), sabor (flavor), and emoción (emotion). Whether the speakers are poking fun at themselves, teasing other members of the group, or telling an unusual tale that involves a cultural other, they are aware of their listeners' expectations and call upon rhetorical strategies that reinforce the personal bonds between them. And whether their stories reaffirm or challenge an element of the group's ideological perspective, members of the group acknowledge that it is all done in fun, in an effort to participate in an important secular ritual that gives their lives meaning and provides them with an opportunity to come to terms with their individual proclivities and the heavy burden of anyone's lived experience.

THE DEMONSTRATION OF PERSONAL KNOWLEDGE THROUGH EXPOSITION

While people unfamiliar with the rhetorical practices of Mexicanos may assume that they are discursively limited to engaging in joking, teasing, and above all performance-oriented storytelling, the evidence we gathered suggests that they are also quite capable of formulating and supporting the kinds of propositional statements that we value in the academy. Despite the assumption among some people that members of social groups with limited formal schooling are incapable of dealing with the complex logic involved in argumentation, members of the social network demonstrate repeatedly their ability to move beyond self-oriented and other-oriented perspectives into a genre whose basis is the propositional statement. In the context of what some may consider an unexpected genre, and may well be surprised to learn is a salient one in the web of genres that makes up their communicative economy, adult members of the social network repeatedly demonstrate their ability to explicate issues and ideas as well as provide evidence for their claims (Toulmin, 1956).

In one wide-ranging conversation about a number of social and religious issues, for example, several members demonstrate their ability to examine abstract issues and take positions on them in an analytical and expository manner. After a member of our research group asks a group of women sitting around Jaime and Rocío's kitchen table to explain why some people within the Catholic Church call themselves *carismáticos* (charismatics), Rosa and Leticia cooperatively discuss the key components that shape what the concept means to them:

Lucía: *Pero eso de los carismáticos, ¿por qué se llaman carismáticos?*
Rosa: *Porque es renovación carismática. Es como si usted vive una vida, la cambia después, conociendo, estando con ellos. Después empieza a ser diferente.*
Leticia: *Ellos dicen que es que creen. Es como una nueva persona. Pero ¿en qué [manera]? ¿Por qué no, uh? Yo digo que ¿en qué es nueva persona? Porque yo digo [que] es nueva persona en los hechos de aquella persona. Si aquella persona, ella le dice, "Yo ya cambié. Soy yo nueva. Soy, ya me," ¿cómo se dice?*
Rosa: *Ya me renové.*
Leticia: *Ya me renové. . . .*

(Lucía: But that about the charismatics, why are they called charismatics?
Rosa: Because it is a charismatic renewal. It's like, if you live a life and then you change it, knowing, being with them, then you start being different.
Leticia: They say that it's that they believe. It's like a new person. But in what [way]? Why not, uh? I say that how is she a new person? Because I say that she's a new person based on the deeds of that person. If that person, she says to you, "I have now changed. I am new, I am, I have," how do you say it?
Rosa: I am renewed.
Leticia: I am renewed. . . .)

In the first excerpt, Rosa and Leticia focus on the faith that leads charismatics to believe that their lives have been changed, have been renewed. Unlike the two narrative-based genres that we examined earlier, the language here seems unsure, unpracticed. Clearly, the narrative-based approaches of their self-oriented and other-oriented genres lend themselves to language forms that sound more polished and rehearsed because the speaker has had extensive experience with joking and teasing or has told the story many times before. In this genre, the language forms are more stilted and rougher as the participants struggle, just like most of us would, to formulate a difficult concept in comprehensible terms.

Later, in the same conversation, members of the group move from defining the term to stating their reasons for questioning or opposing it as an option in their lives:

Leticia: *Bueno, ella dice [que se renovó]. Pero, oiga, entre en la igle[sia], este, ¿cómo le dijera? Entre aquella familia que está adentro de su iglesia [se creen renovados], pero viene usted a su hogar—*
Rocío: *Y son rotundamente /?/*

Leticia: *Y en su hogar es otra vida. Es otra, otra forma de, de vivir.*
Rocío: *Entonces yo no me hago carismática.*
Leticia: *Y por eso, lo que digo yo, mejor no voy porque mejor me quedo así.*
   Porque ¿para qué me voy? Como dice uno, "Mira, en aquel lado ahor-
   ita hay una lumbre. Ahorita están las llamas. Al rato va a ser las bra-
   sas. Después va a ser el respondo. Entonces no hay necesidad de me-
   terse en aquella lumbre, primero porque está la llama, después porque
   están las brazas, y al último porque es el respondo." Pero terco ahí va
   uno a meterse a la llama, a aquella lumbre. ¿Qué pasa? ¡Se quemó! ¿Y
   quién lo mandó? Pos no más porque anda por entremetido, o porque es
   uno ansioso.

(Leticia: Well, so she says [that she is renewed]. But, listen, go into the
   church, uh, how can I put it? Within that family that is inside its
   church [they consider themselves renewed], but then you come to their
   home—
Rocío: And they are categorically /?/
Leticia: And in the home it's a different life. It's another way of living.
Rocío: In that case I'm not going to become a charismatic.
Leticia: And that's why I say, I'd rather not go because I'd rather remain as
   I am. Because why go? As one says, "Look, over there is a fire right
   now. Right now there are flames. Later there are going to be coals.
   Later there's going to be a flame again. So, there's no need to get into
   that flame, first because there is a flame, later because there are the
   coals, and finally because there is a flame again." But hardheaded, you
   go there and get in the flame, in that fire. What happens? One gets
   burned! And who ordered one to go? Well, just because one's being
   nosy, or because one is anxious.)

After having done most of the work of defining the term, Rosa steps back
and lets Leticia explain why she opposes the charismatic movement as Rocío
occasionally chimes in her support. It is not enough, Leticia contends, for
people to say that they've changed; in the end, they must demonstrate it by
behaving at home as they do when they're in church. Leticia concludes her
critique with a provocative metaphor that compares becoming a charismatic
with being drawn into a fire out of curiosity and getting burned in the process.
In short, Leticia argues, those who are drawn to the charistmatic movement
must understand what they're getting into and must be willing to live with the
consequences.

   The second sample text of what I'm calling a propositional statement also
illustrates the kinds of sophisticated analytical and abstract arguments that we
value in the academy. During a visit to the Durán household, I attempt to

persuade Jaime and Francisco Madera, a member of the tutoring group who is not part of the rancho-based social network, to consider pursuing a General Education Diploma (GED) now that they have passed the written and oral exams that are part of the amnesty process. After I read several passages from the GED preparation book and ask them what they want to get out of our sessions, Jaime presents Francisco and me with a "spoken essay" on the three key registers of language. Unfortunately, the tape recorder stops while he is delineating the three registers. During a later conversation that I tape-record, Jaime (with the help of his friend Francisco) reiterates his position and demonstrates why it is important for him and others like him to expand their language skills to the point where they are capable of interacting with people who in his judgement have more sophisticated control of a particular language register:

Jaime: *Porque efectivamente digo, a la mejor yo estoy equivocado, [pero] para mí que hay un inglés de la calle. Ese no hay ni que tenerlo en cuenta. Ese es de la calle. Ni siquiera en la calle lo vamos a usar porque con esa gente ni siquiera cruza uno palabra. En primer lugar sino que lo existe, lo hay, ¿verdad? Todo el mundo lo sabemos que está allí, [pero] ese no lo tomamos en cuenta. Vamos a tomar en cuenta el inglés que utilizamos, por ejemplo, en el trabajo, ¿verdad? El inglés del trabajo y ya luego viene el otro. Ya viene el otro de hablar con gentes más preparadas, más estudiadas, ¿verdad?*

Francisco: *Pues ese es el inglés que se habla en América, lo que [se] dice el inglés mediano, de clase media. Es el inglés que se habla aquí en Estados Unidos.*

Jaime: *Sí, en el ochenta o el setenta por ciento de los estados, se utiliza ese. Siendo que a lo que yo me refiero, que si nosotros podemos, si estamos hablándolo al setenta por ciento y agarramos el diez por ciento más, ¿verdad?, entonces ya estamos mejorando.*

Francisco: *Mejorando en la situación, sí.*

Jaime: *Por ejemplo, [es posible] que en un inglés más avanzado haiga otra manera de llamarle a la botella. Vamos. Ya sabemos que la botella le dice uno en inglés,* Oh, that bottle, *o como sea,* that glass. *Entonces si hay otra manera más correcta, más decente, se le busca. Se llega hasta esa altura y estudiando uno, pues, a su modo, ¿no? Eso sí me gustaría a mí. Avanzar hasta esa altura. Pero para el GED y todo eso, posiblemente no llegue yo porque "Me falta agricultura," dijo Cantinflas.*

(Jaime: That's because in effect I am saying, maybe I'm wrong, [but] for me there is a type of English used in the street. That one you don't even have to take into consideration. That one's from the street. We're not even going to use it in the street because one doesn't share a word with

those people. In the first place, it may exist, it's there, right? We all
know that it's there, [but] we don't take that into consideration. Let's
consider the type of English that we utilize, for example, at work, right?
The English from work and then comes the next type. Then comes the
other one that we use to speak to the better prepared, the better educated, right?

Francisco: Well, that's the English that is spoken in America, what one calls
the English in the middle, of the middle class. That's the English that
is spoken here in the United States.

Jaime: Yes, in eighty or seventy percent of the states, that type is utilized.
Which means that what I'm referring to, that if we can, if we are talking at seventy percent and we pick up another ten percent, right?, then
we are improving.

Francisco: Improving our situation, yes.

Jaime: For example, [it's possible that] in a more advanced form of English
there might be another way of referring to a bottle, let's say. We know
what one calls *la botella* in English, Oh, that bottle, or whatever, that
glass. Then, if there is a more correct form, a more decent form, one
looks for it. You get up to that level, and studying, of course, in one's
own way, no? I would like to do that. To advance to that level. But as
far as the GED and all that, I probably won't get there because "I lack
agriculture," as Cantinflas said.)

In presenting his point of view, Jaime makes use of examples from real life;
these, however, are not presented in narrative form but rather as examples
specifically designed to support a claim or proposition. This process suggests
that he is examining the three levels in abstract terms both in relation to and
apart from their use in everyday life. After naming each level and providing a
variety of examples to illustrate it, Jaime then concludes by voicing his desire
to develop the ability to operate within what he refers to as the top register,
the one used by professional members of our society. After he demonstrates
his ability to do the very thing that he says he hopes to one day be able to do,
Jaime invokes a pun used by a Mexican comedic actor famous for his slapstick
and wordplay and declares ironically that he will never achieve his goal because
like Cantinflas he "lack[s] (agri)culture."

While it is easy for some to accept the argument that different cultural
groups develop "restricted" or "residual" linguistic repertoires as a consequence
of their lack of formal education or their different ways with words (see Bernstein, 1971; Farrell, 1978), the sophisticated analysis of their own rhetorical
strategies that they exemplified during their interviews and the sample texts
of personal narratives and propositional statements that I gleaned from their
everyday use of language mark members of this group as self-aware and highly

articulate. Well, yes, some will argue, oral language use of this kind is not surprising. After all, members of the group have been using oral language all their lives. The question is, are they capable of engaging in the same kinds of sophisticated rhetorical strategies when it comes to written language? The next two chapters, I believe, demonstrate that while most members of the group have very limited formal schooling, the circumstances of their individual lives have made it necessary for them to develop and engage in similar kinds of sophisticated rhetorical strategies in written forms of communication.

CHAPTER 5

Personal Letter-Writing in a Mexicano Context

Despite the fact that it is often the most widely used form of extended written discourse among poor, working-class, immigrant, and Third World groups with limited formal education, the genre of personal letter-writing has received minimal attention as a potential area of research in the field of language and literacy studies (Besnier, 1993; Kalman, 1996). Besnier (1995), for example, laments the fact that despite its importance and ubiquity, letter-writing is not considered a major topic of anthropological or sociolinguistic interest. The few studies he cites (De Rycker, 1991; Mulkay, 1985) have generally focused on letter-writing in middle-class Western settings and "have commonly treated context as unproblematic." Moreover, Besnier notes, scholars who have studied letter-writing within a cross-cultural perspective (e.g., Bennett & Berry, 1991, on the Cree of Northern Ontario; Bloch, 1993, on the Zafimaniry of Madagascar) have presented paraphrases and narrative descriptions or, at best, translated and edited versions. As a consequence, the "voices of letter writers are either stifled completely or are altered through translation and reworking" (Besnier, 1995, p. 73). On the positive side, Brodkey's (1989) reflections on a series of letters exchanged between graduate students in one of her classes and a group of students enrolled in an adult literacy class and Camitta's (1987) and Shuman's (1986) examination of the uses of personal letter-writing, especially in terms of the role that collaboration plays in the process among middle school and high school students in Philadelphia, make use of the kind of approach that Besnier believes is crucial to understanding the role of letter-writing in contemporary contexts. In all three cases, however, the letter-writing being examined takes place in a school setting or between students and teachers.

I begin this chapter with a description of the process I went through trying to obtain letters for the present study, a process made difficult by a general unwillingness among members of the social network to share their personal letters with someone they had come to know as a "*maestro*" (teacher) and, thus, someone who possessed significant differences in their eyes in terms of class and social status. Because I then want to establish a cross-cultural context for my analysis and interpretation of the letters I collected from Mexicanos in

Rancho Verde and Chicago, the second section includes a brief review of the letters that Scribner and Cole (1981) collected among the Vai of Liberia and a more in-depth discussion of the letters that Besnier (1988, 1991, 1993, 1995) collected among Nukulaelae Islanders in the central Pacific. The last and longest section examines the age, gender, and social/familial relationships between letter writers and receivers; the conventional discourse frames letter writers use to begin and end their letters; and the inventive and highly personalized forms of language some letter writers use to represent themselves, their culture, and their relationships with other members of the group.

GAINING ACCESS TO THE PERSONAL
LETTERS OF MEXICANOS

During the initial year of our two-year joint project (1988–1990), the two senior members of our research team (Farr and Elías-Olivares) and I had a relatively easy time collecting samples of oral language use in everyday life. When we asked members of the social network for permission to interview them and to strategically locate tape recorders in their living rooms, dining rooms, and kitchens, they readily assented. Because there was an obvious abundance of oral language in their lives and because most of them felt relatively competent in their ability to use it—despite the fact that some would occasionally denigrate their oral language use by referring to its "substandard" qualities as a rural or rancho form of speech—members of the group rarely censored anything they shared with us. As a matter of fact, in the course of the many months that we spent gathering more than 52 hours of oral language data on tape, there was only one instance when someone asked us to stop a tape recorder and delete a segment.

Members of the group were also readily willing to share the standardized forms and writing associated with their jobs (Farr, 1994b) or religious practices (Farr & Guerra, 1995) and the business and government letters they received written in English (Guerra, 1992). As a matter of fact, more than half of the allusions I make in my field notes to letters have to do with formal letters members of the group received from the Immigration and Naturalization Service (INS) as well as from their children's schools, the legal system, and insurance or mortgage companies. But when it came to the written language they or their relatives and friends generated, the task of collecting samples was complicated by their own representation of themselves as poor writers and of us as accomplished, and potentially critical, readers. Their writing of extended discourse, then, remained relatively invisible, usually hidden away in the private moments when we (the researchers) weren't present. In short, our class differ-

ences, and the ways the larger society positions us all to judge others by their
ability or lack thereof to construct an extended piece of written discourse,
seriously disrupted our ability to collect such material.

According to my field notes, we first became aware of the important role
that personal letter-writing played in their everyday lives as a consequence of
a series of interviews we conducted with 14 adult members about their reading
and writing experiences (*Fieldnotes*, 11 February 1989, p. 152). In the course
of our interviews with several of the men from Rancho Verde, we became
aware of the extent to which they had taught themselves to read and write
through an informal process they call *lírico* (lyrical learning) for the specific
purpose of communicating via correspondence with family members still residing in Mexico. In "*En Los Dos Idiomas*: Literacy Practices Among Chicago
Mexicanos," Farr (1994b) provides an excellent overview of how "a number of
men in their mid-30s and beyond from [Rancho Verde] became functionally
literate essentially without formal schooling" (pp. 18–19). A series of interviews
I conducted in September 1995 with several men in their sixties and seventies
living in Rancho Verde and Textilpa verify Farr's description of how Jaime
Durán, Salvador Durán, and several other men from their generation used
personal letters to learn to read and write. Like the younger men whom Farr
discusses, the older men from Rancho Verde reported teaching themselves to
read and write their own letters to prevent others from taking advantage or
misrepresenting them and to ensure greater privacy in their correspondence.
It is important to note that none of the female members living in Chicago or
either of the two ranchos described a similar learning experience.

Despite the fact that a postal system is available to transport their letters
between Chicago and Mexico, most of the letters sent or received by members
are hand-carried by family members or friends. If the person traveling between
Chicago and the ranchos gives members adequate warning, those who want
to have letters delivered ask the traveler to drop by shortly before departure
to pick them up. If the traveler is unable to provide adequate forewarning, he
or she often is asked to wait while whoever wants a letter delivered can write
it. When that happens, members of the household usually go into their bedrooms or some other unoccupied room to write their letters or to have someone
else in the family write the letters for them. When a departing traveler stops
off to pick up letters from interested members of the social network, he or
she is asked to transport the food, money, goods, and gifts associated with the
letters. Although I carried goods, gifts, and packets of personal letters on my
trips between Chicago and Rancho Verde several times, I was very careful not
to ask members for copies of their personal letters. On the one hand, I was
concerned about the extent to which they considered the letters a private
exchange between the sender and the receiver; on the other hand, I did not
want to put any of them in a position where they would have to turn me down

known as the Ellice Islands" (Besnier, 1995, p. 21).[1] Together, this work reveals some interesting similarities and differences in how and why members of social groups with varying degrees of literacy engage in letter-writing as the principal form of extended written discourse in their communities.

Although they collected more than a thousand letters in Vai script spanning a number of decades,[2] Scribner and Cole (1981) limit their analysis to the content of "fifty letters gathered from a heterogeneous sample of Vai script literates living in upcountry towns." The content of the overwhelming majority of letters they examine focuses on "personal business: family and town news, requests involving deaths, plans for visits, and financial matters" (p. 73). On the basis of their analysis of function and content, Scribner and Cole note that

> three-fourths of all of these communications contain a request of some sort; better than half are written for the sole purpose of asking the recipient to do something, almost always to provide some assistance in the way of money, goods, or people. Information is also communicated; the most common category of news involves announcements of forthcoming visits or reports of family events (births, illnesses, and deaths). (p. 75)

Moreover, the letters written in Vai script are always written between people who know one another well and are very familiar with each other's affairs. Most of the letters are also written to friends and family living in Liberia's capital city of Monrovia or in other upcountry towns; Scribner and Cole make no mention of letters being sent to friends or relatives residing outside the country. Most letters tend to be very short and are written to convey a very specific message. And because "Vai script letters exhibit a businesslike tone over and above the context of the news they transmit," Scribner and Cole "found no examples of chatty letters to the family" (p. 73).[3]

While Scribner and Cole focus on personal letter-writing as but one aspect of the many cognitive and communicative activities in which the Vai engage, Besnier's principal goal is to describe in detail the role that personal letter-writing plays in the lives of Nukulaelae Islanders:[4]

> I show that members of the community use letters to monitor economic transactions with the rest of the world, nurture geographically dispersed networks of reciprocity, and transmit information. Letters are thus deeply embedded in patterns of exchange of both material and symbolic commodities (e.g., goods and gossip), and, as such, they are but one link in communicative networks that straddle the boundary between literacy and orality. Above all, letter-writing is the locus of emotional displays of a certain kind, a characteristic that permeates many of the social roles that letters play. (1995, p. 18)

In his work, Besnier is also interested in demonstrating the limitations of earlier research by scholars (Chafe, 1982; Chafe & Danielewicz, 1987; DeVito, 1966,

1967; Redeker, 1984) who maintained that "written communication is typically less affective than oral communication" (Besnier, 1993, p. 63). Without question, Besnier contends, most of these earlier researchers reached the conclusion that "written language is more 'objective' and less affective than speaking" because the bulk of data on which they based their findings was "academic writing, in which writers are expected to pose as objective and unemotional" (p. 64). Besnier's work, then, is specifically designed to challenge this presupposition (see especially Besnier, 1988) and to demonstrate the degree to which affect is a central element in the kinds of personal letters that Nukulaelae Islanders send to or receive from their relatives and friends in faraway places.

While a few Nukulaelae Islanders send and receive letters through the mail, the overwhelming majority of letters (which often accompany the "food baskets, frangipani garlands, and other packages" associated with them) are entrusted to travelers leaving on the monthly boat and who, in turn, are expected to deliver them "to a vast array of individuals at all ports-of-call" (1995, p. 77). Their relative inability to afford stamps and envelopes seems to be the main reason why most residents of Nukulaelae do not send their letters through the mail (1995, p. 76) and why they instead place "the addressee's address . . . on the folded letter" (p. 80). Most Nukulaelae Islanders also engage in the practice of providing the travelers who have agreed to deliver their letters "with oral messages identical to or elaborating on the content of letters to be delivered" (1995, p. 77). Because of problems associated with poor handwriting and the lack of a unified orthography, Besnier contends that the oral messages are meant to "'help' the recipients understand the letters" (1991, p. 573). Oral messages also come in handy because it is not unusual for travelers to misplace a letter among the many goods with which they often travel or to bring it in contact with some food product and get it soiled to the point of illegibility. Finally, in light of the fact that "a person planning to leave the atoll is often a major motivation for writing letters" (1995, p. 77), Besnier describes how "late on the night before the ship day, women and men of all ages can be seen feverishly filling pages of writing, sometimes with tears rolling down their cheeks, concentrating on a handwriting that gradually becomes looser, disorganized, and lyrical . . . " (1991, pp. 574–575). It is also not unusual, Besnier notes, for them or their relatives on the nearby island of Funafuti to frantically "scribble messages at the wharf as the ship is about to depart" (1995, p. 76).

Like Scribner and Cole (1981), Besnier also is interested in examining the content and function of Nukulaelae letters. Unlike them, however, Besnier delves deeply into the framing and content of the letters to demonstrate how Nukulaelae Islanders use affect to communicate emotions through their letter-writing that they would not ordinarily communicate face-to-face. According to Besnier (1993), the "text of Nukulaelae letters is overtly framed with the help of a number of specific framing markers, which are always present at the beginning and the end of the text" (p. 70). While the opening frames are partially influenced by English letter-writing norms (they often include the writer's address at the top of the letter, as well as the date and salutation in English), the main body usually begins with *taalofa* ("hello," a Samoan borrowing), "followed by references to the health of everyone at the writer's and the recipient's ends, and a sometimes very long series of invocations to God's grace and kindness" (1995, p. 86). The following is an English translation[5] of a typical example:

> Greetings to all of you! Thanks, we are all in good health at this end, and we also have learned from your letters, and have also heard from S and A, that you are in good health. We praise and glorify our Father for ever and ever. (p. 86)

Besnier notes that the closing frames of most letters often demonstrate "evidence of strain in the handwriting, confirming Nukulaelae Islanders' description of letter-writing as physically and mentally strenuous work" (p. 89). Closing frames usually announce the approaching conclusion of the letter and end with a long list of names representing members of the immediate kin group, as in the following example:

> Our conversation will stop here, but let us hope that we shall obtain luck and happiness from God's love for us to meet again in the future. Oolepa, Vave, and Tausegia, Saavali, Aaifoou, Luisa, Uiki, Vaefoou, Fagaua, Aalieta all send their love, but above all, we two, your parents who are useless to you. Goodbye. (p. 90)

Like the general content of the letters, Besnier (1993) contends that these opening and closing frames illustrate the affective intent of the writers through their demonstration and expression of empathy and love.

While Nukulaelae letters may vary slightly as a consequence of the letter writer's age and gender, Besnier's (1991) analysis of their style and content suggests that they generally fulfill "one of only four primary social functions." By far, their most important motive is economic. Such letters often accompany gifts, goods, food, and money or focus on "giving, asking, obligations, and the writer's ability or inability to meet demands." One of them, for instance, reads as follows: "I want to let you know that I have sent along a small package with the old man S. In it are one blue t-shirt, one striped loincloth, one deck of cards, and two belts" (p. 573). A second function is to provide the recipient(s) with narratives of recent personal and social events that manifest themselves in the form of gossip, news about "feasts and other celebrations, games, arrivals and departures," or the political life of the community. A third motivating force involves the giving of advice or the admonishment of younger relatives by older individuals. Finally, no matter what the particular social function of a letter is, the overwhelming majority of letters share one key characteristic: "They are a medium in which affect is given considerable prominence" (p. 107). As we will see shortly, the letters written by members of the social network in Chicago and Rancho Verde tend to be information-oriented like Vai letters, but many are as heavily laden with emotion and affect as Nukulaelae letters.

THE SOCIAL CHARACTERISTICS, DISCOURSE FRAMING, AND TOPICAL CONTENT OF PERSONAL LETTERS

Of the 44 self-initiated letters I collected from members of Jaime and Rocío Durán's social network and examine in this section, 15 were written by residents of Rancho Verde, 6 by a resident of Pinicundo, 19 by residents of Chicago, and 4 by a resident of California.[6] Moreover, 22 different individuals wrote or sent the 44 letters. While it is true that social network members who are unable to write often use informal scribes, all but one of the letters in this collection—the letter that Sandra wrote for her aunt and Graciela transcribed— were written by the persons sending them. On the basis of the dates that appear in 15 of the 44 letters, the earliest letter was written in August 1983 and the latest in September 1995. Although the average length of all 44 letters is 251 words, there is a noticeable difference in length between letters written to and from Mexico. While the average length of a letter written from Mexico to Chicago is 289 words, the longest is 438 and the shortest is 104. In contrast, while the average length of a letter written from Chicago/California to Mexico is 216 words, the longest is 458 and the shortest is 107. In addition to these general characteristics, we need to take into account such issues as the age and gender of letter writers in the social network as well as the social relationships between them. After all, it's important to understand which members are most likely to write letters and why. Moreover, letter writers often make use of framing devices to begin and end their letters that Besnier believes we need to consider seriously because they provide important "'guidelines' for [the] letters' interpretation" (1995, p. 85). Finally, one of the most important characteristics worth exploring is the topical or textual content in the body of the letter, where writers are more likely to break away from the conventions and constraints that guide the framing process.

Age, Gender, and Social Relationships

While the variables that play a role in any social practice are inevitably interrelated in very complex ways, it is sometimes helpful to disentangle them to understand the function of each. It is equally important, however, to acknowl-edge how each immediately is complicated or even called into question once it is examined in a larger context. For example, in terms of age, Scribner and Cole's work among the Vai of Liberia unquestionably suggests that younger men did most of the writing in the group's indigenous script. At the same time, Besnier's (1993, 1995) work implicates the egalitarian values the Nukulaelae share and shows how they encourage people of all ages to engage in the practice of letter-writing. In both cases, their description of the context in which they occur reinforces their conclusions. When we examine the corpus of 44 letters that I collected from among several members of the Mexicano social network, the implications are startlingly different.

In terms of age, the set of letters indicates that most letter writers in the group are neither very young nor very old. Thirty-two (73%) of the letters, for example, were written by persons between the ages of 25 and 50. While 8 (18%) of the letters were written by persons under 25 years of age, only 4 (9%) were written by social network members over the age of 50. Despite these figures, over the course of 9 years, I have observed people under the age of 25 participating in letter-writing to a greater degree than any other group. Does this mean that younger people in the social network write letters more often, or are they simply less concerned about writing in my presence? My guess is that both of these possibilities are likely. This means, then, that Sandra, who is 40, probably played a key role in inadvertently determining the age of the persons willing to share their letters with me. Interestingly, the issue is complicated even further if we take into consideration the age of the persons who received the letters. While 12 (57%) of the 21 letters sent from Mexico were received by persons under the age of 25, 9 (43%) were received by individuals between the ages of 25 and 50. None of the persons receiving a letter from Mexico were over the age of 50. On the other hand, while 7 (30%) of the 23 letters sent to Mexico were received by persons under the age of 25, 5 (22%) were received by individuals between the ages of 25 and 50. Remark-ably, 11 (48%) of the letters sent to Mexico were received by persons over the age of 50. If nothing else, this last figure reinforces the idea that older members of the social network exhibit a greater tendency to stay behind in Mexico.

If we look at the corpus of letters in terms of gender, the same kind of scenario emerges immediately. On the surface, the statistics indisputably sug-gest the feminization of literacy, especially in terms of letter-writing. Of the 44 letters I collected, for example, 35 (80%) were written by women. And of the 9 (20%) letters that were written by men, all but one (2%) were written to women. No doubt the extreme bias toward letter-writing by women reflected in the corpus of letters I collected is also overstated. After all, women were more willing to share their letters with me once Sandra decided to join me in the task of collecting them. While Sandra's role is implicated here again, the scenario involving gender is even more complicated than the one involving age. For example, whenever I announced that I was preparing to travel between their home fronts and that I would stop by to pick up letters that members of the group were writing at the last minute, most of the letter-writing that I observed involved women and children. And in almost every case, the child responsible for acting as an informal scribe for a father or mother who could not or chose not to write was female. To complicate matters further, the principal goal of the lyrical learning by men from Rancho Verde that I mentioned earlier was to develop the ability to read and write their own letters. Unfortunately, the letters they read and wrote are not represented in the corpus for two reasons. First of all, because circumstances have changed as a number of the men have been joined by their families and now have wives and children capable of doing the letter-writing for the family, they have stopped writing as many letters themselves. Second, when I visited a number of men in Rancho Verde with Sandra and on my own in Chicago shortly after the letter collection process began, all of them informed me that whatever letters they may have received or sent had been discarded or destroyed after members of their families had joined them.

Despite the overwhelming, and most likely unrepresentative, bias toward women writers between the ages of 25 and 50 reflected in the letters that I collected, the data provide us with a number of useful insights that we could not attain without them. While the upcoming discussions about discourse framing and the use of rhetorical strategies that emerges in the content of a number of letters are especially significant in terms of language and literacy use among members of the social network, one of the more interesting developments in the analysis of the letters as social phenomena is the varied relationships reflected between letter senders and receivers in Table 5.1. Here, the data on the art of letter-writing among members of the social network illustrate a level of complexity similar to that reflected in terms of age and gender. The number or percentage of letters in each category, I believe, is probably less significant than the total number of different social relationships. For example, of the 7 (16%) letters listed under Godmother to Godson, 6 were written by one of two Godmothers. On the other hand, the 6 (14%) letters written from Cousin to Cousin(s) were exchanged between four different sets of cousins. What is remarkable is that the 44 letters, written or sent by 22 different persons, were exchanged by individuals who shared 15 different kinds of social relationships. This not only suggests that social network members write letters to people who are related to them in a number of ways, but that they are presented with different audiences that demand a significant degree of knowledge about how letters need to be framed and what one is permitted to say to those varied audiences.

TABLE 5.1 Social Relationships Between Letter Senders and Recipients in Mexico and the United States

		Letters	
Sender	*Recipient*	*Number*	*Percentage*
Wife	Husband	4	9%
Mother	Son	1	2%
Father	Daughter	1	2%
Daughter	Mother	3	7%
Sister	Sister	1	2%
Brother	Sister	5	11%
Brother	Brother	1	2%
Aunt	Niece	1	2%
Aunt	Nephew	1	2%
Niece	Aunt	2	5%
Cousin	Cousin*	6	14%
Sisters	In-Law	4	9%
Godmother	Godson	7	16%
Co-mother	Co-Mother**	3	7%
Friend	Friend***	4	9%
TOTAL		44	99%

*4 were female to female, 2 were male to female.
**Equivalent term in Spanish is *comadre*.
***All 4 were female to female.
Note: Due to rounding, columns don't necessarily total 100%.

Discourse Framing in Mexicano Letter-Writing

Besnier (1993) has argued that affect not only occurs in the body of the letters written by Nukulaelae Islanders; it is also "a very salient component of the framing conventions of letters." While we may be tempted, "from an etic perspective, to view this affect as ritualised affect, which would not be 'meant genuinely,' much like the affective connotation of the 'Dear Sir' that frames English letters addressed to complete strangers" (1993, p. 73), Besnier further argues that doing so would be a mistake. I partly agree. In the context of a continuum with conventional devices at one end and inventive ones at the other, I believe the forms of language used by members of the Mexicano social network to frame the openings (introductions) and closings (conclusions) of their letters are fairly conventionalized in lexical, semantic, and syntactical terms. The degree to which assumed conventions are followed, however, seems to vary dramatically. For example, only 9 of the 23 letters sent to Mexico and 6 of the 21 sent from Mexico include the date at the beginning of the letter. Moreover, only three letters sent to Mexico and six letters sent from Mexico include their point of origin. Of the three sent to Mexico, two were written by Doña Cariño Rodríguez's brother in Oceanside, California. These two letters, I should note, also include the date they were written. The two other letters written by him include the date but not their point of origin. I should also acknowledge that all six letters from Mexico that include their point of origin were written by Ignacio Durán's godmother, who lives in Pinicundo.

Although the salutations used by social network members living in Mexico and the United States are relatively conventional in style, there are some interesting differences. For the most part, the letters from Mexico make use of the most limited range of possible salutations. All but three letters, for example, include the name of the person to whom the letter is being sent, although there are significant differences in how the name is framed. Two of the letters simply begin with the first name or full name of the person receiving the letter. Seven of the letters couch the name in a short conventional context like *"Hola Esmeralda"* (Hello Esmeralda) or *"Querido Nacho"* (Dear Nacho). Finally, nine of the letters couch the person's name in a longer conventional phrase that demonstrates a greater degree of affection for the person being sent the letter:

Set 1:

Fernando, mi muy estimado ahijado

(Fernando, my highly esteemed godson) [6FM][7]

Señor Ignacio Durán, mi muy estimado esposo de mi mayor aprecio y cariño

(Mr. Ignacio Durán, my highly esteemed husband who is my greatest appreciation and affection) [1FM]

The remaining three letters use salutations very similar in structure to the preceding set, but do not include a name:

Set 2:

Para mi muy estimada y querida amiga

(For my highly esteemed and beloved friend) [8FM]

Para mi muy estimado sobrino

(For my highly esteemed nephew) [17FM]

The letters sent to Mexico make use of very similar salutations, but a few also use slightly unconventional forms. Five use first names only, and one adds a last name. Another three are simply addressed to *"Mamá."* Moreover, only two are couched in the short conventional frames used in seven letters from Mexico (i.e., Hello Esmeralda). While only two letters couch the name in a longer type of conventional context illustrated in Set 1, eight letters make use of the longer and nameless conventional frame presented in Set 2. The range of social relationships represented in this set, however, is much wider; they include *cuñada* (sister-in-law), *cuñado* (brother-in-law), *hermana* (sister), *prima* (cousin), and *tía* (aunt). Finally, two letters in this set make use of the following unique salutations:

Yo, Anastacia Rosaldo

(I, Anastacia Rosaldo) [5TM]

Te escribo esta carta para ver . . .

(I write you this letter to see . . .) [6TM]

While the salutations used in the letters tend to follow a set of relatively limited conventions, and some even include highly affective terms, their principal goal is to address the person receiving the letter in a way that establishes a degree of familiarity, solidarity, or affection.

Immediately after the salutation but before they address the issues or concerns that have moved them to write their letters, writers sometimes include a sentence or two in which they express their hope that everyone in the recipient's family is well and/or acknowledge that everyone in their own families is doing fine. As was true with the salutations, there are some very interesting differences between letters sent from and to Mexico. Of the 21 letters sent from Mexico, for example, only 5 voice their hope that the addressee and his or her family is doing well but fail to mention the status of their own families. Of the 23 letters sent to Mexico, 7 letter writers use this strategy:

Me dirijo a escribirle esperando se encuentre muy bien en compañía de su familia.

(I direct myself to you in writing hoping that you are very well in the company of your family.) [5FM]

Mucho gusto será para mí que al tomar esta carta en tus manos te encuentres bien gozando de cabal salud como son mis mejores deseos.

(It will be a great pleasure for me if upon taking this letter in your hands you find yourself well enjoying the best of health in keeping with my best wishes.) [13TM]

More often than not, letter writers in both Mexico and the United States extend their best wishes at the same time that they report that their families are doing well through the grace of God. Of the 21 letters from Mexico, the remaining 16 all wish the person receiving the letter the best, report on the well-being of their own families, and acknowledge that their own families are doing well through the grace of God. Interestingly, only 11 of the 23 letters to Mexico do the same. Following are some examples of how they frame this part of their letters:

> *Mucho gusto será para mí al recibir esta carta en tus manos. Espero que te encuentres bien de salud, así como son mis mejores deseos. Nosotros estamos bien, gracias a Dios.*

> (It will be a great pleasure for me when you receive this letter in your hands. I hope you find yourself in good health, in keeping with my best wishes. We are doing fine, thank God.) [17FM]

> *Con el gusto de siempre te contesto la tuya en la que me dices que están bien. Pues me alegro mucho. Que nosotros, bien, gracias a Dios.*

> (With the pleasure I always feel, I answer yours in which you tell me that you're all fine. Well, it makes me very happy. As for ourselves, fine, thank God.) [21TM]

While all the letters from Mexico are limited to the two categories presented above, some of the letters to Mexico fall into two additional categories. Two of them, for example, simply report that the writer's family is doing well through the grace of God. The three remaining letters do not bother to wish the recipient's family the best of health or to report the condition of their own.

One last convention that Mexicano writers use in the opening frame of their letters (as well as in the body of the text) is the transitional device, both to move the reader from the end of the salutation to the body of the text and on occasion to direct the reader through the text itself. Here are several examples of how some writers make use of a particular kind of transitional device to direct the reader's attention to the body of the text:

> *Y después de saludarte, paso a dar contestación a tu carta.*

> (And after wishing you the best, I turn to answer your letter.) [2FM]

> *Y después de un corto y afectuoso saludo, paso a lo siguiente:*

> (And after a short and affectionate greeting, I turn to the following:) [8FM]

> *Después de saludarlos con el cariño de siempre, te hago saber que . . .*
>
> (After giving you all my best wishes with everpresent affection, I want to let you know that . . .) [19TM]

Within the body of the text itself, several letter writers also use a series of transitional devices to move the reader through the text. The most common sequences I came across are the following:

> *Me dices que . . . Cambiando de tema, me dices que . . . Me dices que . . . También te cuento que . . . Me dices que*
>
> (You tell me that . . . Changing the subject, you tell me that . . . You tell me that . . . Also, I tell you that . . . You tell me that) [18FM]
>
> *Me preguntas qué . . . Y me dices que . . . No te cuento nada porque . . . Y, mira, Consuelo . . .*
>
> (You ask me what . . . And you tell me that . . . I don't tell you anything because . . . And, look, Consuelo . . .) [2TM]

Again, it's interesting to note the different degrees to which letter writers in Mexico and the United States use these transitional devices. For example, while only 11 of the 23 letters (48%) sent to Mexico use the long transitional device that leads the reader from the salutation to the body of the text, 14 of the 21 letters (66%) sent from Mexico use it. Moreover, while only 8 of the 23 letters (35%) sent to Mexico make overt use of the shorter transitional devices within the body of the text, 16 of 21 letters (76%) sent from Mexico do the same.

Finally, the letters I collected also make use of a number of conventional closings that demonstrate that a letter is about to end. Like all of the framing devices I have described thus far, these tend to be shared widely by letter writers in the group. While not every writer dates the letter, uses the name of the recipient at the outset, provides the same kind of salutation, or makes use of transitional devices, every writer in the group, with only one exception, invokes much the same kind of closing frame. As the examples below show, there are some variations, but all of the letters in the collection—except for the last example listed below—include the word "*Saludos*" (Greetings) or "*Salúdame*" (Say hello to) before the writers launch into their varied forms of closure:

> *Bueno, Doña Rocío, le mandan muchos saludos Doña Antonia y Julia. Y de mi parte, los mejores recuerdo[s]. Un saludo muy afectuoso para usted que es una de las mejores personas que he encontrado en mi vida.*

Salúdeme a Anita y a su hijo. De mi parte, todos los mejores deseos tanto para usted como para toda su familia. Hasta pronto. Albertina Gómez.

(Well, Doña Rocío, Doña Antonia and Julia send their very best. And on my behalf, best regard[s]. A very affectionate greeting for you who is one of the best persons that I have known in my life. Say hello to Anita and to her son. On my behalf, all the best wishes for you and for your whole family. Until next time. Albertina Gómez) [5FM]

Pues, me saludas a Isabel, los muchachos, y todos los demás. Y a tu esposa. Y los saluda mi papá, Benjamín, Marcos y su familia, Rosita, Gloria, y Graciela. Y me saludas a Leticia, Esmeralda, [y] Lucero. Y de mí recibe el cariño de quien siempre los recuerda y no los olvida. Y cuídate. Lupita Diego.

(Well, give my regards to Isabel, the kids, and all the others. And to your wife. And greetings from my dad, Benjamín, Marcos and his family, Rosita, Gloria, and Graciela. And give my regards to Leticia, Esmeralda, [and] Lucero. And from me accept the love of someone who always remembers you and never forgets you. And take care of yourself. Lupita Diego.) [13FM]

Me saludas a todos y espero que te encuentre[s] bien. Y te mando mis mejores y cariñosos saludos de yo, tu prima, Gloria Durán. Te mandan saludos todos los de aquí—Marcelo, Maravilla, Gato, mi mamá y papá.

(Give my regards to everyone and I hope you['re] doing fine. And I send you my best and most affectionate greetings from I, your cousin, Gloria Durán. Everyone from over here sends their best wishes—Marcelo, Maravilla, Gato, my mom and dad.) [14TM]

Qué Dios los ilumine y los bendiga en todos sus trabajos. Son los deseos de quien los quiere y no lo sabía. Tu papá, Roberto García

(May God enlighten you and bless you in all your endeavors. These are the wishes of he who loves you and didn't know it. Your dad, Roberto García.) [19TM]

Like Nukulaelae Islanders, then, members of the Mexicano social network use affective language to demonstrate their emotional relations with the other members to whom they write letters. Instead of a simple *Hola* (Hello) or *Querido* (Dear), most members of the group expand the extra energy needed to demonstrate their sincere concern about the recipient and his or her family, at the same time that they go to great pains to inform the recipient that their own families are doing well with the help of God. Most letter writers also make an effort to demonstrate the same intensity of feeling and emotion in their closing frames. Many of them, for example, go to great lengths to let the recipient know that they are not simply representing themselves when they write, but, indeed, speak on behalf of a large number of their closest kin.

In the end, these conventional openings and closings, like the array of long and short transitional devices that I discuss, provide the connective tissue that gives their letters a shared form that is easy to read and interpret. Furthermore, I would argue that many of the formulaic patterns they use are so profoundly embedded in the schemas that members of the group share that even individual members who do not know how to write at all can "speak" or "dictate" a letter with relative ease. [8] All this, however, ultimately serves as the mere framing for the content, the substance, the message that the writer embeds within these shared frameworks. It is to these topical issues that I now turn.

The Topical Content of Mexicano Representations

According to Besnier (1995), Nukulaelae Islanders express affect in their letter-writing in overt terms that contrast sharply with the "covertness with which affect permeates everyday discourse in most face-to-face contexts, including damaging gossip." In other words, a license to display affect in letter-writing "seems to be operative that is not found in most face-to-face interactions" (1995, p. 100). Besnier explains this difference by arguing that

> On Nukulaelae, letters are highly "concentrated" communicative events: opportunities to receive and write letters are comparatively few and far between, in sharp contrast with the constant face-to-face socialization that daily life on a tiny crowded islet affords, for better or for worse. The effect that this may have is that, if individuals are going to convey any message in the letters they write, they had better do it in an intensive manner. (p. 111)

Besnier is careful, however, to point out that the kind of "vulnerability and strong positive affect" reflected in letter-writing is also expressed "in one highly marked situation, namely parting interactions" (p. 111). Affect, especially in the form of sorrow, emerges during farewells or "in letters written to loved ones living far away," Besnier concludes, because these instances disrupt the group's shared ideals epitomized in a fulfilling life of "peace," "mutual empathy," and the practice "of performing daily routines together" (p. 112).

The same does not seem to be true about members of the Mexicano social network. As the preceding and current chapter demonstrates, members of the

TABLE 5.2 Range of Topics Discussed in Mexicano Personal Letters

	From Mexico		*To Mexico*		*Total*	
Topic	#	%	#	%	#	%
Personal	65	46%	55	55%	120	50%
Economic	25	18%	27	27%	52	22%
Health	11	8%	7	7%	18	8%
Agricultural	13	9%	4	4%	17	7%
Religious	12	9%	0	0%	12	5%
Community	3	2%	3	3%	6	3%
Interpersonal	3	2%	2	2%	5	2%
Educational	5	4%	0	0%	5	2%
Weather	3	2%	2	2%	5	2%
TOTAL	140	100%	100	100%	240	101%

Note: Due to rounding, columns don't necessarily total 100%.

group seem to use highly emotional language in both their oral and written discourse because it is but one component of the ethos and pathos of their rhetorical practices, which as I pointed out in the preceding chapter include grace, wit, eloquence, taste, and flavor. Although the language forms they use to frame their letters is very rhetorical in nature, the forms tend toward the conventional and formulaic and, thus, lose much of their power in the process. The redundant nature inherent in the choice of words, in their limited meaning through overuse, and in the repeated syntactical constructions saps them of the energy that I would argue emerges in the body of the text, especially in the narratives that individual members of the group purposefully use to share varied experiences in vivid and inventive language with their intended readers. Table 5.2, which lists in order of frequency the topical issues raised in the 44 letters,[9] demonstrates the kinds of concerns members of the group who wrote the letters value and consider worth sharing with one another. Before I present and analyze some extended narratives on economic and personal issues, let me quickly review some of the other concerns that letter writers address in the body of their texts.

Aside from personal and economic issues, which together make up 72% of the topical concerns addressed in these letters, three other areas of interest are religious, agricultural, and health-related issues. The astounding degree to which writers make reference to God in their framing suggests a deeply grounded belief in the Catholic faith that members of the community share. As Table 5.2 indicates, this belief emerges only in the body of the letters written from Mexico. In addition to talk about baptisms, weddings, and priests, writers ask for personal prayers, as in the following passage:

> *Yo le pido, por favor, que cuando usted vaya a sus oraciones, pida mucho por mis hijos que se encuentran cerca de donde usted está. Que yo también le pido a nuestro Señor por usted y por su familia.*

(I ask you, please, that when you go to say your prayers, ask much for my children who are near where you are. And I too ask of our Father for you and for your family.) [5FM]

Agricultural concerns also emerge as a topic of discussion, especially in letters from Mexico, because most social network members who live in Rancho Verde are subsistence farmers who primarily grow corn and beans, although Jaime Durán recently planted a grove of avocados for experimental purposes. Finally, concerns about health emerge because members are generally poor and suffer many of the same health problems as the poor in any country. Writers often inquire after the health of the letter recipients and their families, discuss the need for special herbal and medicinal treatments, and report on the illness or death of a relative or friend.

Because of the economic conditions social network members face in the two countries, a large number of topical discussions, especially in the letters from Mexico, involve talk about exchanging goods and gifts and about the need for money to purchase particular items. Many of the letters from Rancho Verde, for example, acknowledge the receipt of checks or money from Chicago as well as the purchasing or selling of livestock and the payment of bills for local needs. Many of the letters from Rancho Verde also thank the recipients for having sent money and inquire about the employment circumstances of their loved ones in Chicago, especially when someone is unemployed or is getting help from someone in the social network while they look for a new job. In the following passage, Samuel Durán, who lives in Rancho Verde, attempts to persuade his cousin, Ignacio Durán, not to take his 17-year-old son to Chicago with him because Samuel needs his cousin's son to help him with his work:

> *Pues, quién sabe tú que pienses de lo que te voy a decir. Pues, es que yo sé que piensas llevarte a Gustavo. Pues, yo digo que no está bien que te lo lleves porque ¿yo qué voy a hacer solito para trabajar y ir a ver los animales al cerro? Pues, él es el que me ayuda a ir a ver los animales. Pues, ya ves que mi papá no puede ir y hay tú a ver qué piensas. Pero yo solito no puedo andar echando vueltas para el cerro, y yo no quisiera que me dejaran solo. Y ya es cuanto te digo.*

(Well, who knows what you'll think about what I'm going to tell you. Well, the thing is, I know that you're thinking of taking Gustavo with you. Well, I say it's not right for you to take him because, what am I going to do by myself when I have to work and to go see the animals up on the mountain? Well, he is the one who helps me to go see the animals. Well, you know that my father can't go, and so let's see what you think. But I alone can't be taking trips to the mountain, and I wouldn't like to be left alone. And that's all I've got to say.) [16FM]

Unfortunately for Samuel, Ignacio Durán had no choice but to take his son with him because of his own family's need for additional income. While the eloquence of the letter is not lost on Ignacio Durán, economic circumstances limit his options. The letters to Mexico from Chicago, on the other hand, often accompany the sending of money to relatives in Rancho Verde to help their relatives, especially older parents, spouses, and children, pay personal debts and bills or open temporary savings accounts. Some letters also mention that the writers are working too hard and have no time to relax or are hoping to return to Rancho Verde for a visit as soon as they've saved up enough money. In short, the need for money and the things it can pay for or buy are mentioned in most letters sent to and from Mexico.

Above all else, letters to and from Mexico are used to maintain personal relations by constantly making them the central piece of almost every letter. As Table 5.2 indicates, 50% of all topics raised in the letters involve personal matters. While many of these issues are simply mentioned in passing, a number of the letters, especially those written by younger members who are more likely to push the limits and challenge conventions, provide detailed narratives about personal circumstances that often overflow with grace, wit, taste, flavor, and emotion. As is true in any closely knit social network, gossip is always a favorite topic among letter writers:

> *Y lo que me dices de Leticia, que su familia de Marisela te contó para espantarte. Por favor, si yo fuera, hasta vergüenza me había de dar. No sé que le vio Marisela, si está bien feo. A bueno, su dinero ¿verdad? Tiene que ser por el dinero porque no creo que lo quiera. Y sí, como dices tú, el dinero no es todo en la vida. Yo lo que pienso es que no me casaría con alguien porque tuviera dinero si no lo quería. Claro. Porque yo pienso si uno quiere a alguien, no le importa como sea o como esté. De todas formas, ¿se quiere así, o tú qué crees?*

> (And what you tell me about Leticia, what her family of Marisela told you to freak you out. Please, if it was me, I would be so embarrassed. I don't see what Marisela saw in him, since he's so ugly. Okay, his money, right? It has to be because of the money because I can't believe that she loves him. And yes, like you say, money isn't everything in life. What *I* think is that I wouldn't get married to someone just because he had money if I didn't love him. Obviously. Because I believe

if a person loves someone, it doesn't matter what he's like or what he is. Anyway, is that what love is, or what do you think?) [8FM]

In this passage from a letter exchanged between two young women, the language is youthful, playful, and inquisitive. The passage raises the eternal question about whether it is better to marry a man for his looks or for his money. After chastising Leticia for marrying an ugly man for his money, Esther Durán decides that love is more important than money, then ends her letter with a rhetorical question that invites the recipient to continue their written conversation about the nature of love.

Indiscretion, and the price one pays for it, provides the young man who wrote the following passage to his sister in Mexico with a lesson on the power of the written word. The passage also gives him a chance to philosophize and to share a very personal perspective on the battle between the sexes with his younger sister:

Mira, la carta que me mandaste, tocó la mala suerte de que Linda la mirara, y ella se enojó. Ella se va [a] ir, y si un día ella te dice algo acerca de esa carta, no quiero que te vayas a enojar y vaya a ser más problemas. Si te dice algo tú mándame decir, o si estoy yo allá yo mismo la voy a ponerla en su lugar. Pero como te digo, no quiero problemas. Mira, ella entró un día en mi cuarto y miró la carta y la leyó toda. Y ella me dijo que por que tú me decías esas cosas de ella, que tú cuando estabas allá eran muy amigas. ¿Y ahora tú me dices esas cosas? Nos enojamos por eso, pero ya nos hablamos otra vez. Yo le hablo para novia pero nunca me dijo que sí. Dijo que me quería conocer primero. Y después que miró esa carta, ya me dijo que me olvidara. Como quiera, ella no es la única y no es la primera que me dice que no. Yo sé perder y ganar. Yo ya aprendí de todo eso. Son cosas del destino que no siempre se pueda ganar. Y además ella es muy chica. Espero que esto que te digo no se lo digas a nadie. Y no te vayas a enojar, hermana. Cosas pasan y no hay que traerlas en la mente siempre.

(Look, the letter that you sent me, it was bad luck that Linda got to see it, and she got upset. She is leaving, and if one day she tells you something about that letter, I don't want you to get angry and we end up with more problems. If she tells you something you let me know, or if I'm over there I myself will put her in her place. But like I say I don't want any problems. Look, she entered my room one day and saw the letter and read the whole thing. And she told me why you were telling me those things about her, that when you were over there you two were good friends. And now you tell me those things? That's why we

got angry with each other, but now we're talking again. I call on her as
a girlfriend, but she never said yes. She said she wanted to get to know
me first. And after she saw the letter, then she told me to forget it. Anyway, she's not the only one and she's not the first to say no to me. I
know how to lose and win. I've already learned about all those things.
It's a matter of destiny that you can't always come out on top. And anyway, she's very young. I hope that what I'm telling you, you won't tell it
to anyone. And be sure not to get angry, sister. Things happen and
there's no need to keep thinking about them all the time.) [8TM]

Francisco Durán's witty repartee reveals a close relationship with his sister,
which they have been maintaining and building through an exchange of letters.
It is, after all, his sister's letter that gets them both in trouble. The grace with
which he moves through the narrative and the self-conscious eloquence that
eventually gets him to shift from the problem at hand to destiny probably
leaves his sister wanting to hear more.

Finally, like Nukulaelae letters, some of the letters written by members
of the Mexicano social network address the anguish and despair of being alone
and far from those you love and whom you can comfort only from a distance.
In the following passage, Gloria Durán, a woman in her mid-thirties, writes to
a younger cousin whom she left behind in Rancho Verde after moving to
Chicago some four years earlier. Like Francisco in the preceding passage,
Gloria uses the occasion to narrate a moment in her life and then philosophize
about its deeper meaning. This time, however, wit takes a back seat to grace,
eloquence, and emotion:

> *Me la pasé bien en el día de mis cumpleaños. Mira, si tú misma te amar-*
> *gas la vida, nunca vas a ser feliz. No, tú no tienes que hacer así. Tú*
> *puedes hacer[te] feliz. Te voy a decir algo. Mi navidad y año nuevo fue*
> *feliz porque yo lo quise así, no porque Dios lo hizo. Porque yo traté que*
> *fuera los mejores días de mi vida. Aunque lo pasado fue un tiempo mal*
> *para mí porque yo también sufro algo en mi corazón que a nadien*
> *puedo decir. Es algo feo y triste para mí, y no quiero que alguien esté*
> *triste. Pues, de lo que te digo, de que te amargas la vida, por favor trata*
> *de hacer lo que te digo y me cuentas y te sirve porque a mí es lo que*
> *me hace feliz. También olvídate de lo pasado y vete derechito a lo pre-*
> *sente. Este consejo no lo tomes en mal, pero yo estoy preocupada por*
> *eso y nada más quiero ayudar a una prima al cual quiero mucho.*

(I had a good time on my birthday. Look, if you yourself make life bitter, you will never be happy. No, you don't have to be that way. You
can make [yourself] happy. I'm going to tell you something. My Christ-

mas and New Year's was joyful because I wanted it that way, not because God made it so. Because I tried to make it the best days of my life. Although the past was a bad time for me because I too carry a burden in my heart that [I] can't tell nobody about. It's something ugly and sad for me, and I don't want anyone to be sad. Well, about what I tell you, that you make your life bitter, please try to do what I tell you and tell me and it will help you because that's what makes me happy. Also, forget about the past and go right straight to the present. Don't take this advice the wrong way, but I'm worried about it, and there's nothing else I want to do but help a cousin whom I love very much.) [13TM]

Gloria not only offers her cousin hopeful advice; she also reveals that she has a deep secret too "ugly and sad" to share with anyone. She also makes another startling revelation that is generally unexpected among members of her social network: Gloria declares that she, and not God alone, plays a critical role in the decisions that she needs to make in her life. Her stance challenges more than textual conventions; it questions the predeterministic belief implicit in the widely used phrase, "*Si Dios quiere*" (God willing), that she shares with members of the larger Mexicano community. Moreover, Gloria's stance grants her a degree of agency, of free will in her life, that many would consider unconventional among Chicanos and Mexicanos. The passage ends, appropriately so, with Gloria offering herself as distant counsel to her cousin because of her sincere love for her.

While the corpus of letters I collected is probably too small to make any broad generalizations about the personal letter-writing practices of the several hundred members of Jaime and Rocío Durán's social network, it does provide an opportunity for some interesting observations. Members who write letters seem to feel an obligation to follow a set of conventions that helps them organize and present their thoughts using language that, while it varies across a wide range of possibilities, manages to remain close to the well-practiced phrases that they have been reading and writing (or dictating) for most of their lives. These conventions are certainly not unexpected or unwarranted; after all, they provide the connective tissue that makes writing a letter possible in the first place. At the same time, however, the framework within which they operate offers them opportunities to challenge expectations, especially in the body of these texts where they are, ironically, by convention, given room to explore and share their feelings and emotions in ways that demonstrate their ability to manipulate an array of rhetorical practices. It should come as no surprise that much of this more inventive wandering in the body of the text is undertaken by the younger members of the group. It is they, after all, who are in a position to begin to question the conventions that tend to tie many of the older letter writers to very formulaic ways of representing themselves and others to their readers. The next chapter focuses on the elicited writing of three young women who, like members of their social network, cover the range between convention and inventiveness as they work within the genre of autobiography to represent themselves and their culture to imagined audiences of their own choosing.

CHAPTER 6

The Autobiographical Writing
of *Las Tres Marías*

Research on the writing produced by members of marginalized groups in the United States in the course of their everyday lives provides interesting insights into how they represent themselves and their cultures discursively and the extent to which different genres are integral components of their group's communicative economy (Hymes, 1974). The preceding chapter, for instance, illustrates the degree to which personal letter-writing has been conventionalized by members of Jaime and Rocío Durán's social network to serve their communicative needs. At the same time, several of the longer excerpts from the letters that I present as sample texts, especially those written by younger members of the group, challenge some of those conventions by demonstrating how letters can be used for more than the simple exchange of information. These sample texts hint at the possibility that writing elicited from members of the social network may provide additional insights into how they use language in other genres of writing. This is not to suggest that the autobiographical writing I present in this chapter was part of my original plan for this project. As a matter of fact, it was because of the initial frustration that I experienced in trying to obtain personal letters from social network members that I, through happenstance, decided to elicit autobiographical writing from young members of Jaime and Rocío's social network.

The first section of this chapter describes a series of events that led me to shift my focus from collecting examples of letter-writing to collecting autobiographical writing from a group of three young women that I call *las tres Marías*. As I did in the preceding chapter, I examine how such factors as my age, gender, and status as a teacher resulted in long delays between my initial elicitation of the personal narratives, their actual production, and each writer's eventual decision to share them with me. Because of what it taught me about the critical role that gender plays in research, I also discuss how and why my wife, Diane, intervened on my behalf to initiate the collection of autobiographical narratives written by las tres Marías. In light of the fact that the persons who agreed to write personal narratives are all women, the next section reviews some of the key concerns raised by scholars about the place of gender in autobiographical studies, especially in terms of what it means to write about one's self in an era when the notion of an essentialized self is being challenged by an alternative view that suggests that each of us, male or female, mainstreamed or marginalized, consists of an array of fluid, multiple, hybrid, or fragmented selves.

Along with sample texts from the autobiographical writing of las tres Marías, the third and final section provides some biographical information on each of the three writers based on informal conversations and formal ethnographic interviews, as well as my observations of their day-to-day lives in their homes and as members of the social network. This background information, I believe, illustrates the types and degrees of difference that exist among members of any community that outsiders tend to stereotype as virtual copies of one another. And while it is important to consider race/ethnicity, class, and gender as major factors in how a writer represents him- or herself to others, we need to consider an array of other factors that play a critical role in disrupting attempts to essentialize las tres Marías simply as working-class women of color: age, familial configuration, marital status, level of education, length of residency in a particular home front, social standing in the family and the immediate community, personal character, temperament, disposition, and so on. Finally, we need to reflect on the issues that las tres Marías elect to write about, the language(s) they choose to represent themselves and their cultural experiences, and the different ways they position themselves rhetorically in the context of the genre.

FROM PERSONAL LETTERS TO AUTOBIOGRAPHICAL WRITING: AN UNEXPECTED BUT REVEALING SHIFT

Long before the serendipitous moment I experienced during my September 1994 visit to Rancho Verde when Sandra Rodríguez initiated the process that resulted in my collecting the letters I examine in the preceding chapter, I asked a number of young men and women in the social network if they would be willing to establish correspondence with me. Of the nine that I asked, only three young women with whom Diane and I had developed strong and stable relationships expressed a willingness to try. Because Rosa María Durán, María Isabel Durán, and María Guadalupe Ramírez (hereafter referred to as Rosa, Isabel, and Malú, respectively) were all in their late teens, I decided that it would be more tactful if they wrote letters to Diane and me rather than to me alone to avoid some of the problems that differences in age and gender might raise for them or their families. Unfortunately, the kind of momentum necessary to establish correspondence never developed, and my expectations for a smooth exchange of letters evaporated. While Diane and I exchanged a couple of letters with Isabel and Malú over a period of four months, we didn't exchange any letters with Rosa.

By November 1993, I realized that I needed to take a different approach in my efforts to obtain examples of extended written discourse from las tres Marías. In place of the letters, I decided to ask them if they would be willing to write narratives about themselves and the culture that was so much a part of their lives. Because I already had plans to visit her family, I elected to present my new proposal to Isabel first. Despite the fact that she and I had developed one of the closest relationships I had with any member of the social network, Isabel's initial reaction was to say no. No matter what I said to dispel her claims that she didn't know how to write, Isabel remained firm. It was only after her mother interceded by saying that she herself would be interested in doing some writing for me (she never did) that Isabel hesitantly agreed to try it. In a last-ditch effort to withdraw from the obligation, Isabel "voiced some concern about her *ortografía* (spelling)" as she walked with me to the door to say good-bye. The next day I went to visit Malú's family and took advantage of the opportunity "to ask Malú if she would write some narrative pieces about her life for me. To my surprise, she readily agreed. 'Just don't criticize my spelling and my grammar,' she said, as I prepared to leave. I promised that I wouldn't" (*Fieldnotes*, 30 November 1993, p. 583). When I asked Rosa the same question later that week, she told me that she didn't think she would have time in her hectic schedule. After I acknowledged how busy her life was, I told her she didn't have to make any promises; all I asked was that she at least try it out. Like Isabel and Malú before her, she finally agreed but expressed some concern about having her writing judged on the basis of her spelling, punctuation, and grammar. As I had done with Isabel and Malú, I reassured her that I was more interested in other aspects of her writing.

In the course of my next several visits to their homes that month, all three made a point of asking me for detailed instructions about what I expected them to write. Because I wanted to see how each would interpret my request for stories about their lives and the choices each would make on her own, I was purposely vague about the kind of subject matter that I wanted them to address, the language(s) in which it should be written, and the stances that they should take. Despite the fact that each of them pursued the matter to varying degrees, I continued to do everything in my power to avoid giving them the kinds of detailed instructions that I would have given students in my classes. At all costs, I wanted to avoid establishing a student–teacher relationship with them because I was concerned that it inevitably would lead to school-oriented writing. Eventually, I did have to hint that I was interested in having them write about their families, their friends, what schools were like in Mexico and the United States, their personal adventures, and anything else that they thought would appeal to someone interested in learning about their individual lives and how they viewed their cultural experiences.

When I returned to Chicago at the beginning of February 1994, I was anxious to see if any of las tres Marías had started writing their personal narratives. I decided to stop by to see Malú first. After telling me about the rash of personal and health problems that Rosa had experienced, Malú told me about the problems she had been facing trying to cope with life on her own. While her parents and her three younger siblings had stayed behind in Mexico after the Christmas holidays because her mother had become ill, Malú had come back on her own to avoid missing any of her college classes. Besides going to school, Malú also was responsible for maintaining her family's apartment and coping with problems associated with the apartment building her parents owned on the north side of the city. Under the circumstances, I decided not to mention the narrative writing. Almost as soon as I walked in the front door of Isabel's family home the next day, her mother told me that Isabel too had been overwhelmed recently with personal problems. After a month-long trip to Mexico to visit family and get some dental work done, Isabel had come home to discover that she was pregnant with her first child and had been dismissed from her job because she had not given appropriate notice concerning the extent of her absence. Realizing that the lives of las tres Marías were likely to remain complicated for some time to come, I decided at that moment to stop inquiring about their personal narrative writing, at least until my next trip to Chicago.

In late July 1994, eight months after I had introduced my proposal on personal narrative writing, Diane and I returned to Chicago to discover that las tres Marías were not yet prepared to share their work with me. In addition to having to deal with the circumstances of their individual lives, all three were still having difficulty generating text. As I had in the past, I decided to remain patient and hope for the best. Over the next two months, Diane and I continued visiting different families in the social network, always making a special effort to visit Rosa, Isabel, and Malú. Whenever we visited their homes and I inquired about their writing, each of them would remind me that they considered themselves poor writers who had nothing to say and would conclude by reporting that they still had nothing to share. It was clear that the hesitation on their part continued to reflect what I considered their unwarranted fear that I would be disappointed by their writing. Each time they announced that they had nothing to give me, I would nod my head to demonstrate that I understood the difficult position in which I was putting them and would announce that maybe they would have something for me the next time we visited.

Then, without any indication whatsoever that they were going to do it, all three suddenly began to share their personal narratives with me. Although I didn't learn about it until after the fact, Diane—who not only shares their gender but has a very different personal relationship with them than I do—persuaded each of them that their fears about sharing their writing with me were unfounded. During some of our visits, I later learned, Diane took a moment to speak to each of them privately to remind them how important it was for them to write and for me to look at their writing. On the one hand, she explained, the material would provide me with invaluable data that very few other scholars had been able to obtain; on the other hand, I would be able to help them with their writing, something all three had expressed an interest in having me do. In the end, Diane's gender, her less threatening status, and her persuasive temperament helped her coax las tres Marías into sharing their first narratives with me. Despite the fact that I had become an "honorary female" who was granted the privilege of listening to and participating in conversations intended solely for groups of women in the social network, I could not as easily overcome my gender (much less my age and social rank) in my relations with Rosa, Isabel, and Malú. Not even the fact that I had watched them grow up over a number of years and in some ways was also an "honorary member" of the social network proved sufficient. Inadvertently and unexpectedly, Diane and las tres Marías taught me an important lesson about the central role that gender plays in ethnographic research.

THE PLACE OF SELF AND GENDER IN THEORIES OF AUTOBIOGRAPHY

Like literacy, autobiography is a concept that many of us, scholars and laypersons alike, used to take for granted because we believed we could easily identify its boundaries as a genre. Autobiography was, in those simpler days, a piece of writing that represented a person's life written by herself. But like literacy and a plethora of other scholarly terms and concepts used in the academy, over the past three decades autobiography has become a notion difficult to define in terms capable of achieving widespread support (Adams, 1990; Couser, 1989). While a number of scholars acknowledge Gusdorf's (1980) definition of autobiography as a benchmark in modern theories of the genre, in recent years, a number of feminists (Benstock, 1988; Friedman, 1988; Spacks, 1988), multiculturalists (Holte, 1988), postmodernists (Bergland, 1994; Gilmore, 1994), and cultural theorists (Padilla, 1993; Smith & Watson, 1992) have vigorously challenged the parameters that Gusdorf set in his definition of autobiography. Because the concept has so many more rich and varied facets than I have time or space to cover or than I need to touch on in light of the issues I raise in this book, I want to focus my discussion on the controversy surrounding a particular element that I believe will help us situate the autobiographical writing of las tres Marías more meaningfully: the role of gender as a central component within autobiographical conceptualizations of the self. Despite the fact that this chapter and the preceding one suggest the feminization of literacy in the social network, I still think it is important to consider the broad array of factors that play a critical role in the writing of the three young women whose work I elicited and will examine shortly. I also believe that the following discussion about the gender controversy in autobiographical studies will help us understand why the personal narratives of las tres Marías must be examined from a number of perspectives, including a gendered one.

In a groundbreaking essay originally published in 1956, titled "Conditions and Limits of Autobiography," Gusdorf (1980) argues that autobiography

> expresses a concern peculiar to Western man, a concern that has been of good use in his systematic conquest of the universe and that he has communicated to men of other cultures; but those men will thereby have been annexed by a sort of intellectual colonizing to a mentality that was not their own. (p. 29)

Gusdorf further contends that "autobiography is not possible in a cultural landscape where consciousness of self does not, properly speaking, exist" (p. 30). In the course of his essay, Gusdorf posits a highly individualistic concept of autobiography that is based on the idea that, as Olney (1972) also argues, the autobiographer is a figure isolated from those around him by his own consciousness. In autobiography, Olney declares, "Separate selfhood is the very motive of creation" (p. 22). In the course of challenging this essentialist conception of the autobiographical self as autonomous and isolated, some feminists (Friedman, 1988; Mason, 1980) have marshaled a body of evidence into place that suggests that women who write autobiography do so from a very different, even oppositional, stance. In contrast to the autonomous and dispassionate qualities of Gusdorf's and Olney's male autobiographer, Mason (1980) and Friedman (1988), contend, respectively, that among women autobiographers, "the self-discovery of female identity seems to acknowledge the real presence and recognition of another consciousness" (p. 210) that often operates in the context of a "culturally imposed group identity" (p. 34). Consequently, they argue, women autobiographers represent themselves within tightly knit relational contexts that do not allow for the autonomy and individuality posited by Gusdorf and Olney. In the eyes of a number of scholars in the field, such an oppositional approach, however, falls short theoretically because it essentializes women autobiographers in much the same way that Gusdorf and Olney essentialize male autobiographers.

Among recent critics of the essentializing process taking place at both ends of an ideologically gendered continuum, the work of two scholars provides alternative stances from which we can examine autobiographical writing as a provisional undertaking that cannot be contained by any single one of the various elements—race/ethnicity, class, or gender—that have been popularized in the academy over the past 30 years. In an introduction to her edited collection of essays by anthropologists interested in rhetoric's influence on the self, Battaglia (1995), at least on one level, attempts to problematize the issue of gender by broadening the discussion to the larger element of which gender is but one component—the self. Battaglia argues that "under rhetoric's influence, the self cannot be the stable product of its own manufacture" (p. 1). Because contributors to her book focus "on rhetorical practices in contradistinction to finished products of rhetorical activity" (p. 2), Battaglia contends that *Rhetorics of Self-Making* "turns away from the issues of textual eloquence; it is not," she unequivocally argues, "about the 'commanding dominance of the individual personality' in some consummate performance or text. . . . Instead, rhetoric is taken as an uncertain and provisional social project." "Selfhood by this figuration," Battaglia concludes, "is a chronically unstable productivity brought situationally—not invariably—to some form of imaginary order, to some purpose, as realized in the course of culturally patterned interactions" (p. 2).

While I am persuaded by Battaglia's strategic attempts to destabilize essentialist notions of the self, I am concerned about her decision to take the same kind of either/or stance that I described Pratt (1987) taking in my discussion of the home front and the contact zone in the introduction to this book. In the context of the present study, I find it impossible to turn "away from issues of textual eloquence" when members of the social network whose communicative practices I am examining identify eloquence as an integral element of a discourse style they value and admire. Battaglia's contention that we should focus on rhetorical practices rather than rhetorical products reminds me of the long-running debate in composition studies about whether teachers of writing should focus on the composing process or the finished product. Most scholars in that discipline, I believe, have come to the conclusion that teachers must do both. I would argue that the same is true here.

In her essay, "Toward an Anti-Metaphysics of Autobiography," Watson (1983) takes a stance similar to Battaglia's against the essentialism inherent in certain feminist positions in autobiography. After citing Brodzki and Schenck's *Life/Lines* (1988), Watson notes that "They have also emphasized the need for 'resisting reification and essentialism' by feminist theorists who would relocate experimental selfhood from the singularity of the individual to a relational model of alterity" (1993, p. 69). Later in her essay, Watson cites Moraga and Anzaldúa's (1983) *This Bridge Called My Back: Writings by Radical Women of Color* and Minh-ha's (1989) *Woman, Native, Other* as well-grounded examples that theorize and illustrate what Watson calls *bios* (i.e., what for her symbolizes the central question "of what constitutes a 'life' in autobiography" [p. 57]). Watson then turns her attention to Lionnet (1989), whom she notes "privileges voice over word and calls for revising the emphasis in autobiography from *bios* to multiple, irreducible differences." In Lionnet's view, according to Watson, "women's differences cannot be essentialized as gynocriticism, but are inflected by cultural specificities of ethnicity, class, time, and location" (1993, p. 73). I would argue that Rosa's, Isabel's, and Malú's work provides another example in which the writing of women tends to be inflected by a rich array of differences available to them within their situated and multifaceted cultural experiences.

Before we look at their writing in the context of the preceding discussion, it is important to keep in mind that Rosa, Isabel, and Malú represent only some of the options available to young women who are members of their transnational community. Some young women in their community have faced more difficult and tragic lives, while others have managed to surpass all expectations about what anyone born and raised in their social network had the potential to achieve. In that sense, las tres Marías do not represent different points along an ideal continuum. Still, the fact that they are all related and are active members of their community provides us with a unique opportunity to see just how much difference is possible in any community and how individuals, rather than some objectified or homogenized representatives of the culture, use those differences to construct their own lives in discursive terms.

Because I want the reader to meet each of las tres Marías individually and experience their narratives as highly situated reflections of who each of them is, I have elected to present what I learned about each of them and sample texts from their personal narratives individually and in turn. The similarities and differences, as well as the consonances and dissonances, that emerge in the process of reading about their lives both from my point of view and theirs are likely to shift and change for each individual reader and with each individual reading. If I fail to mark adequately the multifaceted differences that have shaped their lives and their written representations of those lives and err in the direction of essentialism or reification, I hope readers will disrupt the tendency by repeatedly acknowledging the rich texture of all lived experience.

COMING TO VOICE: SITUATING THE LIVES AND THE RHETORICAL PRACTICES OF *LAS TRES MARÍAS*

To represent oneself and one's views about the world in which one lives in extended written discourse, as any person who has ever tried it well knows, is an endeavor always fraught with the potential promise of praise and the agonizing fear of failure. Even for those of us who write for a living, attempting to represent ourselves and the world around us—especially in genres like autobiography, which by their very nature verify that intimate details of our lives will be read by more than the few people who might read an entry in our journals or a personal letter—requires the courage to move beyond the limitations inherent in the act itself. Las tres Marías have lived most of their lives in highly segregated environments where they have generally maintained their silence in the face of authority. Not surprisingly, the opportunity that I, a socially and professionally privileged older male, offered them to write about their lives outside a school setting temporarily blocked their ability to take pen to paper and construct a series of discursive representations they would be willing to share with others. That all three eventually managed to overcome their concerns about what I would think about their writing and the equally frightening realization that I planned to publish much of what they wrote demonstrates their courage and willingness to break free from the limitations that fear places on us all. It is in this spirit that I hope readers will approach the excerpts from the personal narratives of las tres Marías that I will be presenting later in this chapter.

Between July 27, 1994, when Isabel gave me her first personal narrative and April 1, 1996, when Malú mailed me her last two, las tres Marías generated autobiographical writing that illustrates the range of possibilities that exists among social network members for representing themselves and others in a written genre with which few, if any (Isabel did report in her interview that she had kept a diary as a young girl in Mexico), have had much experience. True, las tres Marías have been exposed to storytelling and argumentation in their homes and their transnational community from the time they were very small children. And while the extent to which they have done writing in school settings varies, all three have considerable experience writing personal letters to friends and relatives in Mexico and the United States. But in the writing that they generated for me over a period of twenty months, las tres Marías demonstrate an uncanny ability to represent themselves and the world around them while simultaneously using and challenging the rhetorical conventions available to them in their social network, the schools they attended, and their peer groups. Their writing also demonstrates the extent to which a complex variety of factors influenced their use of the different languages and the different organizing schemas available to them. And while they exhibit varied degrees of control over several mechanical aspects of their writing (especially at the levels of spelling, punctuation, and grammar), las tres Marías also reinforce the unassailable fact that they are adapt at using written language as a rhetorical practice in a relatively unfamiliar genre in much the same way that members of their social network use orality and literacy, respectively, as rhetorical practices in their everyday conversational and personal letter-writing activities.

"I Hardly Had Time to Write This"

I first met Rosa, Jaime and Rocío Durán's oldest daughter, on the evening of November 1, 1988, when her father invited me for coffee at a slightly out-of-the-way restaurant that turned out to be his family's home. Thirteen-year-old

Rosa answered the door and later fixed us some something to drink. At that point in her life, Rosa shared the family apartment with her parents, two other siblings (Yolanda and Juan Carlos, ages eight and five, respectively), and Rocío's first cousin (Fernando Vásquez, age 38) and niece (Leticia León, age 22). Because her parents were very strict about letting her date or go out with friends, especially because of the number of gangs in the neighborhood, Rosa spent most of her time in the family apartment while she was growing up. If Rosa ventured out of the house other than to go to school or on a special outing with her family, it was almost always to run a quick errand to a nearby store or to go shopping with her mother or her cousin Leticia. Like her mother and Leticia, Rosa generally accepted the fact that she had to stay home and participate in the cooking and cleaning that young girls her age were expected to do in the households that comprised her family's social network.

Although she was born and has lived in the United States all her life, when I asked at the beginning of our interview in what language she would like us to conduct it, she first said that either Spanish or English was fine. Except for a few moments when we both engaged in code-switching, however, the interview took place entirely in Spanish. No doubt the fact that the interview was done in her family's dining room and her mother was there for the first few minutes played a role in her decision. And yet, when I asked her which language she would prefer if she had to choose between speaking in Spanish or English all of the time, Rosa immediately said, "*Español*" (Spanish). When I asked her why, she said, "*Porque es lo que sé un poco más*" (Because it's what I know a little better). This position was reinforced even further when I provided a variety of options and asked her how she self-identified. Without hesitation, she said, "*Mexicana*" (Mexican). When I asked her why, Rosa said, "*Porque estoy orgullosa de mi nacionalidad*" (Because I am very proud of my nationality). Finally, for most of the year before it was scheduled to take place, Rosa made plans and repeatedly begged her parents to hold her quinceañera (sweet 15 birthday party) at her mother's rancho in Michoacán. In her eyes, I suspect, holding the celebration in Mexico would symbolically reinforce her ties to her Mexican heritage.

As the oldest child with the most formal education in the family, Rosa was expected to deal with literacy-based matters in the household, to serve as a cultural liaison or intermediary between members of her social network and the institutions that required information from them, and to participate on a regular basis in typically adult-only conversations. In terms of literacy-based activities, Rosa would write letters in Spanish for her father; once wrote a note in English for one of her father's cousins; addressed the invitations to a birthday party for her mother's best friend; kept the Christmas grab bag list for the extended family; helped other members, especially older women in the social network, read, interpret, and complete official forms of all kinds in English;

filled out her family's U.S. Census forms; and repeatedly helped her mother go through two boxes full of personal and legal papers to locate necessary receipts or documents. Because of her English-speaking skills, Rosa often accompanied her mother, her cousin Leticia, or other members of the social network to business or government offices to act as a liaison and interpreter.

At the same time that she seemed willing to fulfill many of the social network's traditional expectations of how a girl her age should behave, Rosa was caught in the tension between such expectations on the home front and the seductive draw of the contact zones that found their way into her home, usually through the media, the schools, and her peers. In our interview, Rosa said that she rarely watched television but that she listened to the radio on a daily basis. And while she liked to listen to a particular Spanish station that played contemporary music by artists from all parts of Latin America, Rosa preferred to listen to music in English and had a longstanding desire to go to a rock concert. When she heard that two popular teenage singing groups, The First Edition and New Kids on the Block, were going to be performing in July 1989 at Great America, an amusement park north of Chicago, Rosa convinced her mother to ask Diane and me to take her. Because Rocío often served as Rosa's ally in her daughter's constant negotiations with Jaime, Rocío agreed to ask us. Rocío thought that if we volunteered to go as chaperons, Rosa's father would let her attend the concert. But when Rosa and Rocío presented the idea to him, Jaime refused. By the time the two younger daughters of Rocío's closest family friend were persuaded to go in an effort to reduce the focus on Rosa, Leticia informed us that Rosa was on punishment and would not be able to go after all.

Even more than the pleasure she derived from listening to Top 40 music on U.S. rock stations and her desire to attend concerts, Rosa's growing tendency to code-switch (i.e., use Spanish and English interchangeably) with her peers signaled her increasing acculturation into U.S. culture and deeply disturbed her father's cultural, nationalistic, and linguistic sensibilities. Because she had been born in the United States and had same-age peers of Mexican origin who had also been born in the United States, code-switching was an inevitable by-product of the environment in which she was growing up. Although Rosa and her friends demonstrated their respect for adults in the social network who didn't speak English by speaking in Spanish as much as possible in mixed-group settings, whenever they were having a face-to-face or telephone conversation with one another, they would immediately switch either to English or a blend of English and Spanish. One evening in the midst of a conversation among group members, Jaime made a point of demonstrating his dissatisfaction with the language shift that Rosa was undergoing. At one point, Jaime turned to Rosa and castigated her for speaking English with her girlfriends in the house. He told her in no uncertain terms that he wanted her and her friends to speak Spanish when they were in his home. After a lengthy discussion among those present about the roles of Spanish and English in the lives of Mexicano children, Jaime lamented the fact that kids were forgetting their own language: "*La culpa*" (The fault), Jaime concluded, "*es de los padres por no demandar que sus hijos hablen español en casa*" (is with the parents for not demanding that their children speak Spanish at home) (*Fieldnotes*, 13 June 1989, pp. 309–310).

Rosa's relationship with her parents, as well as her commitment to continue her schooling, the key subjects of the personal narratives that she wrote, finally collapsed when she became pregnant in 1993 and, against her parents' wishes, dropped out of high school before completing her senior year to get married. Although his love for his daughter was beyond question, Jaime was deeply disappointed because of what the sudden change in the status quo meant for the family. The circumstances were probably exacerbated by the fact that Jaime and Rocío had been planning to move back to Mexico with their children as soon as Rosa graduated from high school. As a matter of fact, despite Rosa's decision to drop out of school and get married, Jaime, Rocío, and their other two children went ahead with their plans to move back to Mexico permanently about two months after Rosa's wedding. About a year after the wedding, Diane and I went to visit Rosa to see how she was doing. Rosa told us without hesitation that "If my parents had given me the option of not getting married and living with them, I think I would've taken it" (*Fieldnotes*, 1 August 1994, p. 617). The personal narratives that Rosa gave me all focus on this very difficult period in her life and reflect her attempts to work through the mixed feelings she was having. Writing about these experiences often proved as difficult for her as going through the experiences themselves. In the end, though, I believe her autobiographical narratives illustrate the slow process of her coming to terms with the circumstances of her life as well as with the act of writing about them.

Considering the complicated circumstances of her life at the time, it comes as no surprise that Rosa gave me the least writing of las tres Marías: 3 narratives totaling 11 handwritten pages and 1,305 words. Although she speaks and writes English and Spanish fluently, Rosa wrote all three narratives in English. This decision probably reflects the fact that she was born, raised, and educated in the United States and that, like many Mexicanas who are in transition to a more Chicana or Mexican American lifestyle, she is becoming more comfortable in her use of English over Spanish. It also reflects the fact that she interpreted my request for personal narrative writing as a school assignment intended for an English-dominant teacher and imaginary audience.

Of the writing las tres Marías gave me, Rosa's is most clearly influenced by what she perceives as teacherly expectations and, therefore, reflects a school-oriented or essayist approach to writing. All three of Rosa's personal narratives, for example, indicate that her goal in writing is to answer specific questions that have been put to her. In a sense, the narratives read like responses to short in-class impromptu assignments. Thus, all three narratives begin with thesis-like statements or implied questions for a typical essay assignment that she constructs on her own as a point of departure for her writing:

1. How do I feel about the schools here in Chicago/Mexico?
2. Why I prefer Mexico better than Chicago.
3. My relationship with mom and dad.

Each of these is then followed by an extended explication that in rhetorical terms creates some degree of objectification and distancing between herself as a writer and the issue at hand. In the context of the earlier discussion of the role that gender is said to play in autobiography, Rosa takes what some critics in autobiographical studies would consider a relatively autonomous and nonrelational stance, despite the fact that she is writing about the relationships in her life. I would argue that the rhetorical strategies she uses do not necessarily reflect her gender, but rather a way of positioning herself as a writer that she learned in school and the alienation and isolation that she feels at the time from the institution (school) and persons (parents) that she is writing about.

The first page of her first narrative consists of three false starts that she crossed out in succession, which suggests that Rosa had trouble getting started with her writing. Notice how these false starts illustrate "Engfish," the kind of flat and formulaic discourse that Ken Macrorie (1975) contends students often produce when they are taught to follow the five-paragraph essay format in writing classes:

> The schools here have many different good and bad points/things. (To begin with) some of the good things. I believe (the) teachers have a higher education than teachers from Mexico as an example.

> The (Catholic) schools are good and bad. Good in the way that

> The schools are neither good nor bad. We, the people, the students, teachers and other parts of the staff make it good or bad. Beginning with the students, some go to learn, to achieve their goals, to graduate from high school. Because to many that's a goal. They have to go through gang and drug problems.

The three false starts are followed by a long first paragraph that represents the opening paragraph of a personal narrative on her experiences in school. The paragraph reflects a bitterness in her representation of the roles that the schools and her parents have played in her educational experience. While it is one-sided because she places the blame for her problems in school on others and doesn't share in it, the circumstances I described earlier about how she dropped out of school and how her family moved back to Mexico shortly after she married help contextualize the stance that she takes here.

The second and closing paragraph of her first personal narrative demonstrates Rosa's ability to deal with her experiences in language that conveys the frustration of a young woman who has recently dropped out of high school to marry and have a child:

> I would probably go back to high school to graduate. But there are some problems I have. Who would take care of my son? I want to go in the morning to Villa [High School], but it's hard to leave the baby with just anyone. And if I would go to night school, my husband would come with me to school, so the problem is still the same one. Because in the afternoon when my aunts or cousins get home from work, they fix their homes, cook dinner, and fix their things for the next day, so it's pretty hard for them to baby-sit my son. And besides, nobody has really offer[ed] to take care of him, not even on the weekends, so I'm stuck with him the whole time. I hardly had time to write this that I'm doing because he tries to get the pen or the notebook, and his screaming and crying is pretty annoying, and it's pretty hard to concentrate.

The change in tone from the first to the second paragraphs is dramatic. While she is still bitter about the current circumstances in her life, Rosa is also more pensive and understanding. She still finds someone to criticize, but she is noticeably searching for answers to her dilemma. In the space of four pages of handwritten text, readers witness a transformation in Rosa's writing. As she began the narrative, she was motivated to write as she had in school, but in the process of composing the piece, she intuitively becomes aware of how stiff and uninformative "Engfish" is and switches to a style that is more balanced and detailed. By the end of the first narrative, Rosa is flirting with several of the rhetorical strategies held in high regard by adult members of her social network: emotion, sincerity, even eloquence. Without question, the narrative remains unfinished, but without skipping a beat she lets the reader know why she has to let go of this piece of writing at this point in her day and in her life.

In her third narrative, Rosa focuses on how her relationship with her parents has changed as a consequence of a three-week visit with them and her siblings in Mexico. Ironically, at the time she is writing this third and final narrative, her relationship with her mother has deteriorated while the one with her father has improved. It seems these are consequences of the very action that drove her father to threaten to disown her—Rosa's unexpected pregnancy.

Of the three narratives that Rosa wrote, this one does a better job of integrating the essayist tradition to which she was probably exposed in school and the rhetorical practices valued by social network members. While the piece contains traces of flavor and emotion, its main purpose seems to be to persuade her readers that she and her mother have very different views about how her baby should be raised. In this sense, the narrative is not only eloquent, but attempts to demonstrate to the reader what she has learned from her own experience, another key element in the rhetorical strategies used by adults in her social network.

Even after criticizing her mother's attempt "to take care of the baby, my son, as her own because she thinks I'm still a little girl" in the first paragraph, Rosa uses a highly essayist transitional device ("on the other hand") to begin the second and final paragraph. In it, Rosa compares her parents, shedding a positive light on her father, before she shifts to a concluding statement that indicts both parents and reveals the sense of abandonment that she feels because of how far away they are from her as she is writing:

> On the other hand, my dad was really different. He treated me just as I am, his daughter who is married and a mother of his grandson. My dad wouldn't act like my mom. He would tell me in a different way, like an opinion, that it wasn't good for me to scream at the baby or to spank him. He would ask if he could carry the baby or ask for him (the baby). As with my mom, I had to ask for the baby, but not with my dad. My dad loves the baby a lot, as well as my mom, but my dad accepts the reality now and admits that Tony (the baby) is his grandson and not his son. As with my mom, she thinks the opposite. I would like for my mom to do what she did over there in Mexico, but here instead. But I guess their money is more important to them than coming here and seeing their grandson grow. But I already told them that if they lived here in Chicago, everything would be much different. If they came back, then they'll show me and the baby how much they really care for him (the baby).

In this final passage of her final narrative, Rosa appears to have come to terms with the series of events that led to her alienation and separation from her family, especially her parents. The terrible split between Rosa and her father seems to have been healed. At least as she represents him here, he is now the father she always wanted him to be: caring as well as understanding. As hard as she was on her mother in the preceding paragraph, in this one, Rosa confesses that she would like for her "to do what she did over there in Mexico, but here [in Chicago] instead." Thus, the series of narratives ends with Rosa demonstrating the wisdom that she has gained as a consequence of her experience and expressing an implicit desire to rejoin her family. In September 1995, two months after her parents and siblings resettled in Chicago, Rosa, who had become pregnant in the summer of 1994 and now had two small boys to raise, left her husband temporarily and, acting on her implied desire, moved back in with her family. Shortly thereafter, Rosa's mother—a woman who had worked in Chicago factories for more than twenty years—elected to stay home to baby-sit Rosa's two children while Rosa went to work to support them. Even after Rosa and her husband reconciled a few months later and reestablished a shared household, Rosa continued to take her children to visit her family several times a week. While they may still have their share of problems, the current scenario suggests that Rosa and her family have elected to work them out together rather than on their own or at odds with one another.

"Todo me Parecía Como una Fantasía" (Everything Seemed Like a Fantasy to Me)

About two months after I met Jaime Durán and his family, we set up tutorial sessions for members of their social network who were applying for amnesty through the Immigration Reform and Control Act (IRCA) of 1986. Among those attending the sessions were two of Jaime's cousins, Salvador and Ignacio Durán. Because their families were still in Mexico, the two lived a few blocks away from Jaime with a group of other men from Rancho Verde. After everyone had qualified for permanent residency status in the United States, Salvador and Ignacio asked me if I would help them fill out the forms that would permit their wives and younger children to come live with them in Chicago. Although Diane and I got to meet Ignacio Durán's fifteen-year-old daughter, Isabel, during our first trip to Rancho Verde three weeks after I completed her father's paperwork, Isabel and her family did not join him for another two and a half years.

  In the summer of 1992, when Diane and I went to visit Isabel's family for the first time since they had moved to a small apartment in Pilsen, her mother, Eva Durán, was home alone. We sat and chatted for a while, and she told us that Isabel was planning to get married soon to a young man from *Las Piedras* (see Figure 2.3). Eva told us that the young man had asked for Isabel's hand shortly before the family moved to Chicago. When we returned the next day, Diane and I found Isabel and her siblings at home. In her interview a few weeks later, Isabel described the casual pace she had known and enjoyed in Rancho Verde, where she was free to come and go as she pleased and could spend the afternoon outdoors chatting with her girlfriends. As she describes it, life in that first apartment was the exact opposite:

> *Un día típico aquí en Chicago desde que llegamos es estar allí encer-*
> *rados [en el apartamento]. No salir. Un día especial es el ir al lago, ir*

con toda la familia, convivir un rato con todos, estar a gusto. Pero son muy pocos. . . . La mayoría del tiempo estamos allí encerrados. Nada más platicando y mirando televisión. Y si tenemos que hacer alguna cosa, la hacemos, pero se termina rápido y después pasamos todo el día aburridos.

(A typical day here in Chicago since we arrived is being there, confined [in the apartment]. No going out. A special day is going to the lake, going with the whole family, enjoying each other's company for a while, being content. But they're very few. . . . Most of the time we're confined there. Just chatting and watching television. And if we have to do something, we do it, but it ends quickly and then we spend the whole day bored.)

Within the year, Isabel's parents and two older brothers pooled their resources and bought a building with three apartments in Little Village. During that period of time, Isabel also got married and found a job working with her mother in a factory that produced transistors. Sometime later, after a month-long trip to Mexico, Isabel returned to Chicago to find out that she was pregnant with her first child and had lost her job. By then, Isabel and her husband, a member of a lawn care maintenance crew, had moved out of their own apartment a few blocks away and into an attic apartment that members of Isabel's family had fixed up in their building so that Isabel and the baby would be closer to the family, especially when her husband was working. After losing her job and finding out that she was pregnant, Isabel decided to stay home. Although she explored the possibility of enrolling in adult literacy classes or in a GED program, once her first child was born, Isabel decided to stay at home and help her sisters and mother keep house. And although she and her husband had their own apartment, Isabel spent most of her time with her siblings and parents in their first-floor apartment. This kept Isabel from becoming bored and listless at the same time that it gave members of her family a chance to help care for the baby. When Isabel and her husband had another baby a year and a half later, the second child was immediately integrated into the day-to-day life that Isabel and her first child already enjoyed with her parents and siblings.

Although (or because?) she had the least formal schooling of las tres Marías, Isabel proved a very enthusiastic writer and gave me more than four times as much writing as Rosa and almost as much writing as Malú: four narratives, all in Spanish, totaling 31 handwritten pages and 5,716 words. As will soon become apparent, Isabel's writing is in some ways at the opposite end of the continuum from Rosa's. Probably because she was born, raised, and schooled in Mexico, her writing reflects more directly and emphatically the rhetorical practices described by older members of the social network (see

Chapter 4). Moreover, while Rosa's writing is influenced by some of the essayist traditions that she was probably exposed to in Chicago schools, Isabel's writing reflects the more vivid and flowery style typical of Mexicano discourse in general.[1] Another critical factor is that of las tres Marías, Isabel is the only one who ever kept a diary as a young girl. When I asked her during her interview if she had ever done any out-of-school writing, Isabel said: *"De niña me gustaba escribir todo lo que hacía en el día, pero poco a poco se me fue terminando la costumbre"* (As a child, I used to like to write down everything I did during the day, but little by little, that habit of mine came to an end). When I pursued this line of questioning and asked her why she kept a diary, Isabel responded in this manner: *"Porque pensaba que para que no se me olvidara un día y para recordar y un día leerlo y decir—porque ya cuando no lees las cosas que pasan por un tiempo dices '¿A poco esto hice yo?'"* (Because I thought so that I wouldn't forget it one day and so that I could remember and one day read it and say—because when you don't read the things that happen for a while, you say, 'Is it true that I did this?')

If Isabel had any trouble getting started with her writing in the same way that Rosa did, she did not indicate or demonstrate it. When I asked her about her composing process, she told me that she reflected momentarily on the experience that she wanted to write about and then started writing. After I asked if I could take and xerox her first narrative, Isabel hesitated and asked if she could rewrite it. When I realized that she was concerned that I would have difficulty reading her handwriting, that she wanted literally to rewrite it rather than revise it, I told her that her printed handwriting was actually very easy to read. She hesitated, but eventually agreed to give me the narrative. The four personal narratives that Isabel shared with me focus on three key moments in her life. The first one tells the story of her family's journey from Rancho Verde to Chicago, the third describes her six years of schooling in Mexico, and the second and fourth focus on a series of experiences related to her first trip back to Rancho Verde to attend her second-oldest brother's wedding.

In her first narrative, Isabel provides an extended description of her family's journey from Mexico to the United States after her father, Ignacio Durán, had received permission from the INS to bring his family to this country. Her account is vivid and detailed in ways that reflect a rhetorical tendency among many Mexicanos to write lush and flowery prose; it also reflects her state of mind and the mixed emotions that she experienced as the trip unfolded. Isabel's account begins as follows:

> *Cuando nosotros comenzamos a hacer preparaciones para venir a Estados Unidos todo me parecía como una fantasía. Nunca pensé que eso podría ser realidad. Comenzábamos a arreglar papeles y todo tipo de re-*

quisito que se nos pedía y después llegó mi papá con la cita para ir a Ciudad Juárez. Desde ese momento, aunque todavía no lo tomaba con la seriedad que debiera, pero desde hay comencé a sentir tristezas. Cuando mis amigas me preguntaban que si me iba a venir [a Chicago], no sabía qué contestar porque ni yo misma me sabía dar la respuesta. Y cuando al fin llegó el día tan esperado y a la vez no deseado, ese día en el que comencé a sentir que en menos de 24 horas estaría alejada de mi rancho, el lugar donde nací y crecí, donde están todos mis mejores re- cuerdos, mis amistades—era sentir que algo dentro de mí se estaba apa- gando. Comencé a juntar todas mis cosas que tenían valor sentimental para mí, cosas que en momentos especiales me regalaron personas tam- bién especiales. Sentía que en eso se estaba quedando parte de mi vida y mi forma de vivir porque sabía que ya nada volvería a ser como era. Al momento de comenzar a empacar nuestras cosas, todo lo estábamos haciendo sin ganas, sin deseos. Salíamos a sentarnos afuera de nuestra casa, mirando para todos lados como queriendo que todo esto no fuera más que un sueño, que al momento de despertar todo fuera la vida ru- tinaria que llevamos hoy. Pero no era así. Recuerdo que era un sábado, el 22 de febrero de 1992 a las 12 de la tarde cuando estábamos saliendo de nuestro rancho. Recuerdo que yo salí llorando y pidiéndole a Dios que me permitiera pronto regresar.

(When we started to make preparations to come to [the] United States, everything seemed like a fantasy to me. I never thought that it could be- come a reality. We were starting to arrange papers and all kinds of re- quirements that were asked of us and then my father arrived with the summons to go to Ciudad Juárez. From that moment on, although I still wasn't taking it with the seriousness that I should, but from then on, I begin to feel a great sadness. When my girlfriends would ask me if I was going to come [to Chicago], I didn't know how to respond be- cause not even I myself knew the answer. And when finally the long- awaited and not wished-for day arrived, when I began to feel that in less than 24 hours I would be far from my rancho, the place where I was born and raised, where all my best memories are, my friends—it was as though something inside of me was being extinguished. I started to gather all of my things that had sentimental value for me, things that at special moments were given to me as presents by persons who were also special. I felt that part of my life remained in them and my way of living because I knew that now nothing would ever be the same again. When we started packing our things, we were doing it all without drive, without desire. We would go sit outside our house, looking this way and that as though hoping that all this was no more than a dream, that upon waking up everything would be the routine life that we're living today. But it wasn't like that. I remember that it was a Saturday, the 22nd of February 1992 at twelve o'clock in the afternoon when we were leaving our rancho. I remember that I left crying and asking God to let me return soon.)

Isabel's haunting language is overflowing with the very rhetorical strategies that older members of the social network praise in orators. It appeals to the listener's and the reader's sensibilities because its flavor and emotional qualities are aesthetically pleasing to the eye and the ear. Stylistically, her complex syntactical patterns, especially the repetition and parallelism, fulfill her intended goal of representing a deeply felt moment in her life in eloquent language that is grounded in her lived experience. To United Statesian sensibilities, Isabel's use of language may well seem excessively ornate, even ostentatious. From the point of view of a Mexicano discourse style, however, her ability to conjure up such heartfelt imagery in discursive terms imbues the narrative with a passion that captures their imaginations; it both represents a way of life they recognize immediately and is in a style with which they are intimately familiar.

After exploring her feelings about leaving the rancho, the next part narrates her family's bus trip to the U.S.–Mexican border town of Ciudad Juárez, where they are processed by immigration officials over a period of several days before they are permitted to enter the United States. The next and final excerpt from her narrative describes how, after another long bus trip from the U.S.–Mexican border to Chicago, they finally arrive in Pilsen, the inner-city Mexicano community that has been her father's home for almost 25 years and where, for the first time in her life, Isabel gets to see and experience a world that she has only heard about from others:

> *Al fin, llegamos a Chicago. Todo era tan diferente a como decía la gente. Era una ciudad llena de basura, y adonde nos llevaron primero fue a la casa donde vivía mi tía. Nos bajamos del taxi y lo único que mirábamos era basura, vidrios, y paderes rayadas por gangueros. Entramos a la casa de mi tía y no era como me imaginaba porque vivían como cualquier persona en México pero con las cosas diferentes. Y allí llegaron otra tía y mi prima. Todos nos preguntaron cómo nos había ido y si nos gustaba Chicago. Sin saber qué contestar, pero la verdad es que no nos gustó. Y ese día cayó nieve, cosa que nunca habíamos visto. Nos llamaba la atención pero también teníamos mucho frío. Y al fin la primera noche que llegamos nos quedamos unos en la casa de una tía y otras con la otra. Todavía no nos borrábamos de la mente el rancho y lo que habíamos dejado allá. Pero el día siguiente mi papá se fue con un tío a comprar unas camas y estufa. Nosotros todavía no mirábamos el*

lugar donde iríamos a vivir por un tiempo. Después nos llevaron. Era un sólo cuarto para todos y aparte estaba todo sucio y nada más con lo indispensable para vivir. Yo me ponía a pensar si eso era lo que habíamos cambiado por el rancho, que estaba mejor. Y en [el rancho] teníamos todo más o menos bien o al menos mejor que aquí. En esa casa duramos 9 meses hasta que al fin mis hermanos y mi papá pudieron comprar una casa.

(Finally, we got to Chicago. Everything was so different from what the people said. It was a city full of garbage, and where they took us first was to the house where my aunt lived. We got out of the taxi, and the only thing we saw was garbage, broken glass, and walls scrawled on by gang members. We went inside my aunt's house and it wasn't as I had imagined because they lived like any person in Mexico but with different things. And another aunt and my cousin came by. They all asked us how things had gone and if we liked Chicago. Without knowing what to answer, but the truth is that we didn't like it. And that day snow fell, something that we had never seen before. It caught our attention but we were also very cold. And at the end of the first night that we got there some of us stayed in the home of one aunt and some of us with the other. We still had not erased the rancho from our minds and what we had left there. But the next day my father went with an uncle to buy some beds and stove. We still had not looked at the place where we were going to live for a while. Then they took us there. It was a single room for all of us and, besides, it was all dirty and had only the most indispensable things to live. I started to wonder if that was what we had exchanged for the rancho, which was better. And at [the rancho] we had everything, more or less, or at least better than here. We lasted nine months in that house until finally my brothers and my father were able to buy a house.)

The rhetorical strategies reflected in this second excerpt are very different in a number of ways from those used in the first excerpt. To begin with, Isabel's description and language style both seem toned down, more in keeping with the kind of language that Rosa used in her third personal narrative. Moreover, Isabel effectively encourages readers to empathize with her circumstances by rendering Chicago as a place very different from what she had imagined or had been described to her. The language is still vivid, detailed, and flavorful, but the passion and the emotion that she expresses in the first excerpt give way to the beginning of a slow, resistant acculturation into a new way of life, something that I suspect demands a different style of language to represent it.

The second and fourth personal narratives, which together comprise slightly more than half of the writing I obtained from Isabel (2,970 out of a total of 5,716 words) and whose story I inadvertently interrupted when I asked her to write a piece on her educational experiences, focus on a very important event in her life: the 10 days of her first trip back to Rancho Verde to attend the wedding of her second-oldest brother, Samuel. In the first part of the fourth narrative, Isabel describes how she and her older brother Martin flew from Chicago to Mexico, where her mother and Samuel were already making arrangements for his wedding. She reflects on her feelings about being back in the land of her birth, about her family's visit to the bride's home, as well as her brother's wedding and the dance afterwards. The next two excerpts I present are taken from the fourth narrative, which explores many of the same themes as the second, but provides an expanded version that again reflects the rich and flowery language of her first narrative. The first excerpt describes Isabel's arrival in Rancho Verde in the middle of the night and the visiting that she did the following day:

Al final llegamos a casa. Hogar dulce, hogar [en el cual] paz y tranquilidad se respiraba. Aunque todo lo miraba más bonito, yo sé que la casa se miraba abandonada y mal arreglada. Pero eso realmente no me importó. Llegaron mis tres tías a saludarnos. Me dio mucho gusto verlas y más que nos recibieron con calabaza cocida con piloncillo. Y después de saludarnos y una buena botana, nos fuimos a dormir y descansar un rato porque casi amanecía. Dos o tres horas más tarde, me desperté al cantar de los gallos y me levanté a ver el amanecer, que hacía tiempo no veía. Di una ligera barrida, me bañé, y después nos fuimos a recorrer el rancho y entregar todas las cartas que llevábamos. A mitad del camino nos encontramos a mi abuelita que nos iba a saludar y a invitarnos a almorzar. La saludamos y lloramos de alegría y emoción de volvernos a ver.

(Finally we got to the house. Sweet home, a home [in which] one could breathe peace and tranquility. Even though I saw everything as more beautiful, I knew that the house looked abandoned and out of sorts. But that really didn't matter to me. My three aunts arrived to greet us. And I was so glad to see them and even more glad because they received us with cooked squash in brown sugar. And after sharing greetings and a good appetizer, we went to sleep and rest a while because it was almost morning. Two or three hours later, I awoke to the singing of the roosters, and I got up to watch the sunrise, which I had not seen for some time. I quickly swept the floors, took a bath, and then we went to walk around the rancho and deliver all of the letters that we

had brought with us. In the middle of the street, we ran into my grand-
mother who was on her way to visit us and to invite us to lunch. We
greeted her and cried with the joy and emotion of seeing each other
again.)

As in the first excerpt from the first personal narrative, Isabel represents herself
and the world around her in lush language that captures the spirit of her coming
home. Again, she uses very complex syntactical constructions that, by making
use of repetition and parallelism, present a litany of recollections and create
a seductive cadence and rhythm in her narrative. Isabel's use of poetic language
and evocative imagery manages to turn a simple visit back home into a spectacle
full of awe and wonder.

Without question, one of the most significant events during her visit to
Mexico was what Isabel sees as her last chance to enjoy the company of young
men before her own marriage. In the following excerpt from the latter part of
her fourth and final personal narrative, Isabel provides an extended description
of what she refers to as her rite of passage from life as a single woman to life
as a married one. In short, Isabel has a final flirtatious fling at the dance after
her brother's wedding that breaks all the rules. It is her last chance to enjoy
the attention of young men who fancy her before she gets married and settles
down to raise a family of her own:

> *Aunque yo ya estaba pedida en matrimonio, y después de eso las mucha-*
> *chas no pueden bailar más que con el novio, pero como yo no lo tenía*
> *allí me olvidé de eso y comencé a bailar sin parar hasta que terminó.*
> *Ese día me divertí de lo más bonito bailando con todos. Yo lo tomé*
> *como una despedida de soltera. Bailé con ex-novios y amigos. Hubo al-*
> *gunos que como me miraban bailando creyeron que no tenía ningún*
> *compromiso y me comenzaban a pretender. Y yo como pensé que no iba*
> *a tener más oportunidades, le seguí la corriente. Pero el que más las-*
> *tima me dio fue un muchacho que me quería mucho y comenzaba a olvi-*
> *darme. Pero en cuanto me miró bailando, él me comenzó a pedir que*
> *fuera su novia otra vez. Y le seguí la corriente, tanto que me visitó*
> *todos los días mientras estuve en el rancho. Y nunca le dije que todavía*
> *estaba comprometida. Él siguió yendo a verme, y yo con tal de no pasár-*
> *mela aburrida, le seguía la corriente. Platicaba con él y él pensó que*
> *volveríamos a ser novios. Y lo mantuve con las esperanzas hasta que pa-*
> *saron los días y le dije que yo estaba todavía comprometida. Él no lo*
> *podía creer y se sentía ofendido. Y con mucha razón. Pero como yo no*
> *estaba enamorada de él pues no me dolió mucho. En fin, después de*
> *que me la pasaba todas las tardes con mis amigas platicando de todo lo*
> *que había pasado en el rancho desde que me fui y lo que me había pa-*

sado a mí en Chicago, se pasaron los días y mi mamá decidió que nos teníamos que venir.

(Although I was already engaged to be married, and after that young women can't dance except with the fiancé, but since he wasn't there, I forgot about that and started to dance without stopping until it was over. That day I enjoyed myself to the maximum dancing with everyone. I took it as a farewell to my life as a single woman. I danced with ex-boyfriends and friends. There were some who because they saw me dancing thought that I had not made a commitment, and they started to court me. And because I thought that I would not be having any more opportunities, I went with the flow. But the one I felt most sorry for was a young man who used to love me very much and had started to forget me. But as soon as he saw me dancing, he started to ask me to be his girlfriend again. And I kept going with the flow, so much so that he visited me every day while I was at the rancho. And I never told him that I was still committed. He continued going to see me and because I did not want to get bored, I kept going with the flow. I would speak to him, and he thought that we would become boyfriend and girlfriend again. And I kept him hoping until the days went by and I told him that I was still engaged. He could not believe it and felt offended. And with good reason. But since I was not in love with him, well, it didn't hurt me much. In the end, after spending every afternoon talking with my girlfriends about everything that had happened at the rancho since I had left and that had happened to me in Chicago, the days went by and my mother decided that we had to come back.)

Just as she did in an earlier passage, Isabel tones down her use of the fecund language that is representative of a Mexicano rhetorical style and focuses on the logic behind the choices that she made on the night of her brother's wedding. While the language is less conventional in terms of Mexicano rhetorical practices, it is her decision to challenge social convention—to dance and have a good time, to lead a young man on despite the fact that she is engaged, to "go with the flow," as she puts it—that is most salient. Like the woman in the preceding chapter on personal letter-writing who breaks with tradition by declaring that she is just as responsible as God for what happens in her life, Isabel makes a choice here that eventually leads others in her social network to see her as irresponsibly flirtatious and to gossip about it among themselves. In the long run and in the eyes of social network members, her saving grace is that she eventually marries her fiancé, has several children, and settles down to raise a family.

"It Is as If My Story Repeats Itself"

In August 1989, some 10 months after I met Jaime and Roció Durán, Rocio's older sister, Olga Ramírez, and three of her four children moved back to Chicago from San Jacinto, the rancho where the two women had grown up. Olga immediately found a job and started contributing to her family's economic welfare. Olga's husband, Arturo, and their oldest child, Malú, had remained behind in Mexico. Olga's family had moved back to their home in Mexico four years earlier after her mother had become very ill. Like too many other Mexicano families who have tried to resettle in their rural homes, Olga and Arturo ran out of the money they had saved and were forced to return to Chicago, where the two of them had lived for almost 20 years before their departure and where all four of their children were born. Although the Ramírez family owned a two-apartment building on the north side of Chicago where they had lived for many years before their return to Mexico, Olga decided to resettle in the Pilsen area to be closer to her sisters and other members of their social network. When Jaime and Rocío learned that Olga and her family were moving back to Chicago, they prepared one of the smaller apartments for them in the rear building. Olga and her three younger children moved into the apartment, but despite the physical proximity to Rocío's family, after a few days, Olga and her children felt lonely and isolated. After some discussion, Jaime and Rocío agreed to have Olga and her three children move in with them, their own three children, Rocío and Olga's cousin Fernando, and their niece Leticia. Four months later, Olga's husband, Arturo, returned to Chicago, joined his family in Jaime and Rocío's apartment, and got back the factory job that he had held several years earlier. The following summer, after Olga and Rocío's younger sister, Teresa Pérez, and her three children left one of the two apartments upstairs to move into a house that Teresa had bought in Little Village, Olga, Arturo, and their three children moved into the vacated apartment. Shortly thereafter, Malú returned from Mexico and moved in with her family.

Although Diane and I had met Malú during her occasional visits to Chicago, we didn't establish a relationship with her until the summer of 1993. At first, Malú struck me as a very timid and shy individual. During my first few visits to her family's home, Malú would stay in the background, quiet and barely noticed. I decided to work hard to establish a relationship with her, mainly because she was one of the few social network members going to college with whom I thought I had a chance to establish a close relationship.[2] I also had an ulterior motive that emerged from my interest in letter-writing among members of the social network. The fact is, a few days before I started visiting Malú on a regular basis, I had decided to ask her to join Rosa and Isabel in corresponding via letter-writing with Diane and me. Once I had established a relationship with her and reestablished one with the rest of her family, I made an effort to visit them on a regular basis during the following two years, often taking time to help Malú and her siblings with their homework when I wasn't chatting with Malú or her parents in the kitchen.

As I learned when I interviewed her, Malú was the quintessential middle point that I had been looking for in a continuum represented by Rosa at one end and Isabel at the other. Of las tres Marías, Malú was the only one who had attended school in Chicago and her family's rancho in Mexico. At the age of 11 and shortly after she completed fifth grade in Chicago, Malú moved to Mexico and attended school there for the next four years. When I first met her in Chicago in October 1989, she was still living with an aunt and uncle in her parents' rancho and was about to move back to live with her parents and siblings. Although she considers herself a Mexicana in the same way that Rosa and Isabel do, during her interview, Malú is the only one who demonstrates any degree of hesitancy about national identity. When I asked her if she ever thought of herself as a Chicana or Mexican American, her response was, "*A veces sí, pero siento que estoy más acostumbrada a México*" (Sometimes, yes, but I feel that I am more accustomed to Mexico). And while she was very definite about having the interview conducted in Spanish, like Rosa, she occasionally would code-switch and include some English phrases or sentences in our conversation. Although all three women were about the same age, unlike Rosa and Isabel, who were already married and had children, Malú said that she didn't plan either to get married or to have children. When I asked her why not, Malú replied, "*No me gustan los niños*" (I don't like children). When I pressed her about whether or not she would one day like to have some children, Malú said, "*Adoptarlos, sí, pero míos, no*" (Adopt them, yes, but my own, no). As far as marriage is concerned, Malú informed me that she planned to get married someday—well after she had turned 50.

Of las tres Marías, Malú gave me the most writing: six narratives totaling 37 pages and 6,131 words. In linguistic terms, Malú's writing was also the most varied of the three: the first, fourth, and sixth were written in English, the second and fifth in Spanish, and the third in a combination of the two languages. Like all of Rosa's and Isabel's narratives, Malú's first four were handwritten, but the last two were typed. Finally, while the first three were written specifically for me, the last three, all personal narratives dealing with the very same issues, were written for different teachers and different classes at the university.

Like Rosa, Malú also drafted some of the narratives that she gave me. Unlike Rosa's, though, her first drafts did not consist of a series of false starts. Instead, they reflected Malú's struggle with finding the appropriate language to frame her narrative. The original text of the first narrative, for example, contains extensive additions and deletions as she searches for the voice that will represent a particular childhood experience. The relative polish of the last three narratives, all of which she wrote for university writing classes, indicates that they too underwent a series of drafts as she struggled to find ways to represent her experiences in discursive language and to fulfill different sets of teacherly expectations. As will soon become apparent, Malú's writing is in many ways an intricate mix, in linguistic, rhetorical, and discursive terms, of the kinds of writing generated by Rosa and Isabel. Because her lived experience and the options she chooses are very different from those of the other two Marías, what Malú elects to represent discursively—as well as the blending not only of the two languages but of two very different rhetorical styles, the rich and florid Mexicano style and the more direct and analytical essayist one—illustrates the greater degree to which she has ventured into and been influenced by the discourse styles present in a greater variety of contact zones.

Because I will not have space and time enough to provide excerpts from all six of Malú's personal narratives, I want to present a brief overview of the first three personal narratives that she wrote for me; I will discuss the last three that she wrote for teachers later. In the first of the three narratives that she produced for me, Malú writes in English about "the feelings of confusion I had on my first day in kindergarten." The narrative, which is very linear and straightforward, describes the moment-to-moment experience of getting ready for school, feeling out of place there, and finally settling in to the point of wondering why a boy who joined her class was crying when, in her words, "it's kind of fun here." The second narrative, written entirely in Spanish, begins with a detailed description of a house she and her parents are walking through with a real estate agent, then shifts in the middle to how an older woman that she learned to love dearly took on the responsibility of baby-sitting her while her parents went to work. The third personal narrative, which begins in English and shifts to Spanish and then back to English, describes the reasons why she decided to go to college and the positive roles that her parents and girlfriends played in motivating her to stay in college despite the difficulties that she encountered there.

In the opening passage of her third personal narrative, Malú not only establishes a clear thesis reminiscent of those that Rosa used; it also proves to be a more complex and multilayered one. In the course of presenting *"las razones por las que decidí ir al colegio"* (the reasons why I decided to go to college), Malú contrasts what she calls *"las ilusiones de una niña"* (the illusions of a child) with a desire to *"dejar la ignorancia"* (leave ignorance behind). The highlight of this opening passage is Malú's vivid description of her visceral reaction and the embarrassment she feels when a teacher asks her to answer a question in a university setting:

> *Me siento mal cuando alguien me pregunta de algo y yo [no] lo en-*
> *tiendo, o tengo la menor idea de lo que está hablando, o cuando no*

puedo expresar lo que siento cuando me preguntan. Me da coraje con-
migo misma de pensar que como uno puede saber tanto y yo tan poco.
Realmente ni yo misma me entiendo. Al sentirme ignorante me siento
menos. Y ese sentimiento no me es nada agradable. Yo sé que nunca voy
a saber todo o siquiera tanto como otros, pero quiero que llegue el día
en que alguien me pregunte algo y yo sepa cómo responderle sin tener
temor. Como el otro día, cuando un maestro me preguntó algo de la lec-
ción, me puse roja, me empezaron a temblar por dentro las piernas y
manos, sentí un calor que me llegó hasta las orejas, el corazón me latía
más y más, mi lengua se me trabó, y la boca me temblaba cuando ha-
blé. Me dio vergüenza conmigo misma.

(I feel bad when someone asks me about something and I do [not] understand it, or I have the slightest idea about what someone is talking
about, or when I cannot express what I feel when they ask me. I become angry with myself to think that someone else can know so much
and I so little. In reality, I don't understand myself. Whenever I feel ig-
norant, I feel small. And that sentiment is not pleasant for me at all. I
know that I'm never going to know everything or at least as much as
others, but I want the day to come when someone asks me something
and I'll know how to respond without being afraid. Like the other day,
when a teacher asked me something about a lesson, I turned red, my
legs and hands began to tremble inside, I felt a heat that went all the
way to the ears, my heart was throbbing more and more, my tongue
got stuck, and my mouth trembled when I spoke. I was ashamed of myself.)

Interestingly, several of the rhetorical strategies appreciated by adult members
of her social network find their way into the text. Like some of the passages
from Isabel's personal narratives, this excerpt is vibrant with emotion, solidly
grounded in personal experience, and expresses a sincerity that is unusual in
academic writing. At the same time, ironically, the honesty that she expresses
and the fact that she is describing an act in which she has participated gives
the passage an eloquence that we find in the best of student narrative writing
in a university setting.

In the middle of her third narrative, right before she switches to English
and describes the important role that her girlfriends have played in supporting
her university studies, Malú describes in vivid and detailed terms the role that
her parents, especially her father, have played in making sure that she obtains
the kind of education she needs to get into college and makes an extra effort
to stay in school once she has been admitted. Throughout the first part of the
passage, Malú acknowledges her father's role in her education as he pushed

all his children to excel in school, sometimes even making up his own homework assignments for them despite the fact that he had very little schooling himself. Malú also praises him because while she knew that he was one of the people in her life who wanted her to go to college, *"él nunca me obligó"* (he never obligated me). While her description of her father's role in her education is fairly routine and low-keyed, her description of her mother's response when Malú ponders dropping out of school and Malú's bilingual representation of it are priceless:

> *Mi mamá, también, ha sido de gran ayuda para mí porque desde antes que yo entrara [en la universidad] ella me decía que entrara, que no tuviera miedo. Un día de por curiosidad le pregunté que haría si yo dejara el colegio. Ella me contestó, "Si te sales porque realmente tu mentalidad no te alcanza y no puedes, está bien. Yo lo acepto. ¿Qué se va hacer? Pero si te sales por huevona, te chingo!"*

> (My mom has also been of great help because even before I entered [the university] she would tell me to enroll, not to be afraid. One day, out of curiosity, I asked her what she'd do if I were to quit college. She answered me, "If you leave because in reality you don't have the mental capacity and you can't, that's fine, I'll accept it. What is one to do? But if you leave out of laziness, I'll get you!") And she smiled. With those words she told me everything, that everything was up [to me]. If I wanted to fail, I'd fail. If I wanted to succeed, I would succeed.

While the first part of Malú's third narrative presents her as an isolated, and at times alienated, individual caught in the clash of cultures and discourses that members of marginalized communities often experience in university settings, the second part locates her as the child of parents who are deeply involved and concerned about her education. Interestingly, however, she does not portray her parents as individuals who are simply interested in an education for its own sake. Instead, she dramatically illustrates their position that it is Malú who must decide whether or not she wants to go to college and who must exert herself if she is going to succeed. The shift from Spanish to English at the end of the second passage further complicates an already complicated representation as she signals a shift in languages from the one she shares with her parents to the one she must master if she wishes to succeed in college.

As I noted earlier, the last three personal narratives that Malú gave me were written for three different classes at the university. In them, Malú illustrates the struggles that she is experiencing as one of the few members in her group who has made the leap from a tight-knit social network to the open-ended social spaces of a university setting. Her fourth and fifth narratives—the first of which

is handwritten in pen and in English and the second of which is typed, titled
¿Español o Inglés? (Spanish or English?), and written in Spanish—focus on
the struggles she has faced in trying to move back and forth between the
languages of her social network and of the larger society in which she is hoping
to succeed. They both cover much the same territory, telling about her back-
and-forth movement between schooling in the United States and Mexico. The
final paragraph of her fourth narrative captures this conflict in language that
again melds the rhetorical styles of her Mexicano social network and the essayist
tradition that she has been learning in school. It also dramatically summarizes
the particular circumstances and difficulties that she continues to struggle with
to this very day:

> Every summer when school was over, my cousin and I would come to
> Chicago for vacation. After I had finished my last year in junior high,
> my parent[s] decided I should stay in Chicago to further my education.
> My cousins who lived in Chicago told me I should stay and go to the
> same high school they did. I had to repeat again my experience of en-
> tering a school with no friends but my two cousins and to an educa-
> tional system in which English was now again the first language. When
> I entered high school, I was placed as a sophomore but with a fresh-
> man's English. During my three years in high school, it was as if I was
> in the same situation as before, but now it was backwards. I was more
> fluent in Spanish than in English. It is as if my story repeats itself over
> and over again. I had trouble expressing my ideas in English during
> high school, and I am still having them in college. I have problems with
> my grammar, spelling, and putting my ideas together, but here I am
> again trying to recover and confront all my changes.

Because she has attended school in Mexico and the United States and has
decided to venture into the multiple contact zones that a university setting
provides, Malú faces the most pronounced struggle of las tres Marías. This is
not to say that Rosa and Isabel may not be headed in the same direction,
especially as their own choices lead them further away from their home front
in Chicago and into the contact zones represented at work, and if they get the
opportunity, in college. Of the three, however, Malú is the only one who is
having to acknowledge and is in a position where she is expected to analyze
complex transitional experiences.

In her sixth and final narrative, which she titled "Caught Between Two
Cultures" and which was not only written for a university teacher but went a
step beyond the other narratives I have presented by using an outside source,
Malú shifts her focus from the difficulties that linguistic change has forced her
to face to the difficulties that cultural change has brought to her daily life.

While this book is primarily about the discursive practices that members of Malú's social network struggle with as they attempt to fulfill their group's discursive conventions at the same time that some of them challenge them, it is important to note that social and cultural issues have forced them to do the same thing. In effect, Malú's final narrative illustrates the extent to which language and culture are inextricably bound. In the first two paragraphs of the narrative, Malú demonstrates her understanding of the role that conventions play in the day-to-day survival of social networks like hers and of the need that individual members sometimes have to challenge them when they consider them too constraining. A few paragraphs later, the desire of the individual member to break free of the group, to find a way to exert the personality of his or her individual self despite the possible consequences, serves as the other side of the dialectic between one's community and one's self:

> I'm not trying to act like the perfect child because I know I'm not. There are things I have done without the consent of my parents, like when I cut my hair and got a tattoo. When I told my mother I was going to cut my hair, she really didn't protest, but it took me 19 years to convince her. However, when I told her I wanted a tattoo, she said, "No!" I had completed my part by asking for her permission. It was up to her if she wanted to give or not give permission, but I was still going to get it. I didn't ask my father for permission because I already knew he was never going to give it to me. I'd rather surprise him and then face the consequences. When I cut my hair, he stopped talking to me for a week. The image my father has of a pure Mexican girl is with long hair, so he makes my sister and me have long hair like my mother did. And the tattoo? I hope he never finds out, but if he does, we'll just have to deal with it. The reason I cut my hair and had the tattoo was not only because it was something I wanted, but also to demonstrate to my parents that I'm growing up and can make my own decisions. When I decide to do something, it's because I know it's not going to hurt my family or me.

Like Rosa and Isabel before her, Malú finds the need on occasion to "demonstrate to my parents that I'm growing up and can make my own decisions." While Rosa's rebellion is the more extreme of the three and causes her and members of her family a prolonged agony, Isabel—who incidentally gave birth to her third child in March 1998—demonstrates her need to assert her personal independence by going through what she refers to as her rite of passage into marriage, a final chance to demonstrate that she will not always be bound by the conventions and constraints that any social group imposes on its members. By cutting her hair, an open and obvious form of rebellion that is readily acknowledged, Malú lets her parents and other older members of her social network know that she has a right to challenge their traditional expectations. Her tattoo, on the other hand, although hidden from sight, may eventually surface as an act of defiance with a set of repercussions that she says she is willing to face when the time comes. As Malú writes in language filled with the power of someone who has found her voice and is willing to take a stance: "And the tattoo? I hope [my father] never finds out, but if he does, we'll just have to deal with it." At the same time that they reveal different forms of resistance to their social network's discursive and cultural expectations, the personal narratives of las tres Marías also challenge theoretical attempts to essentialize the work that women do as writers by verifying Watson's (1993) contention that women's differences and their writing "are inflected by cultural specificities of ethnicity, class, time, and location" (p. 73). Equally important, their autobiographical writing serves to illustrate the sophistication and eloquence inherent in the rhetorical and discursive practices of marginalized groups in the United States. Unfortunately, these are not recognized often enough because members of such groups are rarely encouraged to represent their lives in writing outside of school settings or in genres not generally considered part of their communicative repertoires.

CHAPTER 7

Conclusion

In 1949, I was given birth by an immigrant and brought into the world by a midwife in a south Texas labor camp established to house Mexican laborers deliberately recruited by North American interests (Portes & Rumbaut, 1990) to do the work that many United Statesians were unwilling to do. Four years later, my mother, my stepfather, my two older Mexican-born sisters (age 8 and 10 at the time), and I moved into a brand-new and highly segregated federal housing project on the western edge of Harlingen, Texas, called *Los Vecinos* Homes (i.e., Homes of the Neighbors), where another six siblings were born. Of the six oldest children in my family, five dropped out or were pushed out of school before they reached the ninth grade; I was the only survivor of our town's public school system, one in which Chicano/Mexicano children had no choice but to learn English long before bilingual education was introduced as an option and were held in detention or sent home if they were caught speaking Spanish on school grounds. I eventually graduated and later, through a series of random but fortunate circumstances, went off to college. Over time, my five siblings earned their high school equivalency diplomas and one of them, Berta, also received an undergraduate college degree. As a consequence of an improvement in schooling opportunities at the college level for members of racial and ethnic minority groups in the United States that took hold in the 1970s, the three youngest children in my family had a chance to attend college and earn degrees. Not surprisingly, the types of jobs that my siblings and I have today are divided along class and professional lines: those among us who never went to college work as laborers or in the service industry, those who earned college degrees work in education, government, and high-tech industry.

Whether I would have gone to college after graduating from my hometown high school is something I'll never know. In the summer before my senior year, I left Harlingen and moved to Chicago to live with my sister Berta, who had moved there a few years earlier with the help of one of our cousins. My move to Chicago signalled an unprecedented shift in my own life. After having lived in a highly segregated Chicano/Mexicano community all my life, I was suddenly thrust into the racial and ethnic mix of what to this day is still the most segregated city in the United States. Because Berta lived in an all-white neighborhood composed primarily of Polish and German immigrants and their

U.S.-born children, as well as a scattering of families that had migrated from Appalachia, I daily faced the challenge of living in a community very different from the only one I had ever known. Because Berta and I are among the more fair-skinned siblings in our family, Berta must have known intuitively that we would be able to survive if we remained as unmarked as possible. Before I went to bed on my first night in that community, Berta told me something I had never expected to hear: "Listen, Juan, if anybody in the neighborhood asks you what your name is, tell them it's John." While I might have given her a quizzical look, I was in no position to challenge her. For the next two years, in the factory where I worked closely with European American, Puerto Rican, and African American men and women for the first time in my life, in the large and overwhelmingly white high school I attended in the company of no more than 10 or 12 other Latino students, and at the University of Illinois at Chicago, where I enrolled in 1968 as one of no more than 30 or 40 Latino students after unexpectedly receiving a scholarship, I introduced myself to everyone as John. It wasn't until the father of a young woman in the neighborhood, both of whom I had come to know very well, stopped speaking to me after he found out I was Mexican that I angrily and defiantly changed my name back to Juan and, despite my ability to pass, marked myself as linguistically and culturally different.

While this brief autobiographical sketch illustrates how much circumstances have changed in this country for large numbers of people who were born and raised in marginalized communities, my work among Jaime and Rocío Durán's social network demonstrates how far we still have to go. On the one hand, like my mother, my two older sisters, and their peers, the Mexican-born members of their social network have had to struggle with the difficulties that come when the continuing problems of economic, linguistic, and racial/ethnic segregation isolate groups of people and make it difficult for them to interact with members of other groups, much less have the opportunity to immerse themselves in and learn the language of power in the United States. On the other hand, the young adults in the group, but especially the U.S.-born children, have had more opportunities to enter a variety of contact zones and, as a consequence, have learned to respond to and deal with them in numerous ways. Unlike myself, who grew up in a different era and in a rural part of the country where our roles in life were clearly demarcated and rarely challenged, these young people live in an urban center where crossing borders from one ethnic neighborhood to another is sometimes a daily occurrence. To survive, younger members of the group in particular have learned to equip themselves with a number of different skills and sensibilities. What I didn't know while I was growing up but have learned since, especially in the course of the research project that informs this book, is that members of groups like Jaime and Rocío's and the one in which I grew up don't enter contact zones as blank slates, much less as the illiterate and inept individuals that the news media sometimes labels them in the midst of the current anti-immigration hysteria. Instead, they come to this country equipped with a range of social, linguistic, and rhetorical abilities that human beings born into any language and culture inevitably develop, not only to function and survive in everyday life, but to progress and thrive under typical and unexpected circumstances.

The range of communicative practices across oral and written genres that I illustrate in the preceding three chapters demonstrates a particular group's rich repository of rhetorical strategies and the varying degrees to which they are used by different members. Because no single person in the group possesses the complete cache available to the community, we can safely say that the communicative practices are an example of communal rather than individual property. More specifically, these communicative practices can be said to belong to the community in the truest sense of the word because members who possess a certain array share it by acting as intermediaries when the need arises, teach it as part of the lyrical learning process, exchange it through personal letter-writing, or enact it in everyday conversation. While it is important for readers to appreciate how the social network's conventions place limits on the ways members choose to communicate with one another within the boundaries of their transnational community, it is also important for them to keep in mind that members are drawn to varying degrees into the multiple contact zones that lie within and beyond its borders. In short, they not only communicate with others outside their usual social space, but are likely to enact many of the communicative practices they learn when they return and interact with other social network members.

In this concluding chapter, I discuss the implications of my research on Mexicano communicative practices in terms of theory, policy, curriculum, and pedagogy. I am especially interested in discussing them in terms of a variety of schooling contexts available to the younger adults, who increasingly challenge the social, cultural, linguistic, and discursive parameters within which most of the older adults in the social network operate. As researchers, it is important for us to continue to enter a variety of social settings so that we can better understand how different groups of people cope with life, language, and literacy. It is also important for scholars who specialize in theorizing to understand the implications of what we learn about people's lived experience in marginalized communities on these theories. In addition, elected and appointed government officials, public and private funding agencies with an educational research agenda, members of school boards, program administrators, and school principals need to realize that the policies they formulate must not only be sensitive to and address the needs of the varied populations they serve; they also need to help those who work under their guidance and supervision find ways to educate a citizenry and prepare a work force that, because of its unparalleled demographic growth, is becoming increasingly responsible for the continuing prosperity of everyone in this nation. Finally, teachers in K–12, adult literacy, and college settings must continue to familiarize themselves and become more aware of the many ways in which the "funds of knowledge" that members of marginalized groups bring into ideologically constrained schools and classrooms can best be integrated into their curricula and pedagogy.

THEORIZE IN PARADISE, PRACTICE ON EARTH

Within the academic community, there is probably no issue more intractable than finding ways to overcome the historical split between theory and practice. Such internationally renowned scholars as Freire and Bourdieu, for example, have struggled with this conundrum and have offered their own ideas about how to overcome it. Both have grounded their ideas in the practices of everyday life in which people engage as they struggle to come to terms with the political nature of their circumstances in their own discourses rather than in the often sterile and objective discourses privileged by the academy. In his work, especially in *Pedagogy of the Oppressed* (1970), Freire has consistently argued that theory must not be imposed on the practices of people but instead must emerge from and in turn inform those very practices. Through his close affinity with the poorest and most illiterate citizens of Brazil, Freire developed a practice-based approach to the teaching of reading and writing that blends his theoretical interpretations with those very practices in what he refers to as *praxis*. Praxis is that in-between space where theory and practice become one, where the two inform each other in dialogical terms to the point where they become indivisible.

Because of his dissatisfaction with the ongoing battle between those who privilege objectivity (theory) and those who privilege subjectivity (practice), Bourdieu (1991), too, has struggled with their dichotomization by arguing, as Freire does, that we must move beyond dichotomizations that paralyze our thinking and prevent us from understanding how the practices of people unfold in their everyday lives. Despite Freire's and Bourdieu's Herculean efforts to overcome the split, I would argue that most of us, theorists and practitioners alike, continue to be held in the dichotomy's stranglehold, especially when it comes to the division of labor between scholars in the academy and teachers in the public schools.

In the work that I have presented in this book, I continue to find myself caught in that stranglehold. Do the theoretical ideas I propose emerge from my analysis and interpretation of the practices that I observe, or are they imposed by me on those practices in ways that inevitably privilege the theoretical over the practical? The answer is probably a combination of the two. After all,

I cannot escape or ignore the academy's expectations that I theorize any more than I can escape or ignore the practices that I have observed in the field and in my own life. I would like to suggest that while Freire, Bourdieu, and others have generally succeeded in overcoming the split between the two in terms of theory (paradise), I have yet to encounter work by anyone who has managed to overcome it in terms of practice (earth). What I think we can talk about in more productive and meaningful terms is how the two inform one another and how we can use each as a framework or a lens to interpret the other. For whether or not we ever manage to overcome the split between theory and practice in the context of lived experience is not as important as how we conceptualize them, especially how we write up what we have learned through our subjective experience in the field about the nature of practice and how it, in turn, informs or is informed by our scholarly need to objectify it to one degree or another. Inevitably, then, we return to the two central issues that I raise in the introduction and engage throughout this book: the extent to which our conceptions of the social spaces in which we study orality and literacy, as well as the nature of and relationship between orality and literacy, determine what we see in the field and what we say in our writing.

Like Pratt (1987), Bourdieu alerts us to the dangers of idealizing the nature of speech communities. As Thompson, the editor of Bourdieu's *Language and Symbolic Power* (1991), puts it:

> Under the guise of drawing a *methodological* distinction, the linguist surreptitiously makes a series of *substantive* assumptions. For the completely homogeneous language or speech community does not exist in reality: it is an idealization of a particular set of linguistic practices which have emerged historically and have certain social conditions of existence. This idealization or *fictio juris* is the source of what Bourdieu calls, somewhat provocatively, "the illusion of linguistic communism". . . . [The] ideal language or speech community is an object which has been *pre*-constructed by a set of social-historical conditions endowing it with the status of the sole legitimate or "official" language of a particular community. (p. 5)

As much as I may have tried to disrupt this tendency in my formulation of a home front, because I contend that any discourse community is at least partially governed by a set of conventions, I am automatically guilty of falling into this same trap. Thus, while I demonstrate the extent to which some members of Jaime and Rocío Durán's social network challenge and destabilize the group's conventions, I end up supporting a critical aspect of the position that Pratt and Bourdieu staunchly denounce. I do it, however, in an attempt to correct what I see as a relentless shift in focus over the last several years toward conceptualizing social spaces worthy of study as contact zones without acknowledging the fact that the participants in those contact zones often come from the many highly segregated social, cultural, economic, political, and linguistic home fronts that exist in the United States. If nothing else, I want to press the issue and argue that we must broaden the range of social spaces worth studying to include the home front and the contact zone. As I see it, fruitful research *can* take place in both of these social spaces, and especially in the multiplicity of social spaces that lie along a continuum between the two.

Like the unending confrontations that we face in regard to how we theoretically formulate the social spaces where the communicative practices we examine take place, our conceptions of orality and literacy and their relationship to one another are also fraught with challenge and controversy. And yet, again, we cannot easily step away from this difficult set of circumstances. Just as the way we formulate in theory the social spaces that we study in practice affects what we choose to study, how we conceive of orality and literacy influences not only what we choose to accept as valid data, but what we choose to ignore. While most scholars in the field of language and literacy studies currently acknowledge the idea that orality and literacy are social practices, there are still differences of opinion in how we conceptualize their relationship. Scholars, for example, are still motivated by Heath's (1982) contention that we must examine the oral and written language practices that take place during what she refers to as "literacy events," those moments when members of a community simultaneously interact with a piece of written text and with one another in conversation as they analyze and interpret it. That certainly continues to be a central arena worth exploring in what Street (1993) refers to as the "oral/literate mix." I would argue, however, that orality and literacy can be said to mix, not only when the two occur simultaneously, but whenever rhetorical, generic, or ideological aspects of one emerge in the practice of the other.

LIFE ON THE "CULTURE WARS" FRONT

As complicated and intractable as the theoretical issues we face in the academy may seem, they pale in comparison with the more difficult task that policymakers face in making sense of the data and information available to them and that educators at all levels face when they enter increasingly diverse classrooms of adults or children who make their way there from increasingly segregated communities. It certainly comes as no surprise that the policymakers who must make excruciatingly difficult decisions and the teachers who face the daily grind of finding ways to help the students in their classrooms often put little faith in the theories that scholars develop and the research that we undertake in the academy. And who can blame them? At conference after conference, in the company of freshly minted scholars as well as internationally renowned ones, I have witnessed the difficult struggle that we all experience in our attempts to translate what we have learned from our research with social groups in homes, schools, communities, and workplaces and from the analyses and interpretations we have undertaken in our offices and at home. Despite (or because of ?) my 25 years as a teacher and scholar in the academy, I continue to be amazed by how much we have in common with our colleagues in the medical community. As much as members of the two fields of research currently know about their respective areas of interest, and we know a lot, especially as a consequence of unprecedented theoretical and technological advancements and breakthroughs, we both still have so much to learn. Despite what some members of our society may want to believe, teaching and learning are not the cookie-cutting experiences that, if they were, would dramatically simplify how we go about doing them. If anything, the acts of teaching and learning are as complex as brain surgery itself.

Can we, then, take what we have learned out in the field as researchers and in our university classrooms as teachers and translate it in ways that policymakers and educators on the front lines of our culture wars will find meaningful and applicable? Despite some nihilistic tendencies that I periodically share with a number of my colleagues (who among us, after all, has not at one time or another in frustration thrown his arms up in the air?), I know that in the end our purposes and goals demand that we do what we can to assist teachers and policymakers in developing and implementing curricular and pedagogical strategies that will lead to an improvement, rather than a simple change, in the lives of the students whom we all have dedicated our lives to educating. That is a challenge that scholars continually face, and that I, in particular, as I continue to struggle with what I have learned about how rhetoric and ideology manifest themselves in the genres of oral and written language used by members of Jaime and Rocío Durán's social network, must now address.

The Critical Role of Policymakers in the Educational Process

More than ever, policymakers at all levels of the decision-making process—elected and appointed government officials interested in educational issues, educational research funding agencies, school board members, program administrators, and principals—are inundated with multifarious and at times contradictory proposals about how best to deal with the problems in the schools under their jurisdiction. In recent years, the difficulties they face have been compounded by the unprecedented numbers of immigrants who have entered the United States from Asian and Latin American countries and have brought with them a variety of cultural values, language and literacy practices, and educational expectations. The anti-immigration hysteria surrounding this tremendous demographic shift has certainly contributed to the vitriolic nature of the culture wars, which in turn has resulted in widespread fears about the future direction of the United States. Not surprisingly, these are fears that U.S.-born citizens as well as newly arrived immigrants face on a continuing basis. Like many of the fears that emerge in our personal and public lives, these fears are often fed by the misrepresentation of facts, the demonization of whole groups of people, and a general misunderstanding of the degree to which what we currently face is in many ways nothing new at all.

Throughout U.S. history, the large influx of immigrants has always raised nativist fears about its impact on the status quo, future generations, and the shifting political winds. What is new this time around is the fact that the wave of immigration that began in 1965 has been predominantly composed of non-European peoples who in many cases have relocated to the United States because of the impact of U.S. federal policies on the immigrants' nations of origin. To an extent unacknowledged by most United Statesians, the role of the U.S. government in the social, political, economic, and military affairs of other countries over the past several decades has, in a sense, come home to roost. In light of the seemingly irreversible ramifications, especially the unprecedented and continuing flow of immigrants and refugees into the country, the pertinent question for us to ask is, What can policymakers do about the educational challenges that the current influx of immigrants presents to us all at this point in the process?

One obvious response to the increasing number of immigrants settling in the United States is for policymakers at all levels to familiarize themselves with the multiple histories and characteristics of the various immigrant groups so that they can make informed decisions that will contribute to the welfare of all instead of the welfare of the few. Because the tremendous demographic shifts taking place in the student makeup of our schools began 30 years ago, as scholars, we have only recently begun to examine their ramifications. In addition to reading varied perspectives and views on the lived experience of different immigrant groups and doing a better job of educating themselves, policymakers also need to identify what they see as areas of concern, then encourage and fund research projects by scholars in the academy and teachers in the schools that will tackle those problems and look for better ways to address them. While extensive research has been undertaken and must be continued on racial and ethnic groups (Chicano, Puerto Rican, Native American, African American, and Asian American) with long histories in the United States, as scholars, we are only now coming to terms with the tremendous impact that newly arrived immigrant groups (Mexicanos, Central Americans, Asians, Pacific Islanders, etc.) are having on the educational system. This study is an attempt to demonstrate that members of the immigrant groups currently transforming the complexion of this country bring rich caches of social, cultural, linguistic, and discursive values and practices that have the potential to enrich rather than impoverish the nation as a whole.

But policymakers also need to understand the particular contexts in which immigrant-related educational issues are being debated. At present, the manifestation of the culture wars in education is best represented in two principal ways: 1) an "English Only" movement that wants to strip immigrants of their native languages, and 2) the continuing battle between those who argue for a return to phonics, on the one hand, and those who argue for a whole language approach, on the other. In terms of language policy, attempts to force immigrants to give up their native languages will inevitably impoverish the nation as a whole, resulting in a monolingual entity unable to communicate or compete with developed and developing nations that are increasingly instituting multilingual policies. As far as the teaching of phonics is concerned, the data in this book show that social network members understand the importance of mastering the basic skills that many educators consider key aspects of a standard language: spelling, punctuation, mechanics, and grammar. At the same time, however, the data repeatedly demonstrate the extent to which members of the community, including those whom some experts would consider illiterate or semiliterate at best, have learned to position themselves rhetorically and to develop sophisticated syntactical constructions that rival the intricate forms we value in the academy. Finally, despite the seemingly insurmountable obstacles that members of the social network have had to face, their desire to pursue an education as adults and to support the education of their children is beyond question. More often than not, opportunity rather than desire is what is lacking in their hectic lives.

While it is important for policymakers to learn as much as they can about the rich and complex lives of members of different immigrant groups in the United States and about the political controversies their presence creates, an equally important task is to find ways to provide teachers with the time and the training they need to handle the unprecedented challenges they face and are likely to face for many years to come. Just as teachers are often prone to stop reading or listening to academic scholars whose work they see as relatively removed from their daily lives in the classroom, they often feel hampered by top-down policies that rob them of the time they need to become well informed and of the opportunities to use their expertise to experiment with different curricular and pedagogical approaches. Policymakers also need to find ways to encourage scholars and teachers to work together on their mutual goal of improving educational options and opportunities for everyone, both adult and child, in the United States. While more and more scholars are working hand-in-hand with teachers, the schism that remains between theory and practice also represents a division of labor that fails to fulfill the needs of the students that we serve. Obviously, policymakers alone cannot bridge the distance between scholars and teachers; the latter two must also make an effort to understand the nature of their respective cultures and the constraints within which each group operates. Fortunately, the administrations and schools of education at more and more universities located in urban areas, the universities of Arizona at Tucson, California at Los Angeles, Illinois at Chicago, and Washington at Seattle among them, are working hard to overcome the split between the urban university and the local schools. Policymakers at all levels, however, are in a position to facilitate and expand what out of necessity must become a closer working relationship between the two groups.

Curriculum, Pedagogy, and Lived Experience

As important as the theories and research that scholars produce and the policies that representatives from the various educational policymaking bodies implement may be, neither supersedes the significant and undervalued work that teachers undertake every day in their increasingly diverse classrooms. Because scholars and policymakers, respectively, tend to operate within hierarchical frameworks that place greater value on theory than practice, on policymaking than implementation, teachers are understandably suspicious about what they sometimes perceive as sanctimonious pronouncements sent down from above. In the adult literacy classes and the primary, middle school, and secondary classrooms that I have visited over the past several years, I have witnessed a continuing disillusion with the top-down nature of our educational system at both the national and local levels. While efforts have been made to ease the constraints on teachers and clarify both local and national standards and expectations, in my conversations with them, teachers have clamored for better and more comprehensive training, the time to share their ideas with one another, and the opportunity to gain greater control over the curricular and pedagogical practices that schools expect them to institute in their classrooms. No book in recent times better demonstrates the high hopes that come from active participation and engagement in the process of education and the disillusion brought about by the imposition of standardized educational practices from above than Heath's *Ways with Words* (1983). The closing chapter of her book vividly and depressingly illustrates what I have observed in a variety of classrooms. Teachers want to teach. Like any of us, they want greater control over their working lives. What is still lacking is the kind of framework that allows for the necessary give and take among scholars, policymakers, and the teachers on the front lines of our educational system.

In the adult literacy classrooms I have visited, for example, teachers are invariably underpaid for their labor, rarely receive the kind of training they need and want in order to do their jobs, and use outdated and unproductive curricular and pedagogical approaches imposed from above. Traditional programs of this kind are often based on the assumption that language is made up of highly discrete and interconnected elements that must be transmitted to students in linear fashion before the students can learn to apply them (i.e., first a student must learn the letters of the alphabet, then join them into words, sentences, paragraphs, and finally into an extended discursive piece of readable or written language). Because these approaches are based on the assumption that language is a set of discrete bits of predetermined information that teachers simply need to transmit for learning to take place, the activities that are part and parcel of these approaches often numb, bore, or paralyze students. This is not to suggest that administrators and teachers are unaware of the terrible constraints under which they have to operate. Still, for a variety of reasons that are almost always beyond their immediate control—the overcrowded class-rooms, the high turnover rate among language teachers, and the lack of ongoing and effective preservice training—they are often forced to stumble along and do the best job they can within the worrisome constraints that they and their students repeatedly face.

There are, however, a number of adult literacy programs from which we all have much to learn and that operate under dramatically different circumstances. While the policies instituted along with the funding in some of these programs also require that they operate within highly constrained curricular and pedagogi-cal circumstances, the administrators and teachers still find ways to move beyond such policies. Sometimes, administrators and teachers in these programs are even fortunate enough to operate within an institutional culture that trains them and encourages them to look for ways to integrate the lived experience of their students into their curricula and pedagogy. One of the more provocative and successful adult literacy programs ever implemented, researched, and written about in scholarly journals is the Boston English Family Literacy Pro-gram affiliated with the University of Massachusetts at Boston. Unlike tradi-tional "deficit-based" approaches that start "with mainstream ways of using literacy and transmitting them to families" and then blame the students' families for their school-related problems, researchers who use what Auerbach (1989) refers to as a "social-contextual approach to family literacy" look "at community practices as the basis for informing and modifying school practices" (p. 176). In light of what my data suggest about the sophisticated language strategies used by members of Jaime and Rocío Durán's social network, in both oral and written contexts, such an approach offers individuals like them an unprece-dented opportunity to build on what they know instead of demanding that they ignore the funds of knowledge available in their families and communities and began the process of learning from scratch.

As they begin to understand the dialogical relationship between what students learn at home and from their peers and what they are expected to learn in school settings, more and more scholars and teachers are experimenting with different curricular and pedagogical approaches to the problems that they face in programs at all levels of the educational system. Historically, this approach grows out of Dewey's (1899, 1900) unyielding support for progressive education. As most educators know, Dewey contends that learning in formal settings is likely to be more effective and meaningful if it is somehow connected to the lived experience of students outside the classroom. While a number of theorists have developed highly politicized versions of much the same perspective in recent years (Giroux, 1983; Kutz & Roskelly, 1991; Williams & Snipper, 1990), the individual work of Freire (1970) and Shor (1980), as well as their work together (Shor & Freire, 1987), has been credited with reaffirming Dewey's stance in their respective areas of interest—adult education and basic writing. In light of the work that I present in this book on oral language use in everyday life, personal letter-writing, and autobiographical writing among members of Jaime and Rocío Durán's social network, it is important to acknowledge the ways in which these particular genres have been and can be used in classrooms to frame a variety of fruitful learning opportunities based on lived experience.

Because of certain widely accepted assumptions about the oral language practices of Mexicanos as a group, assumptions not very different from those ascribed to Native American, Asian American, and other Latino groups, teachers and laypersons often assume that adult Mexicanos and their children are quiet, timid, and nonparticipatory in classroom discussions because of their social and cultural training. While there is probably a smidgen of truth to this myth, the reality is generally quite different. Mexicanos of all ages in Jaime and Rocío Durán's social network, for example, repeatedly looked forward to the secular ritual I described in Chapter 4 known as "echar plática" (to chat). There is, in other words, a culturally based disposition to engage in rich conversational exchanges in group settings that is obviously highly context-bound. Thus, something clearly changes in the context of the classroom. In one of the excerpts from her narratives, for example, Malú describes in vivid detail the physical reactions she experienced when she was asked to speak in one of her college classes. A personal experience I had with one of Rosa's closest family friends and an intimate member of the social network early in my research illustrates this further. The year before I first met Jaime Durán and the other members of his social network, Rosa's friend Dora was a student in a Saturday College writing class for students of color that I taught at the University of Illinois at Chicago to eighth graders interested in pursuing a higher education. At the time, I tried to coax Dora into speaking with me on a one-to-one basis and in the workshop groups to which I had assigned her. In the several months that we spent together in class, Dora never uttered a single word. One evening, shortly after I had met Rosa's family and was visiting them at their home, Dora unexpectedly walked into their apartment with her mother and sisters. A review of my field notes from that period presents a picture of a Dora who spoke almost incessantly with her friends, her family, and me. The problem, then, is not that individuals like Malú or Dora lack the skills or are somehow incapable of participating in classroom discussions; the problem is that we as teachers need to develop more effective and culturally appropriate opportunities in the classroom that will invite them to speak more freely and in their own voices.

As I attempted to show in the description of my efforts to gather the letters and autobiographical narratives from members of Jaime and Rocío Durán's social network, their initial unwillingness to share their writing with me reflects their mutual assumption that they don't know how to write well and the fear that someone in a position of authority is only interested in verifying it. In this sense, teachers face the challenge of trying to get students to produce written text when students consistently argue that they are not capable of it. At the same time, teachers must try to come to terms with the differences in class and power that stand between them and their students. This, then, means that teachers at any level of the educational system cannot simply surrender to their students' or their own impulses not to pursue the matter further. While patience is a prerequisite, care also must be taken to ensure that new problems are not created by trying to force recalcitrant students to share with their teachers their written work in particular genres. But if what I have discovered in the course of my research is true—that Mexicanos are generally well equipped to construct complex pieces of writing—then we must also look for ways to create classroom environments in which such students feel safe enough to share the funds of knowledge that they bring into the classroom so that we then have something on which to build. While the kind of writing represented in the two genres that I examine is considered highly problematic in school settings because of the extent to which they often reveal personal aspects that may prove uncomfortable for both the student and the teacher, a number of scholars and teachers are currently exploring different ways in which these two genres can be used in classrooms at all levels of the educational system (Gale, 1994; Hadaway, 1992; Naumann, 1991; Peterson, 1991) as the bases for improving a student's self-esteem as well as gaining insights into the linguistic and discursive competencies that students from marginalized communities bring into the classroom.

As I noted at the beginning of this chapter, translating theory and research into practice is one of the biggest challenges that anyone in the field of education is ever likely to encounter. At one time or another, we all face what seem like insurmountable obstacles in trying to share what we have learned in our particular professions as educators with others in related professions who need to understand the work that we are doing in order to do their own work more effectively. This applies across the board to scholars, policymakers, and teachers. In the end, no one group has more to teach the others. Our work as scholars is bound to remain ineffectual if policymakers and teachers find it either inaccessible or irrelevant. At the same time, the work of policymakers and teachers will fail to improve our theories and our research if we continue to think of the process as a one-way street. My commitment to my work with members of Jaime and Rocío Durán's social network over the last 9 years, I would like to think, verifies my belief that it has the potential to contribute to the overall improvement in the opportunities educators will make available to the fastest-growing minority group in the United States. I know from experience that my colleagues in the academy think the same thing about the work in which they too invest so much of their time and energy. Policymakers and teachers undoubtedly feel the same way. The problems we face as educators are enormous, and little of value is likely to come from our isolated efforts. Somehow, we need to reduce the distance that separates us. And we need to learn to work together more closely and more effectively to fulfill the implicit goal that we all share: to improve to the best of our abilities the educational options and opportunities available to the rich variety of students we serve in our respective capacities.

Notes

CHAPTER 1

1. For a historical review of the concept of community in anthropology, see Chavez, 1994.

2. Milroy (1987), who differentiates between "closeknit" and "looseknit" social networks, notes that close-knit networks "function in society as a norm enforcement mechanism. This pressure may result in the maintenance of a set of norms—including linguistic ones—which then flourish in opposition to publicly legitimized norms" (p. 106).

3. My use of "transnational community" acknowledges the fact that, as Chavez (1994) sees it, immigrants "can imagine themselves to be part of their communities 'back home,' and they can also imagine places for themselves in their 'new,' or host, communities. An immigrant is not necessarily restricted to an either/or classification when imagining his or her community or, more accurately, communities" (p. 68). In the context of my discussion, we can take it a step further and complicate the use of the plural form of community, when appropriate, by using the term "home fronts" in its place.

4. Between November 1988 and November 1997, I spent 491 days engaged in field research.

5. A word of caution is warranted here. While Anderson applies the term "imagined communities" to nation-states, Pratt (1987), Chavez (1991, 1994), and I sometimes use it to refer to communities of a few hundred people. Our mutual goal, however, is to highlight the "style of imagining" that researchers and residents use, respectively, to invent the communities they study or in which they live.

6. I am using the term "discursive" in the sense suggested by Fairclough (1992): "Any discursive 'event' (i.e., any instance of discourse) is seen as being simultaneously a piece of text, an instance of discursive practice, and an instance of social practice" (p. 4).

7. Except for the names of my wife (Diane J. Guerra), my sister (Berta), and the co-principal investigators (Marcia Farr and Lucía Elías-Olivares) with whom I worked as a research assistant (1988–1990), all the names used in this book are pseudonyms.

8. I occasionally adopt the Mexicano practice of using the term "United Statesian" (*estadounidense*), which I believe more accurately reflects how many of the Mexicanos that I have met position themselves vis-à-vis U.S. citizens in general.

9. Aside from occasional visitors who came to service utilities and consumer products, or because of their association with government agencies, the schools, or the Catholic church, the only non-Mexican–origin adults that I know of who regularly visited the social network households that I frequented were: my wife, Diane J. Guerra, an African American; Marcia Farr and her husband, both of whom are European American;

Lucía Elías-Olivares, a Chilean; Mary Ann Gómez, a European American married to a member of the social network who lives in Waukegan, Illinois; Marisela Padilla, a Puerto Rican friend of Rocío Duran's; and Miriam Williams, a European American woman who worked as a secretary at Jaime Durán's place of employment.

10. Puerto Ricans and Chicanos/Mexicanos are less segregated on the north side of Chicago, where the latter settled in what was once a predominantly Puerto Rican community (Betancur, 1996). Research on residential segregation among Chicanos/Mexicanos, Puerto Ricans, and Cubans, however, suggests that they are often as segregated from one another as each is from European Americans and African Americans (Massey & Denton, 1989).

11. I generally use the terms "Chicano" to identify Mexican-origin people born in the United States and "Mexicano" to identify Mexican-origin people born in Mexico or the U.S.–born children of people born in Mexico who self-identify as Mexicanos or Mexicanas. I also use the term "Mexican American" in place of "Chicano," especially when the term is invoked by a scholar I'm citing.

12. While I use the actual names of the neighborhoods, towns, and cities in the Chicago area where members of the social network reside (e.g., Pilsen, Little Village, Chicago) and for big cities (e.g., Mexico City and Guadalajara) and states (e.g., Guanajuato, Michoacán) in Mexico, I use pseudonyms for the ranchos, towns, and cities (San Jacinto, Rancho Verde, Pinicundo, Textilpa) in the region where members of the social network originate.

13. When a child or young adult undergoes a rite of passage in the Roman Catholic Church, parents use the occasion to solidify or expand their social network through the practice of *compadrazgo* by asking individuals to serve as the child or young adult's godfather (*padrino*) or godmother (*madrina*) and, simultaneously, as the parents' co-father (*compadre*) or co-mother (*comadre*) (West, 1988).

CHAPTER 2

1. Two decisions—the federal government's decision to engage in extensive highway construction in the area in the 1950s; and Mayor Richard J. Daley's decision to have the University of Illinois at Chicago built in the heart of the Near West Side's residential community in the 1960s—decimated what at that point was one of the oldest and largest Chicano/Mexicano neighborhoods in the city. While many of the area's Italian residents survived the upheaval and established what today is known as "Little Italy," most of the community's Mexican-origin residents were pushed or steered by real estate agents south into Pilsen (Betancur, 1996).

2. Contrary to popular belief, except for the Poles, none of the European American ethnic groups that settled in Chicago at the turn of the century lived in "ghettos." Unlike the highly segregated African Americans and Chicanos/Mexicanos in Chicago today, most Eastern and Southern Europeans lived in what Massey and Denton (1993) refer to as "ethnically diluted" communities where no one group represented a majority (p. 33).

3. Pilsen and Little Village (or *La Villita*) are officially referred to, respectively,

as the Lower West Side and South Lawndale by the Chicago Department of Planning and Development as well as other government agencies (Garza, 1994a; Reardon, 1992).

4. Using 1990 U.S. Census data, Reardon (1992) identified three Hispanic "mega-neighborhoods" that together contain 83% of all Latinos in the city and 54% of all Latinos in the metropolitan area. Figure 2.2 is based on my analysis of the Chicago census tract data for Chicanos/Mexicanos only.

5. In terms of size, the five largest suburban Latino populations reside in Cicero (24,931; 37% of the total population), Aurora (22,864; 23%), Waukegan (16,443; 24%), Elgin (14,576; 19%), and Joliet (9,741; 13%) (Reardon & Montaña, 1991).

6. Between September 1988 and June 1990, I worked as a research assistant for the Mexican American Language and Literacy Project (MALLP) at the University of Illinois at Chicago. During the first three months of the project, I spent much of my time serving as an ESL tutor and substitute teacher at two community centers, *La Casa de Unidad* (The House of Unity) in Pilsen and *El Esfuerzo del Pueblo* (The Power of the People) in Little Village. (The names of the community centers are pseudonyms.) In addition to providing a free service to members of the local community, I used my position as an opportunity to meet potential contacts for a Mexicano social network.

7. Because the overwhelming majority of adults who attended ESL classes in the late 1980s were enrolled in lower-level classes, the few advanced classes tended to be relatively small.

8. In this section I focus on Rancho Verde primarily because it is the rancho that I visited more regularly and where I established the strongest working relationship with local members of the social network. As I noted earlier, except for the names of states and big cities in Mexico, the names of the ranchos and towns are pseudonyms.

9. For a discussion of the social and psychological impact that the immigration of Mexicano men to the United States has had on the women and children left behind in rural communities similar to Rancho Verde, see Salgado de Snyder (1993).

10. I tabulated all of the numbers and percentages presented in this section using Chicago census tract information available on Chicanos/Mexicanos from the U.S. Bureau of the Census (1940, 1950, 1960, 1970, 1980, 1990). The figures, of course, are problematic. The most recent, for example, were challenged in the courts because they were thought to undercount African Americans and both documented and undocumented Latinos, especially in inner-city neighborhoods like Pilsen and Little Village (Davis, 1994; Reardon & Kaplan, 1990). Thus, while they probably represent the best data available from any source on the growth of the Chicano/Mexicano population in the city of Chicago, a degree of caution is in order.

11. A number of community leaders in Pilsen believe that history is about to repeat itself. In their view, the University of Illinois at Chicago's (UIC) $300 to $400 million "South Campus Development Project" threatens to decimate the neighborhood by accelerating the process of gentrification currently taking place in the area. According to Marx (1997), some community leaders "fear that a larger, more upscale UIC could threaten the character of Pilsen, a primarily Mexican immigrant neighborhood, and nearby African-American communities by displacing local residents and businesses" (p. 1). One community leader in particular "described the new development as only a 'train-trestle' away from Pilsen, the predominantly Mexican-American neighborhood

that came to house many of those who were displaced by the original UIC construction in the mid-1960s" (Garza, 1997, p. 3).

CHAPTER 3

1. Throughout this chapter, I observe Lakoff and Johnson's (1980) convention of representing metaphors in capital letters.

2. For a detailed discussion and defense of the dichotomous perspective, see Goody & Watt, 1968; Olson, 1977; and Ong, 1982.

3. For incisive reviews and critiques of the dichotomous approach to orality and literacy, see Brandt, 1990; Gee, 1994; Street, 1984; and Walters, 1990.

4. Cook-Gumperz and Keller-Cohen (1993) also encourage a dialectical approach: "We join talk to writing in this theme issue because of a growing appreciation that the spoken and written word are dialectically related in literacy interactions. This understanding has become critical to any discussion of alternative literacies since the speech-writing matrix varies depending on the community in which it is embedded" (p. 283).

5. I did not engage in an exhaustive search of the metaphors available in literacy studies. I simply kept track of the metaphors that emerged in the course of reading the scholarly work that informs this study.

6. The metaphors I have identified vary along a continuum from literal to figurative. Lakoff and Johnson (1980) argue that definitions are forms of fossilized metaphors. In other words, most if not all definitions begin their lives as metaphors, but as they become more conventionalized and familiar, their figurative characteristics become submerged.

7. To avoid redundancy, I present only the source domain of each basic-level metaphor in the lists. The reader should keep in mind that each word in these lists is assumed to fill the blank line in the frame "LITERACY AS _____."

8. See my earlier discussion of Therborn's views, which suggests that ideology always addresses three central questions: What exists? What is good? What is possible?

9. Stewart (1995) is vehemently opposed to the use of the term "representation" because "the symbol [read, semiotic] model embraces a representationalism rooted in the Cartesian-Kantian distinctions between subject and object. . . . [It] treats language as a tool or instrument humans use to accomplish their goals" (pp. 125–126).

CHAPTER 4

1. In the fall of 1992, an incident caused hurt feelings among social network members that disrupted the degree to which they interacted. As wounds have healed and misunderstandings have been clarified over the course of several years, members have returned to a semblance of their previous and frequent patterns of interaction.

2. The sample texts presented in this chapter were culled from 14 interviews conducted in the interviewees' homes and 52 hours of "natural speech" recorded primar-

ily in Jaime and Rocío Durán's home by members of the MALLP (Marcia Farr, Lucía Elías-Olivares, Edith Ortega, and me) between January 1989 and August 1990.

3. I do not include the autobiographical narratives here because those were elicited rather than self-generated, but I would argue that the rhetorical and discursive principles associated with oral language and personal letters operate in them as well.

4. Miller (1984) provides an interpretation of genre that I believe adds depth to Hanks's definition: "What we learn when we learn a genre is not just a pattern of forms or even a method of achieving our own ends. . . . We learn to understand better the situations in which we find ourselves and the potentials for failure and success in acting together. As a recurrent, significant action, a genre embodies an aspect of cultural rationality. For the critic, genres can serve both as an index to cultural patterns and as tools for exploring the achievements of particular speakers and writers; for the student, genres serve as keys to understanding how to participate in the actions of a community" (p. 163).

5. Like all ethnographers, I had varied forms of access to different social settings based on my age, gender, temperament, professional status, etc. Moreover, in writing this book, I had to select from a plethora of field notes, informal conversations, tape recordings of sociolinguistic interviews and natural speech, personal letters, and autobiographical writings what I thought would best represent my interpretations of life, language, and literacy in the transnational community I chose to study. While the personal letters and autobiographical writings reinforce my observations of a tendency in the group toward the feminization of literacy, the excerpts of natural speech do not seem to represent or illustrate a tendency I observed toward the masculinization of orality, especially in mixed-gender settings. More research needs to be undertaken to verify or dispute these observed and documented tendencies.

6. In Table 4.1, I present (in alphabetical order based on their first names) some pertinent background information on the social network members whose interviews and natural speech are excerpted throughout this chapter.

7. For a discussion of how some of these rhetorical strategies are used in public speaking by Mexicanos and contrasted with essayist literacy, see Farr (1993).

8. While Rosa's and Leticia's public conspiracy against Rocío is clearly feigned, it brings into question the strong ideological bonds that I observed among women in the social network, especially in relation to their power struggles with men. For example, as the only male sitting with a group of women in someone's kitchen, I once witnessed two women berating a third for allowing her husband to humiliate her publicly. As soon as a man walked into the room, they shushed and changed the subject. While the traditional academic assumption is that women in Mexicano homes are powerless in the context of their culture's patriarchical structure, anecdotal evidence of this kind illustrates the private power that they wield individually and as a group.

CHAPTER 5

1. In his work, which builds directly on Besnier's, Vetter (1991) examines a corpus of 60 Tuvaluan-language and 30 English-language letters with the expressed goal of

substantiating Ostler's (1986) and Kaplan's (1972) argument that "when individuals write in languages other than their native tongue, they tend to continue using their native patterns of discourse" (1991, p. 125). Because all of the letters I am examining are in Spanish only, I did not include Vetter's work in my discussion of letter writing.

2. Except for anecdotal evidence that suggests very similar uses in letters written in Vai script and English, Scribner and Cole do not provide any detailed analysis of letters written in English. And because people were reluctant to share letters written in Arabic, they never collected a large enough corpus to compare with those written in Vai script.

3. Like the letters that Besnier and I examine, Vai personal letters follow a distinct organizational format: a formulaic greeting announcing the name of the recipient, a short body that provides the subject matter in the fewest words possible, and a formulaic closing.

4. Besnier also talks about the sermon, but it is a secondary issue because fewer people engage in it than in letter-writing, a genre that almost every member of the community practices.

5. The examples of Nukulaelae letters that I present here were originally written in the Tuvaluan dialect, with a few borrowings from English and Samoan.

6. The six letters from Pinicundo, which is only a few kilometers from Rancho Verde (see Figure 2.3), were written by Ignacio Durán's godmother; the four letters from California were written by Doña Cariño Rodríguez's brother. They follow the same general patterns of all the other letters in the corpus.

7. TM denotes letters sent "To Mexico"; FM denotes letters sent "From Mexico." The number that precedes the two-letter designation denotes each letter's place in its respective sequential set.

8. When I interviewed Carolina Durán, a woman in her forties who now lives in Chicago, and asked her about her letter-writing experiences, she told me she was familiar with the alphabet, but had never learned to put letters together into words effectively enough to write a letter. All of the letters she has ever "composed" were written for her by her sister, her cousin, or her daughter. To demonstrate her experience with composing letters orally, Carolina described, then dictated a "sample letter" during our interview.

9. After I organized the letters sequentially into two groups (From Mexico and To Mexico), I identified individual topics on the basis of any topical shifts that I noticed within each letter. I then named the topics on the basis of their content and placed them in categories that seemed consistent across the corpus of letters.

CHAPTER 6

1. For a discussion of the theory behind and illustrations of these two rhetorical styles as they were used by several members of the Little Village community in

a public setting, see Farr's "Essayist Literacy and Other Verbal Performances" (1993).

2. As of 1995, at least seven other individuals that I knew of who were associated with the social network had attended or were currently attending college: two of Malú's cousins and Lucinda Cabrera's five daughters.

References

Adams, T. D. (1990). Introduction: Design and lie in modern American autobiography. In T. D. Adams (Ed.), *Telling lies in modern American autobiography* (pp. 1–16). Chapel Hill: The University of North Carolina Press.

Aiken, R. (1980). *Mexican folktales from the borderland*. Dallas: Southern Methodist University Press.

Anderson, B. (1991). *Imagined communities: Reflections on the origin and spread of nationalism*. London: Verso.

Año Nuevo Kerr, L. (1976). *The Chicano experience in Chicago: 1920–1970*. Unpublished doctoral dissertation, University of Illinois at Chicago.

Anzaldúa, G. (1990). *Haciendo caras, una entrada*: An introduction. In G. Anzaldúa (Ed.), *Making face, making soul (Haciendo caras): Creative and critical perspectives by women of color* (pp. xv–xxviii). San Francisco: Aunt Lute Foundation Books.

Auerbach, E. R. (1989). Toward a social-contextual approach to family literacy. *Harvard Educational Review, 59*(2), 165–181.

Bakhtin, M. (1981). *The dialogic imagination: Four essays by M. M. Bakhtin* (C. Emerson & M. Holquist, Trans.). M. Holquist, Ed. Austin: University of Texas Press.

Bakhtin, M. (1986). *Speech genres & other late essays* (V. W. McGee, Trans.) C. Emerson & M. Holquist, Eds. Austin: University of Texas Press.

Bartholomae, D. (1985). Inventing the university. In M. Rose (Ed.), *When a writer can't write: Studies in writer's block and other composing process problems* (pp. 134–165). New York: Guilford Press.

Bashi, V. I., & Hughes, M. A. (1997). Globalization and residential segregation by race. *Annals of the American Academy of Political and Social Science, 551*, 105–120.

Battaglia, D. (1995). Problematizing the self: A thematic introduction. In D. Battaglia (Ed.), *Rhetorics of self-making* (pp. 1–15). Berkeley: University of California Press.

Bennett, J. A., & Berry, J. W. (1991). Cree literacy in the syllabic script. In D. Olson & N. Torrance (Eds.), *Literacy and orality* (pp. 90–104). Cambridge, UK: Cambridge University Press.

Benstock, S. (1988). Authorizing the autobiographical. In S. Benstock (Ed.), *The private self: Theory and practice of women's autobiographical writing* (pp. 10–33). Chapel Hill: The University of North Carolina Press.

Bergland, B. (1994). Postmodernism and the autobiographical subject: Reconstructing the "other." In K. Ashley, L. Gilmore, & G. Peters (Eds.), *Autobiography and postmodernism* (pp. 130–166). Amherst: The University of Massachusetts Press.

Berlin, J. A. (1988). Rhetoric and ideology in the writing class. *College English, 50*, 477–494.

Berlin, J. A. (1991). Poststructuralism, cultural studies, and the composition classroom: Postmodern theory in practice. *Rhetoric Review, 11*, 16–33.

Bernstein, B. (1971). *Class, codes, and control: Theoretical studies towards a sociology of language* (Vol. I) (2nd ed.). London: Routledge & Kegan Paul.

Besnier, N. (1988). The linguistic relations of spoken and written Nukulaelae registers. *Language, 64*(4), 707–736.

Besnier, N. (1991). Literacy and the notion of person on Nukulaelae atoll. *American Anthropologist, 93*(3), 570–587.

Besnier, N. (1993). Literacy and feelings: The encoding of affect in Nukulaelae letters. In B. V. Street (Ed.), *Cross-cultural approaches to literacy* (pp. 62–86). Cambridge, UK: Cambridge University Press.

Besnier, N. (1995). *Literacy, emotion, and authority: Reading and writing on a Polynesian atoll*. Cambridge, UK: Cambridge University Press.

Betancur, J. J. (1996). The settlement experiences of Latinos in Chicago: Segregation, speculation, and the ecology model. *Social Forces, 74*(4), 1299–1324.

Bizzell, P. (1982). Cognition, convention, and certainty: What we need to know about writing. *Pre/Text, 3*, 213–243.

Bizzell, P. (1988). Arguing about literacy. *College English, 50*, 141–153.

Bizzell, P. (1994). Opinion: "Contact Zones" and English Studies. *College English, 56*, 163–169.

Bloch, M. (1993). The uses of schooling and literacy in a Zafimaniry village. In B. V. Street (Ed.), *Cross-cultural approaches to literacy* (pp. 87–109). Cambridge, UK: Cambridge University Press.

Bourdieu, P. (1991). *Language and symbolic power* (G. Raymond & M. Adamson, Trans.). John B. Thompson, Ed. Cambridge, MA: Harvard University Press.

Brandt, D. (1990). *Literacy as involvement: The acts of writers, readers, and texts*. Carbondale: Southern Illinois University.

Briggs, C. L. (1988). *Competence in performance: The creativity of tradition in Mexicano verbal art*. Philadelphia: University of Pennsylvania Press.

Brodkey, L. (1989). On the subjects of class and gender in "The literacy letters." *College English, 51*, 125–141.

Brodkey, L. (1991). Tropics of literacy. In C. Mitchell & K. Weiler (Eds.), *Rewriting literacy: Culture and the discourse of the other* (pp. 161–168). New York: Bergin & Garvey.

Brodzki, B., & Schenck, C. (Eds.). (1988). *Life/lines: Theorizing women's autobiography*. Ithaca, NY: Cornell University Press.

Bruffee, K. (1984). Collaborative learning and the "conversation of mankind." *College English, 46*, 635–652.

Camitta, M. P. (1987). *Invented lives: Adolescent vernacular writing and the construction of experience*. Philadelphia: University of Pennsylvania.

Campa, A. L. (1976). *Hispanic folklore studies of Arthur Campa*. New York: Arno Press.

Cardoso, L. A. (1980). *Mexican emigration to the United States, 1897–1931: Socioeconomic patterns*. Tucson: The University of Arizona Press.

Chafe, W. L. (1982). Integration and involvement in speaking, writing, and oral literature. In D. Tannen (Ed.), *Spoken and written language: Exploring orality and literacy* (pp. 35–54). Norwood, NJ: Ablex.

Chafe, W., & Danielewicz, J. (1987). Properties of spoken and written language. In R.

Horowitz & S. J. Samuels (Eds.), *Comprehending oral and written language* (pp. 83–113). New York: Academic Press.

Chavez, L. (1991). Outside the imagined community: Undocumented settlers and experiences of incorporation. *American Ethnologist, 18,* 257–278.

Chavez, L. (1994). Power of the imagined community: The settlement of undocumented Mexicans and Central Americans in the United States. *American Anthropologist, 96,* 52–73.

Cintron, R. (1993). Wearing a pith helmet at a sly angle: Or, can writing researchers do ethnography in a postmodern era? *Written Communication, 10,* 371–412.

Cintron, R. (1997). *Angels' town: Chero ways, gang life, and rhetorics of the everyday.* Boston: Beacon Press.

Cook-Gumperz, J., & Keller-Cohen, D. (1993). Alternative literacies in school and beyond: Multiple literacies of speaking and writing. *Anthropology & Education, 24,* 283–307.

Couser, G. T. (1989). Introduction: Authority, autobiography, America. In G. T. Couser (Ed.), *Altered egos: Authority in American autobiography* (pp. 13–27). New York: Oxford University Press.

Davis, R. (1994, August 10). Ruling gives city chance to see census count rise. *Chicago Tribune,* Section 2, p. 2.

Delgado-Gaitan, C., & Trueba, H. (1991). *Crossing cultural borders: Education for immigrant families in America.* New York: Falmer.

De Rycker, T. (1991). Turns at writing: The organization of correspondence. In J. Verschueren & M. Bertuccelli-Papi (Eds.), *The pragmatic perspective: Selected papers from the 1985 international pragmatics conference* (pp. 613–647). Amsterdam: John Benjamins.

DeVito, J. A. (1966). Psychogrammatical factors in oral and written discourse by skilled communicators. *Speech Monographs, 33,* 73–76.

DeVito, J. A. (1967). Levels of abstraction in spoken and written language. *Journal of Communication, 17,* 354–361.

Dewey, J. (1899). *The school and society.* Chicago: University of Chicago Press.

Dewey, J. (1900). *The child and the curriculum.* Chicago: University of Chicago Press.

Durand, J., & Massey, D. S. (1992). Mexican migration to the United States: A critical review. *Latin American Research Review, 27*(2), 3–42.

Espinosa, A. M. (1985). *The folklore of Spain in the American southwest.* Norman: University of Oklahoma Press.

Fairclough, N. (1992). *Discourse and social change.* Cambridge: Polity Press.

Farr, M. (1990). *Oral folk texts and literacy practices among Mexican immigrants in Chicago.* Proposal to the Spencer Foundation. Chicago: University of Illinois at Chicago.

Farr, M. (1993). Essayist literacy and other verbal performances. *Written Communication, 10*(1), 4–38.

Farr, M. (1994a). Biliteracy in the home: Practices among *Mexicano* families in Chicago. In D. Spener (Ed.), *Adult biliteracy in the United States* (pp. 89–110). McHenry, IL: Center for Applied Linguistics and Delta Systems Co., Inc.

Farr, M. (1994b). *En los dos idiomas*: Literacy practices among Chicago Mexicanos.

In B. J. Moss (Ed.), *Literacy across communities* (pp. 9–47). Cresskill, NJ: Hampton Press.

Farr, M., & Guerra, J. C. (1995). Literacy in the community: A study of *Mexicano* families in Chicago. *Discourse Processes, 19*(1), 7–19.

Farrell, T. J. (1978). Developing literacy: Walter J. Ong and basic writing. *Journal of Basic Writing, 2*(1), 30–51.

Finnegan, R. (1988). *Literacy and orality: Studies in the technology of communication.* New York: Basil Blackwell.

Flower, L., & Hayes, J. (1981). A cognitive process theory of writing. *College Composition and Communication, 32,* 365–387.

Foucault, M. (1982). *The archaeology of knowledge and the discourse on language* (Rupert Swyer, Trans.). New York: Pantheon.

Freire, P. (1970). *Pedagogy of the oppressed.* New York: Continuum.

Frey, W. H. (1980). Black in-migration, white flight, and the changing economic base of the central city. *American Journal of Sociology, 85*(6), 1396–1417.

Friedman, S. S. (1988). Women's autobiographical selves: Theory and practice. In S. Benstock (Ed.), *The private self: Theory and practice of women's autobiographical writing* (pp. 34–62). Chapel Hill: The University of North Carolina Press.

Gale, X. L. (1994, March). Personal experience and academic discourse: Teaching writing through autobiography. Paper presented at the Conference on College Composition and Communication. Nashville, Tennessee. [Ed372393]

Galindo, R., & Brown, C. (1995). Person, place, and narrative in an Amish farmer's appropriation of nature writing. *Written Communication, 12*(2), 147–185.

García, J. R. (1996). *Mexicans in the Midwest, 1900–1932.* Tucson: The University of Arizona.

Garza, M. M. (1994a, July 17). To their health. *Chicago Tribune,* Section 5, pp. 1, 6.

Garza, M. M. (1994b, August 19). Mexico's election: Campaign trail this year makes a Chicago stop. *Chicago Tribune,* pp. 1, 20.

Garza, M. M. (1997, January 15). Groups decry UIC's plans to expand campus. *Chicago Tribune,* Section 2C, p. 3.

Gates, H. L. (1992). *Loose canons: Notes on the culture wars.* New York: Oxford University Press.

Gee, J. P. (1994). From *the savage mind* to *ways with words.* In J. Maybin (Ed.), *Language and literacy in social practice* (pp. 168–192). Clevedon, Avon, UK: Multilingual Matters Ltd.

Gilmore, L. (1994). The mark of autobiography: Postmodernism, autobiography, and genre. In K. Ashley, L. Gilmore, & G. Peters (Eds.), *Autobiography and postmodernism* (pp. 3–18). Amherst: The University of Massachusetts Press.

Giroux, H. (1983). *Theory and resistance in education: A pedagogy for the opposition.* South Hadley, MA: Bergin & Garvey.

Goody, J. R., & Watt, I. (1968). The consequences of literacy. In J. Goody (Ed.), *Literacy in traditional societies* (pp. 27–68). Cambridge, UK: Cambridge University Press.

Graff, G. (1993). *Beyond the culture wars.* New York: Norton.

Green, G. M. (1982). Colloquial and literary uses of inversions. In D. Tannen (Ed.),

Spoken and written language: Exploring orality and literacy (pp. 119–153). Norwood, NJ: Ablex.

Greene, M. (1994). Postmodernism and the crisis of representation. *English Education, 26*(4), 206–219.

Grillo, R. D. (1989). *Dominant languages: Language and hierarchy in Britain and France.* Cambridge, UK: Cambridge University Press.

Guerra, J. C. (1992). *An ethnographic study of the literacy practices of a Mexican immigrant family.* Unpublished doctoral dissertation, University of Illinois at Chicago.

Guerra, J. C. (1996). "It is as if my story repeats itself": Life, language, and literacy in a Chicago *comunidad. Education and Urban Society, 29*(1), 35–53.

Guerra, J. C., & Farr, M. (in preparation). Writing on the margins: The written discourse of *Mexicanas* in the community. In G. Hull & K. Schultz (Eds.), *School's out!: Literacy at home, at work, and in the community.*

Gusdorf, G. (1980). Conditions and limits of autobiography. In J. Olney (Ed.), *Autobiography: Essays theoretical and critical* (pp. 28–48). Princeton, NJ: Princeton University Press.

Gutiérrez, D. G. (1995). *Walls and mirrors: Mexican Americans, Mexican immigrants, and the politics of ethnicity.* Berkeley: University of California Press.

Hadaway, N. L. (1992). Letters to literacy: Spurring second language development across the curriculum. *Childhood Education, 69*(1), 24–28.

Hanks, W. (1987). Discourse genres in a theory of practice. *American Ethnologist, 14,* 668–692.

Harris, J. (1989). The idea of community in the study of writing. *College Composition and Communication, 40,* 11–22.

Harvey, I. E. (1987). Foucault and language: Unthought metaphors. In R. E. Haskell (Ed.), *Cognition and symbolic structures: The psychology of metaphoric transformation* (pp. 187–202). Norwood, NJ: Ablex.

Havelock, E. A. (1963). *Preface to Plato.* Cambridge, MA: Harvard University Press.

Heath, S. B. (1982). Protean shapes in literacy events: Evershifting oral and literate traditions. In D. Tannen (Ed.), *Spoken and written language: Exploring orality and literacy* (pp. 91–117). Norwood, NJ: Ablex.

Heath, S. B. (1983). *Ways with words: Language, life, and work in communities and classrooms.* New York: Cambridge University Press.

Herrera-Sobek, M. (1982). Chicano literary folklore. In E. García, F. Lomelí, & I. D. Ortiz (Eds.), *Chicano studies: A multidisciplinary approach* (pp. 151–170). New York: Teachers College Press.

Hirsch, E. D. (1987). *Cultural literacy: What every American needs to know.* Boston: Houghton.

Holte, J. C. (1988). Introduction: Personal voices from the new world. In J. C. Holte (Ed.), *The ethnic I: A sourcebook for ethnic-American autobiography* (pp. 1–8). New York: Greenwood Press.

Hutcheon, L. (1989). *The politics of postmodernism.* New York: Routledge.

Hymes, D. (1974). *Foundations in sociolinguistics: An ethnographic approach.* Philadelphia: University of Pennsylvania Press.

Jargowsky, P. A. (1996). Take the money and run: Economic segregation in U.S. metropolitan areas. *American Sociological Review, 61*(6), 984–998.

Johnson, M. (1987). *The body in the mind: The bodily basis of meaning, imagination, and reason*. Chicago: The University of Chicago Press.

Kalman, J. (1996). Joint composition: The collaborative letter writing of a scribe and his client in Mexico. *Written Communication, 13*(2), 190–220.

Kaplan, R. B. (1972). Cultural thought patterns in intercultural education. In K. Croft (Ed.), *Readings on English as a second language* (pp. 245–262). Cambridge, MA: Winthrop Publishers.

Kennedy, D. M. (1996, November). The price of immigration: Can we still afford to be a nation of immigrants? *The Atlantic Monthly, 278*(3), 52–54, 56, 58, 61, 64, 66–68.

Kozol, J. (1985). *Illiterate America*. Garden City, NY: Anchor Press/Doubleday.

Kutz, E., & Roskelly, H. (1991). *An unquiet pedagogy: Transforming practice in the English classroom*. Portsmouth, NH: Boynton/Cook.

Labov, W. (1972). *Language in the inner city: Studies in the Black English vernacular*. Philadelphia: University of Pennsylvania Press.

Lakoff, G. (1987). *Women, fire, and dangerous things: What categories reveal about the mind*. Chicago: The University of Chicago Press.

Lakoff, G., & Johnson, M. (1980). *Metaphors we live by*. Chicago: The University of Chicago Press.

Lakoff, R. B. (1982). Some of my favorite writers are literate: The mingling of oral and literate strategies in written communication. In D. Tannen (Ed.), *Spoken and written language: Exploring orality and literacy* (pp. 239–260). Norwood, NJ: Ablex.

Lévi-Strauss, C. (1966). *The savage mind*. Chicago: University of Chicago Press.

Lionnet, F. (1989). *Autobiographical voices: Race, gender, self-portraiture*. Ithaca, NY: Cornell University Press.

Lu, M.-Z. (1992). Conflict and struggle: The enemies or preconditions of basic writing? *College English, 54*, 887–913.

Lunsford, A. A., & Ede, L. S. (1984). Classical rhetoric, modern rhetoric, and contemporary discourse studies. *Written Communication, 1*(1), 78–100.

Lyon, A. (1992). Re-presenting communities: Teaching turbulence. *Rhetoric Review, 10*, 279–290.

McLaren, P. (1986). *Schooling as a ritual performance: Towards a political economy of educational symbols and gestures* (2nd ed.). New York: Routledge.

Macrorie, K. (1975). Strangling the Engfish. *Media and Methods, 12*, 12, 14, 55.

Marx, G. (1997, March 12). Opposition brewing to UIC expansion. *Chicago Tribune*, pp. 1, 13.

Mason, M. G. (1980). The other voice: Autobiographies of women writers. In J. Olney (Ed.), *Autobiography: Essays theoretical and critical* (pp. 207–235). Princeton, NJ: Princeton University Press.

Massey, D. S., & Denton, N. A. (1989). Residential segregation of Mexicans, Puerto Ricans, and Cubans in selected metropolitan areas. *Sociology and Social Research, 73*(2), 73–83.

Massey, D. S., & Denton, N. A. (1993). *American apartheid: Segregation and the making of the underclass*. Cambridge, MA: Harvard University Press.

Miller, C. R. (1984). Genre as social action. *Quarterly Journal of Speech, 70*, 151–167.

Miller, E. K. (1973). *Mexican folk narrative from the Los Angeles area*. Austin: University of Texas Press.

Miller, R. (1994). Fault lines in the contact zone. *College English, 56*, 389–408.

Milroy, L. (1987). *Observing and analysing natural language*. New York: Basil Blackwell.

Minh-ha, T. T. (1989). *Woman, native, other*. Bloomington: Indiana University Press.

Moll, L. C., & Díaz, S. (1987). Teaching writing as communication: The use of ethnographic findings in classroom practice. In D. Bloome (Ed.), *Literacy and schooling* (pp. 55–65). Norwood, NJ: Ablex.

Moore, S. F., & Myerhoff, B. G. (1977). Secular ritual: Forms and meanings. In S. F. Moore & B. G. Myerhoff (Eds.), *Secular ritual* (pp. 3–24). Amsterdam, The Netherlands: Royal Van Gorcum.

Moraga, C., & Anzaldúa, G. (Eds.). (1983). *This bridge called my back: Writings by radical women of color*. New York: Kitchen Table Press.

Mulkay, M. (1985). Agreement and disagreement in conversations and letters. *Text, 5*, 201–227.

Myerhoff, B. G. (1982). Rites of passage: Process and paradox. In V. Turner (Ed.), *Celebration: Studies in festivity and ritual* (pp. 109–135). Washington, DC: Smithsonian Institute Press.

Naumann, J. A., Jr. (1991). Letter writing: Creative vehicle to higher-level thinking. *Social Education, 55*(3), 198.

Novek, E. M. (1992). Read it and weep: How metaphor limits views of literacy. *Discourse and Society, 3*, 219–233.

Olney, J. (1972). *Metaphors of the self: The meaning of autobiography*. Princeton, NJ: Princeton University Press.

Olson, D. R. (1977). From utterance to text: The bias of language in speech and writing. *Harvard Educational Review, 47*, 257–281.

Ong, W. J. (1982). *Orality and literacy: The technologizing of the word*. London: Methuen.

Ostler, S. E. (1986). English in parallels: A comparison of English and Arabic prose. In U. Connor & R. B. Kaplan (Eds.), *Writing across languages: Analysis of second language text* (pp. 169–184). Boston: Wesley.

Padilla, G. M. (1993). *My history, not yours: The formation of Mexican American autobiography*. Madison: University of Wisconsin Press.

Paredes, A. (1956). *"With his pistol in his hand": A border ballad and its hero*. Austin: University of Texas Press.

Peterson, L. H. (1991). Gender and the autobiographical essay: Research perspectives, pedagogical practices. *College Composition and Communication, 42*(2), 170–183.

Polyani, L. (1982). Literary complexity in everyday storytelling. In D. Tannen (Ed.), *Spoken and written language: Exploring orality and literacy* (pp. 155–170). Norwood, NJ: Ablex.

Portes, A., & Rumbaut, R. G. (1990). *Immigrant America: A portrait*. Berkeley: University of California Press.

Pratt, M. L. (1987). Linguistic utopias. In Nigel Fabb et al. (Eds.), *The linguistics of writing: Arguments between language and literature* (pp. 48–66). New York: Methuen.

Pratt, M. L. (1991). Arts of the contact zone. *Profession 91* (pp. 33–40). New York: Modern Language Association.

Prus, R. (1996). *Symbolic interaction and ethnographic research: Intersubjectivity and the study of human lived experience*. Albany: State University of New York Press.

Puente, T. (1995, September 22). Mexican-Americans stake claim on past: Families trace Midwest roots to before turn of the century. *Chicago Tribune*, pp. 1, 12.

Quinn, N. (1991). The cultural basis of metaphor. In J. W. Fernandez (Ed.), *Beyond metaphor: The theory of tropes in anthropology* (pp. 56–93). Stanford, CA: Stanford University Press.

Rader, M. (1982). Context in written language: The case of imaginative fiction. In D. Tannen (Ed.), *Spoken and written language: Exploring orality and literacy* (pp. 185–198). Norwood, NJ: Ablex.

Reardon, P. T. (1992, September 16). Communities defy racial patterns of city. *Chicago Tribune*, Section 8, pp. 13–14.

Reardon, P. T., & Kaplan, J. (1990, April 20). Census to miss many, count some twice. *Chicago Tribune*, pp. 1, 22.

Reardon, P. T., & Montaña, C. (1991, March 18). Hispanic presence booms in suburbs. *Chicago Tribune*, pp. 1, 13.

Redeker, G. (1984). On differences between spoken and written language. *Discourse Processes, 7*, 43–55.

Rorty, R. (1979). *Philosophy and the mirror of nature*. Princeton, NJ: Princeton University Press.

Rosales, F., & Simon, D. T. (1987). Los trabajadores Chicanos en la industria siderúrgica y el sindicalismo en el Medio Oeste de 1919 a 1945. In J. G. Quiñones & L. E. Arroyo (Eds.), *Origenes del movimiento obrero chicano* (pp. 146–157). Mexico, D.F.: Ediciones Era.

Salgado de Snyder, V. N. (1993). Family life across the border: Mexican wives left behind. *Hispanic Journal of Behavioral Sciences, 15*(3), 391–401.

Schön, D. A. (1979). A generative metaphor: A perspective on problem-setting in social policy. In A. Ortony (Ed.), *Metaphor and thought* (pp. 254–283). Cambridge, UK: Cambridge University Press.

Scollon, R., & Scollon, S. B. K. (1981). *Narrative, literacy, and face in interethnic communication*. Norwood, NJ: Ablex.

Scribner, S. (1988). Literacy in three metaphors. In E. R. Kintgen, B. M. Kroll, & M. Rose (Eds.), *Perspectives in literacy* (pp. 71–81). Carbondale: Southern Illinois University Press.

Scribner, S., & Cole, M. (1981). *The psychology of literacy*. Cambridge, MA: Harvard University Press.

Severino, C. (1992). Where the cultures of basic writers and academia collide: Cultivating the common ground. *Journal of Basic Writing, 2*, 4–15.

Shor, I. (1980). *Critical teaching and everyday life*. Boston: South End Press.

Shor, I. (1986). *Culture wars: School and society in the conservative restoration, 1969–1984*. London: Routledge and Kegan Paul.

Shor, I, & Freire, P. (1987). *A pedagogy for liberation: Dialogues on transforming education*. South Hadley, MA: Bergin & Garvey.

Shuman, A. (1986). *Storytelling rights: The uses of oral and written texts by urban adolescents*. New York: Cambridge University Press.

Siems, L. (1992). *Between the lines: Letters between undocumented Mexican and Central*

American immigrants and their families and friends. Hopewell, NJ: The Ecco Press.

Smith, S., & Watson, J. (Eds.). (1992). *De/colonizing the subject: The politics of gender in women's autobiography.* Minneapolis: University of Minnesota Press.

Spacks, P. M. (1988). Female rhetorics. In S. Benstock (Ed.), *The private self: Theory and practice of women's autobiographical writing* (pp. 177–191). Chapel Hill: The University of North Carolina Press.

Spellmeyer, K. (1993). *Common ground: Dialogue, understanding, and the teaching of composition.* Englewood Cliffs, NJ: Prentice Hall.

Stahl, S. (1983). Personal experience stories. In R. Dorson (Ed.), *Handbook of American folklore* (pp. 268–276). Bloomington: University of Indiana Press.

Sternberg, R. J. (1990). *Metaphors of mind: Conceptions of the nature of intelligence.* New York: Cambridge University Press.

Stewart, J. (1995). *Language as articulate contact: Toward a post-semiotic philosophy of communication.* Albany: State University of New York Press.

Street, B. V. (1984). *Literacy in theory and practice.* Cambridge, UK: Cambridge University Press.

Street, B. V. (Ed.). (1993). *Cross-cultural approaches to literacy.* Cambridge, UK: Cambridge University Press.

Street, B. V. (1995). *Social literacies: Critical approaches to literacy in development, ethnography and education.* London: Longman.

Stuckey, J. E. (1991). *The violence of literacy.* Portsmouth, NH: Boynton/Cook Publishers.

Sullivan, F. J. (1995). Critical theory and systemic linguistics: Textualizing the contact zone. *Journal of Advanced Composition, 15*(3), 411–434.

Szwed, J. (1981). The ethnography of literacy. In M. Farr Whiteman (Ed.), *Variation in writing: Functional and linguistic-cultural differences* (pp. 13–23). Hillsdale, NJ: Erlbaum.

Tannen, D. (1982). The oral/literate continuum in discourse. In D. Tannen (Ed.), *Spoken and written language: Exploring orality and literacy* (pp. 1–16). Norwood, NJ: Ablex.

Taylor, D., & Dorsey-Gaines, C. (1988). *Growing up literate: Learning from inner-city families.* Portsmouth, NH: Heinemann.

Therborn, G. (1980). *The ideology of power and the power of ideology.* London: NLB.

Thompson, J. B. (Ed.). (1991). Editor's introduction. In P. Bourdieu's *Language and symbolic power* (pp. 1–31). Cambridge, MA: Harvard University Press.

Toulmin, S. (1956). *The uses of argument.* Cambridge, UK: Cambridge University Press.

Urban, G. (1989). The "I" of discourse. In B. Lee & G. Urban (Eds.), *Semiotics, self, and society* (pp. 27–51). The Hague, Netherlands: Mouton de Gruyter.

U.S. Bureau of the Census. (1940). *16th census of the United States: Population and housing* (Vol. 1). Washington, DC: U.S. Government Printing Office.

U.S. Bureau of the Census. (1950). *U.S. population: Census tracts* (Vol. 3, pt. 1). Washington, DC: U.S. Government Printing Office.

U.S. Bureau of the Census. (1960). *1960 U.S. Census of Population and Housing Census Tracts* (Pts. 26–30). Washington, DC: U.S. Government Printing Office.

U.S. Bureau of the Census. (1970). *1970 U.S. Census of Population and Housing Census*

Tracts: Chicago IL SMSA, No. 1 (Vol. 1, pt. 43). Washington, DC: U.S. Government Printing Office.

U.S. Bureau of the Census. (1980). *1980 U.S. Census of Population and Housing Census Tracts: Chicago IL SMSA* (Pt. 119, sec. 1). Washington, DC: U.S. Government Printing Office.

U.S. Bureau of the Census. (1990). *1990 Census of Population and Housing Census Tracts. Chicago PMSA* (Vol. 113B, pt. 1). Washington, DC: U.S. Government Printing Office.

van Slyck, P. (1997). Repositioning ourselves in the contact zone. *College English, 59,* 149–170.

Vásquez, O. A., Pease-Alvarez, L., & Shannon, S. M. (1994). *Pushing boundaries: Language and culture in a Mexicano community.* New York: Cambridge University Press.

Vetter, R. (1991). Discourse across literacies: Personal letter writing in a Tuvaluan context. *Language and education, 5*(2), 125–145.

Walters, K. (1990). Language, logic, and literacy. In A. A. Lunsford, H. Moglen, & J. Slevin (Eds.), *The right to literacy.* New York: Modern Language Association.

Watson, J. (1993). Toward an anti-metaphysics of autobiography. In R. Folkenflik (Ed.), *The culture of autobiography: Constructions of self-representation* (pp. 57–79). Stanford, CA: Stanford University Press.

Weiher, G. R. (1991). *The fractured metropolis: Political fragmentation and metropolitan segregation.* Albany: State University of New York Press.

West, J. O. (1988). *Mexican American folklore: Legends, songs, festivals, proverbs, crafts, tales of saints, of revolutionaries, and more.* Little Rock, AR: August House.

Williams, J. D. (1992). Politicizing literacy. *College English, 54,* 833–842.

Williams, J. D., & Snipper, G. C. (1990). *Literacy and bilingualism.* New York: Longman.

Young, R., Becker, A., & Pike, K. (1970). *Rhetoric: Discovery and change.* New York: Harcourt Brace Jovanovich.

Index

About the Author

Juan C. Guerra, an associate professor in the Department of English at the University of Washington (UW), teaches courses on literacy, ethnography, writing, the teaching of writing, and Chicana and Chicano autobiography. For 15 years before he joined the faculty at UW, he worked as a Lecturer in English Composition at the University of Illinois at Chicago and taught writing to minority and economically disadvantaged students, a professional interest that has continued to the present day. In 1997, his work with students recruited through academic opportunity programs culminated in the Modern Language Association's publication of a collection of original essays that he coedited with Carol Severino and Johnnella E. Butler, *Writing in Multicultural Settings*.

His latest project, titled *Bridges and Barriers: A Binational Study of Schooling and the Mexican Immigrant Family* and supported by a Spencer Postdoctoral Fellowship Award granted by the National Academy of Education at Stanford University, signals a shift in focus from studying the uses of oral and written language within a Mexicano family and community context to studying their uses in a binational schooling context. The project involves field work in several public schools and adult literacy programs in the same three home fronts represented in this book. The goals of the new project are: 1) to undertake a comparative analysis of schooling practices (theories of education and the development of curriculum and pedagogy, as well as their influence on learning and teaching styles), and 2) to investigate the personal, familial, and educational ramifications of these schooling practices on the adults and children who continually move back and forth between Mexico and the United States.